COMMUNITY EFFECTS

OF LEADERSHIP DEVELOPMENT

EDUCATION

VOLUME THREE

RURAL STUDIES SERIES

SPONSORED BY THE

RURAL SOCIOLOGICAL SOCIETY

OTHER VOLUMES IN THE SERIES:

VOLUME ONE:

Rural America in a Globalizing World:
Problems and Prospects for the 2010s

CONNER BAILEY, LEIF JENSEN, AND ELIZABETH RANSOM

VOLUME TWO:

California Dreaming: Boosterism, Memory,
and Rural Suburbs in the Golden State

PAUL J. P. SANDUL

Community
Effects of Leadership
Development
Education

Citizen Empowerment
for Civic Engagement

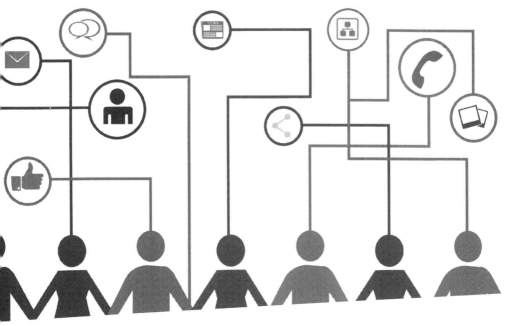

Kenneth Pigg Stephen Gasteyer

Kenneth Martin Godwin Apaliyah **Kari Keating**

West Virginia University Press   Morgantown 2015

West Virginia University Press 26506
Copyright 2015 West Virginia University Press
All rights reserved
First edition published 2015 by West Virginia University Press
Printed in the United States of America

22 21 20 19 18 17 16 15   1 2 3 4 5 6 7 8 9

ISBN
HC: 978-1940425-57-3
PB: 978-1-940425-58-0
EPUB: 978-1-940425-59-7
PDF: 978-1-940425-60-3

Cataloging-in-Publication Data is available from the Library of Congress.

Book and cover design by Than Saffel.

Contents

Preface

As an experienced author told us several years ago, "Writing a book to tell your story is probably the right decision, but it is not the easiest way to go about it." At the time, little did we know how right he was. This specific book has now been several years in development with revisions and rewrites, reorganizations and reformulations, and too many cleanups to count. At one point, there were so many stages of different chapters across so many different computers that it was difficult to make sure we were working with the most current version. We fully appreciate that a first book is a learning experience, and we believe we can take away many lessons that will likely be useful in our futures.

The research reported in this book began as a study of the community effects of leadership development activities. We wanted to discover whether we could empirically identify and measure these effects in ways that could guide the organizers of leadership development programs and demonstrate that their work was meaningful. As researchers, we were also interested in testing a specific research approach using recognizably reasonable and reliable methods. This lent itself to a comparative approach that pitted communities with leadership development programs that were actively offered to residents against communities without such programs to better determine the effects of leadership development activity. Of course, many contextual factors affect rural communities as well.

As rural sociologists, we were especially interested in the rural population of community-based leadership development programs; we were also interested in the empirical results' implications for rural and community development. From the beginning, it was clear to us that the leadership development programs being offered, despite their diverse sponsors, aimed to create a cadre of leaders who could tackle the challenges of maintaining viable rural communities in a global environment. While leadership development is not the only activity intended to achieve this purpose, most of the others depend on the quality of leadership in a community for successful implementation. This was the basic presumption from which we launched this research project.

That said, it is frequently difficult to account for or predict where a specific research task may lead as the work progresses. While we were aware from the beginning that leadership was a complex idea from an intellectual standpoint and that community leadership in particular had been largely neglected as a focus of reported research, we did not anticipate precisely where our investigation would eventually lead us. We had some ideas about how we wanted to proceed, but acknowledge that some of the research was exploratory in nature as we discovered unexpected things. We also did not begin our research with a definitive definition of community leadership, although we were aware of many that might have been relevant. While we had some basic ideas that undoubtedly colored our approach and our interpretations, our strategy was to focus on community leaders and see how they behaved in the community context as they acted to improve the places in which they chose to live. We aim to determine whether leadership development activities produce desired outcomes at the community level and open some discussions about the nature and purpose of community leadership and how it may be improved. Readers may read this book and reasonably come to different conclusions than we did, but we feel confident that the empirical research supports our interpretations of community leadership's nature and process. (We welcome feedback on your own interpretations; contact the senior author at piggk@missouri.edu.)

We want to take a small amount of space to tell those who have assisted and supported us during this work a very sincere "thank you." We benefitted from the our families' support and encouragement, especially when family members were too young to understand exactly what was going on but tolerated our absences anyway (we think). Maybe they were just too young to know how to complain adequately! Our spouses were most supportive, although we frequently heard plaintive questions of, "Aren't you done with that yet?" Without their understanding encouragement (most of the time), we might not have stuck to it to the finish.

We also wish to thank the reviewers of the several drafts of the book, namely the members of the Rural Sociological Society's Rural Studies Series Editorial

Committee, for their willingness to support our proposal and for their continuing interest in the finished product. Added to that list is the new Series publisher's representative, Carrie Mullen, who patiently waited for us to finish with a listening ear to all our challenges and good advice for getting the work done. Without the reviewers' and Carrie's support and guidance, our product would have been less than satisfactory.

Lastly, we thank the US Department of Agriculture's National Research Initiative staff (now National Institute For Agriculture) for the generous financial support it gave us to conduct this research.[1] Sincere appreciation is extended to the Bush Foundation in St Paul, Minnesota, for their financial support in helping to prepare the final manuscript. Thanks also go to our respective institutions for their willingness to give us the time necessary to complete the work, as they received little compensation for our time away from other educational responsibilities.

As with many projects of this sort that wind up in educational institutions, we took every opportunity to share what we were doing with students and colleagues on campus and in professional meetings of various types. More often than not, we received constructive questions and lots of encouragement for this work. Many people have been waiting on the publication of this volume, and we sincerely hope it will stimulate among them continuing efforts to address the leadership needs of rural communities and their residents.

Introduction

De Tocqueville (2000; 1836) called the American habit of forming associations, of working collectively toward community solutions, the "Mother Science." The term reflected his understanding of the fundamental role that citizen participation played in the governance of a democratic society in which equality and liberty were core values. In the early nineteenth century, de Tocqueville's visits to the new American states gave him ample evidence that Americans routinely found ways to join together and create citizen leaders for community benefit. Many times these relationships spawned formal associations, some of which still function today. But just as often, they were transitory and arose to meet a specific need or interest in the community. After accomplishing their objective, participants returned to their routine lives. This habit has been studied and codified into the field known today as community development.

As Wren (2007) explains, the Mother Science required a new form of leadership suited to a democratic society where sovereignty remained in the hands of people rather than in those of the ruler or the elites. In many ways, this form of leadership continues to evolve as the context in which our democracy operates grows more complex and the population more diverse.

Developing community leaders is an important element of preserving our democratic way of life in the United States (Poston 1976; Boyte 2009). De Tocqueville (2000) was among the first to note that Americans seemed "naturally engaged" in civic life, as they joined all sorts of associations and acted in a collective manner on many kinds of issues. He observed that it was at the local level that the real dynamics of this new democratic experiment actually played out. Many new community associations quickly became more organized and replicated themselves across other communities. Their organizational structures became more formal, as did the procedures that each of their chapters followed. In many cases, the people who served as associational leaders learned valuable skills that translated into local community politics. As the nation grew and matured, things changed (Skocpol 2003). These changes have mostly occurred during the twentieth century and may account for some of the difficulties facing many communities, especially smaller ones, in building the civic capacity to manage public affairs. Residents frequently do not have the skills, motivation, or knowledge about how things work in their community; what they perceive to be substantial personal and structural barriers keep them from pursuing leadership roles in public life.

Interventions, such as community leadership development (CLD) programs, that are designed to increase citizens' capacity for civic engagement have been considered central to communities' future viability for a number of decades (Moore 1988). These programs are designed to fill gaps in what people know about governance and its processes, especially at the community level. It may be sufficient for a high school civics class to teach students about the federal, state, and local systems of governance, but it seems there are few opportunities for similar learning about how non-governmental organizations, associations, and informal networks operate and influence local governance systems. And since what goes on in this context is extremely important for the well-being of each citizen of the community, knowing how the community is governed is a fundamental part of engaged citizenship.

The work of many people in the field of leadership development is a response to the recognition that, in smaller, rural communities and disadvantaged neighborhoods, the skills and aptitudes citizens need to be successful leaders are often missing or underdeveloped. Secondary school civics class simply does not adequately prepare people to function in the highly complex environment of today's communities. In modern life, global structures impinge on local processes in numerous ways, which suggests that another difficulty is the lack of a civic infrastructure that can satisfactorily address increasingly complex issues. Further, growing population diversity brings diverse agendas and values that complicate pathways to successful development. We do not need another academic course to address this deficit. On the other hand, it is not often possible to learn everything necessary through experience alone. Therefore, many institutions, foundations, and organizations have developed and sponsored what have become known as CLD programs. These programs may parallel, in part, the kind of curricula found in corporate leadership and management programs. More often, they deal with unique subject matter and are organized and managed by local sponsors to meet specific local needs for increasing local leaders' capacity. Here, we document the valuable new evidence of return-on-investment made by these community-based programs for individuals, organizations, and communities.

In this volume, we address the deficit in our understanding of the community effects of leadership development efforts by sharing the results of a five-year effort to track CLD programs' community-level effects in several states. We document, as others have, the individual effects of program participation. Relevant and recent discussion of these effects in the existing literature often narrowly focuses on the individual-level effects of leadership development programs often operated by the state-level Cooperative Extension Service (e.g., Allen and Morton 2006; Basset and Barron 1988; Earnest 1996; Ehmke and Shipp 2007; Hughes 1998; Langone 1994; NCRIN 1984; Ohnoutka et al. 2005; Paxson et al. 1993; Ricketts and Place 2009; Schauber and Kirk 2001; Tackie et al. 2004; Black 2007). To measure these effects, we not only use survey data to construct indices in a manner similar to a number of previous studies, but also show how individual effects relate to one another. We examine the specific curriculum elements that are related to these effects. Then, we link the individual effects to new roles in organizational leadership as well as to community activism and change. To conclude, we provide an empirically based model of change that links individual-level capacity to community change, and note the antecedents of civic engagement as well as the instrumental variables that affect the outcomes.

In this volume, we offer readers two important ideas. First, CLD programs really do produce the kinds of change in communities that sponsors commonly desire. We demonstrate this in some detail in the first part of this volume as we identify the important outcomes of the leadership development efforts for individual participants, the outcomes that accrue to the community, and the organizational changes that also relate to individual-level effects. We also delve briefly into the specific educational design aspects of CLD efforts to get an idea of what works to produce these outcomes.

Second, we propose rethinking what CLD programs accomplish, how they do it, and why. Our research reveals some unexpected results that strongly suggest we should change how we think about community leadership and leadership development. Our proposal is not particularly radical, but it is one of the first empirical efforts to link to some important conceptual work in leadership and leadership development that has appeared in the last decade or so. In presenting this second idea, we offer some practical suggestions for implementing leader development practice, as well as some concrete ideas for linking that practice to the new concepts that see leadership as an attribute of social processes rather than of individuals.

Community Development

Community development, or the improvement of community residents' well-being, is a term that some use to describe a self-development process (Littrell and Hobbs 1989) and others use to describe structural change (Young 1999). Some describe the process as involving improvements in the economic and/or human capital assets of the community, and may even include the social, cultural, natural, and built assets (Flora and Flora 2008). Others argue that community development is the result of community organizing to gain access to typically unavailable resources (Gittell and Vidal 1998).

Whatever its definition, the process involves residents' engagement in public processes of negotiation, mobilization, organization, and action, which often broadly represent the community as a whole and involve a diverse cross section of residents who act in their roles as citizens. Community development as it is typically practiced in the United States is, at its roots, a democratic process (Poston 1976). While early observers of the American community like de Tocqueville (2000) did not interpret what they saw as community development, they did observe unique community democratic and civic activity at the local level.

In practice, community development is often segmented by a focus on specific needs such as health care, education, infrastructure, planning, and economic improvements (Green and Haines 2002). Rural communities have seen the quality of these services significantly decline in the face of economic changes resulting from agricultural industrialization and job outsourcing to low-wage countries (Besser 2009). Local leaders may need to implement unique tactics in each area if development is to be successful. Many CLD efforts often focus on learning about these tactics, along with some practical tools and basic community leadership ideas such as collaboration and participatory approaches to needs assessment and planning. Field theorists (e.g., Wilkinson 1991) argue that, if these segmented efforts are not based on approaches that build stronger attachment to and capacity for the community field, community development will not occur despite improvements in specific areas. We return to this perspective several times in this volume. What is important to remember is that, to achieve success, all of the tools that underscore the practice of community development require residents' engagement and skills deployment.

Community Leader Development

Readers may rightfully ask what the research base says about community leadership needs and how to effectively meet them. In a field of such recognized importance, readers might expect to find a rich resource of available research. Unfortunately, the reverse is true. Community leadership, as a social and political concept, is largely understudied (Pigg 1999). As extensive reviews of the research literature (Vandenberg, Fear, and Thullen 1988; Rost 1991) document, there is very little to draw upon. Nearly all the relevant research focuses on the "structure of power" and "patterns of participation" in communities (e.g., Hunter 1953; Dahl 1982; Gaventa 1980). Much of the work is not only outdated, but also provides little guidance for educational program development. The most relevant recent work is that Reinelt and associates (2002) conducted for the W. K. Kellogg Foundation, in which they surveyed program sponsors. However, most sponsors were from the non-profit sector, thus omitting many relevant providers of leadership development programs at the local level.

The most directly relevant piece of work may be *Public Leadership*, a small book written by Wendell Bell, Richard Hill, and Charles Wright in 1961 for the Fund for Adult Education. Bell, Hill, and Wright (1961) reviewed over 600 references to determine recommendations for leadership development training. While some of their recommendations are still relevant, others are not. For example, their review indicated, "in the world of public affairs, it is men who dominate leadership positions in the United States" (1961, 53). Almost anyone involved in leadership development today knows that this is not as relevant now as it was in 1961, as women increasingly take up the challenges of community leadership (Brown and Nylander 1998; Lowndes 2004; Whitaker 2006). They also reviewed ethnic leadership prior to the era of civil rights activism, and their suggestion that Lewin's (1948) periphery theory of ethnic leadership represents contemporary leadership in the United States finds little current support in the literature (Molnar and Lawson 1984). However, Bell, Hill, and Wright pointed out a large number of unexamined, unanswered questions that research has not yet addressed — particularly in regards to community leader development in particular.

Most of the leadership research of the past forty years has been conducted in large, formal, complex organizations, either businesses, government bureaucracies, or the military.[1] The limited amount of this research that is relevant mostly deals with personal and inter-personal skills and knowledge—face-to-face skills that are important in any context. Further, most of the theories of leadership derive from these research settings. In short, there is a limited research base and little theoretical treatment of leadership in community contexts.

It is useful to digress a bit and consider the notion that a community is analogous to a large organization. Both are concerned about long-term viability. Both are concerned with adapting existing structural components, goals, and so on to reflect internal and external environmental changes. Those in leadership positions in communities and organizations must consider how to coordinate and integrate the structure's various parts, as leaders must modify existing tasks and procedures in order to improve outcomes. Both communities and large organizations are also the scenes of repeated conflict, which leaders must effectively manage in order to use differences constructively (Dubin 1979; Pigg 2001). These kinds of similarities in function mean that some of the research on leadership in formal organizations is relevant. Leadership—and research on it—that focuses on function and action is often termed "transactional" leadership (Burns 1978). For Burns, transactional leadership refers to a leader-follower relationship in which a leader provides direction for a task and a follower uses those directions to complete the task in exchange for some kind of reward, often a salary. In this view, transactional leaders use their control over resources and authority to modify procedures as required to manage followers' productivity.

Despite these similarities, communities differ from large organizations in both structure and process (Pigg 1999; Ricketts 2005). For this volume, we consider community as Wilkinson (1991) defines it: a bounded place of social interaction where people share common norms and values. For leadership concerns, community structure consists of both the explicit component organizations in the community, such as volunteer associations, civic groups, local government agencies and commissions, and numerous other groups that handle community residents' perceived needs, and also the implicit set of social norms that provide the procedural guidelines for individual behavior and relationships. Examples of such norms include the notorious sundown laws historically practiced in the rural South or the selection of candidates for public office based on relationships, business practices, or membership in the right clubs. Community process refers to how the community works, or how things get done in it. The process applies to many kinds of activities, and is generally analogous to a procedures manual in a formal organization. The process determines the relationships between component organizations in the community and the domain of responsibility and authority of each.

The challenge for community leaders, even if they are experienced in formal organizations, is that most community structures and processes are implicit and informal, embedded in the routines of previous leaders and community residents, and are therefore hard to learn. The rules are not written down. Learning effective community leadership is often like wandering in a forest or wading through a swamp. Learning is usually accomplished over a long period of residence in the community and through practicing leadership in various types of local organizations. Leadership *in* the community is more common than leadership *of* the community (Gardner 1968). Nevertheless, experience does translate into learning where leadership is concerned (Pigg et al. 2009).

Obviously, a number of factors affect this representation of community. One is size. Size is related to complexity, and the simpler the community structure and process, the easier it is to learn leadership lessons. Another is distance, as greater distance decreases interaction between places, simplifying learning and behavior. Yet another is resource availability, as the resources available to support leaders' decisions affect the kinds of decisions they make and are likely related to local innovation (Flora and Flora 1988). The possible variety across these elements and many others makes it unlikely that there is a general case for CLD. In other words, no model of leadership development can address local leadership development needs alone.

We must consider another factor before proceeding. Frequently, community leadership suffers from an "attribution" mystique (Pigg 1999). Many researchers study the processes, problems, and results of community change. Typically, the chosen independent variable(s) (e.g., educational attainment) will not explain the nuance in the selected change variable (e.g., change in employment). As a result, researchers usually attribute some of the remaining variation to the quality of community leadership. While few would deny the causal quality associated with leadership, its specific contribution remains unknown. Without analytical research that explicitly includes variables to measure the nature of leadership in the community, this situation will not improve. Not only does our knowledge suffer as a result, but our efforts to develop and improve the quality of leadership remain without adequate foundation. In this sense, present leadership development programs represent ad hoc normative approaches rather than a design based on relevant research.

We also admit to a bias toward the primacy of local leadership in the context of development. Our reasons for this transcend any philosophical rationale. The local community provides the initial training ground for the largest number of public leaders in the United States (Skocpol 2003). It is in this arena that individuals who have leadership aspirations or are committed to a better quality of life often learn first-hand the demands of leadership, the skills and knowledge required of leaders, and ways to get things done. Another reason is that, for individuals, the local community is less psychologically threatening than any other. In such an environment, they have personal relationships that will not likely fail if they make unsuccessful initial leadership attempts. In fact, friends are likely to lend their support and encouragement, and may even become part of the "team." In this sense, too, lessons come much easier and potential leaders may often find a mentor to show them the ropes (Lovell 2009). Even a cursory review of various biographies of respected and recognized leaders usually indicates the importance of these initial leadership attempts at the hometown or local level. In fact, these may even come in youth, in programs such as Scouting or 4-H (Gardner 1995).

Local leaders also make decisions that lead to some of the most important changes regarding the course and pace of development. Even in areas where the initiative may rest with state agencies, the decision to participate and the basis for that participation occur locally. Transportation issues are an excellent example. Although local governments manage city and county roads, the decision to build or improve a state or federal highway or bridge on a particular roadway is often influenced by local leaders in such areas as scheduling, responsibilities for maintenance, funding sources, and so on.

Finally, our research suggests that the fundamental processes that underlie community change can be captured in our understanding of civic engagement and social cohesion. We understand Berger's (2011) argument that the term "civic engagement" has been used to cover so many ideas it may no longer have real meaning. However, we like the term, with the understanding that there is an important political element to civic actions and that the basic notion of "civic" relates to "public" or the common good. In our work, civic engagement has become a cornerstone of our thinking about leadership development efforts and outcomes. Social cohesion, another key element in our analysis, speaks to the notions of social relationships and networks of interaction on which leadership is founded in this new way of thinking.

How This Volume Is Organized

In this volume, we present several core ideas regarding community leadership, leadership development, and the practice thereof. We also discuss the theory and practice of CLD and its effects when implemented in rural communities. We argue:

- CLD has community level effects that are measurable;
- CLD is linked to community change and development activities;
- Community change is often a civic activity (in the context of Boyte's [2004] "public work") and involves political engagement, related skills, and confidence;
- Community changes are often the result of groups of leaders who work together, rather than the result of one leader who works alone;
- Community leadership culture needs to change if long-term capacity to deal with increasingly complex problems will develop or grow; and
- CLD program designs need to change in order to support and encourage transformations in leadership culture.

In part 1 of this volume, we present our analysis of data collected on CLD programs' effects on communities using the sources described above. Since we determine that civic engagement is necessary for leaders to affect their community, we feel it is necessary to understand the foundation of the concept of civic engagement in the US democratic system. In part 2, we address this need, and build on key authors who examine why and how citizens become engaged. We ask: how do CLD programs relate to civic engagement, power and empowerment, diverse networks of generalized trust and shared vision, and, ultimately, community change? In addition, we offer important lessons from this research that affect the design and delivery of CLD programs, ways to grow communities' capacity for change, and the relationship between leadership and community change. Readers may choose to skip part 2 if they feel they fully understand the concept and practice of civic engagement in contemporary American society and/or the application of bridging social capital (social cohesion) for leadership effects.

In chapter 1, we describe the contents and purpose of this volume, and the overall direction readers will take. We also briefly review some of the related literature in this field, and note the comparative absence of relevant work that focuses on community leadership specifically. In addition, we link the implementation of CLD efforts to the intent to produce community development outcomes, noting these outcomes are often not explicit or understood. While we do not explore the reasons for this lack of explicit exploration, the connection in all the programs we investigated was obvious.

In chapter 2, we describe the results of our online survey data collection and analysis, which demonstrate the effect one CLD program has on its participants. We demonstrate that these effects are not dissociated, but actually form a structured pattern of relationships that are important for the production of community effects. A number of studies show that CLD participation leads to more involvement in organizations. In chapter 3, we further demonstrate that such participation means not only that individuals take on more responsibility in organizations in which they were already active, but also that they seek out new organizations in which to become involved.

In chapter 4, we explore new investigative areas and the ultimate purpose of this research: the effects CLD participation have on the community itself. Using civic engagement as one of the links between individual participation effects and community effects, we demonstrate a significant relationship to various kinds of community activities as captured by the elements of the community capitals framework (CCF) (Flora and Flora 2008). In chapter 5, we examine how these effects relate to the design of CLD programs, especially in terms of content elements and the time spent considering them. In addition to those effects from community and participation, sponsorship also has an effect on the individual changes, and so we explore how different sponsors affect program outcomes as well as the participant group's composition. In chapter 6, we link the empirical results in part 1 to the questions the research raises for CLD programs' practitioners, evaluators, and sponsors. We discuss how these results might apply to program design and implementation, from recruitment to post-program mentoring and community projects. We also address implications for sponsors, including benefits, as well as some guidelines for determining funding priorities. We offer a number of suggestions we believe will improve these programs, their design, and their effectiveness.

We also want help practitioners and others understand the basic ideas this research highlights. While improving practice is important, we think it can best be accomplished when paired with some deeper conceptual understanding of these ideas. Therefore, in part 2, we consider more broadly what our research and results might mean for future CLD efforts. In chapter 7, we examine how civic engagement relates to leadership development in theoretical and practical ways. In chapter 8, we discuss our concept of social cohesion, its relationship to bridging social capital, and how these ideas support community leadership and make it more effective. In these two chapters together, we deepen our earlier discussion of the basic ideas of our research.

Many people who conduct leadership programs or evaluate their effects lament the lack of a theory of change for community leadership (e.g., Reinelt et al. 2002). We take up this challenge in a very preliminary fashion in chapter 9 with a discussion of how leaders contribute to making changes in communities. We use civic engagement and social cohesion as the link pins that connect individuals to community activity and argue for an understanding of the social and political dynamics that underlie the community's civic infrastructure. This discussion underscores our early thinking about a general theory of community leadership. We also transcend much of the current discussion of leadership as skills, knowledge, attributes, or other personal characteristics, and argue instead for a relational definition of community leadership.

In this volume, we challenge the social sciences to use some of the newest research tools available in, for example, network analysis and multi-level analysis, as well as to apply improved qualitative research methods to the study of community leadership and community change. The futures of communities, especially small ones, may depend on the quality of their citizens' leader corps as they endeavor to carve a niche for themselves in a global society and economy. In all communities, citizens who deal with governance issues, individually and collectively, face the challenge of the growing complexity and diversity of modern life (Boyte 1989). To the extent that we claim that finding solutions is a function of leadership, it behooves us to better understand how leaders most effectively identify and act on solutions.

It should be clear by now that we intend this volume for practitioners, sponsors, and those engaged in activities related to evaluation research for CLD programs. We include considerable information that could help practitioners who organize and implement these programs to review and improve their methods. Although we do not provide a specific curriculum, the ideas we explore and the relationships among them should provide a reasonable starting point for curriculum design and redesign.

We have two lessons for CLD program sponsors. First, the work they sponsor really does produce community change. Second, the nature and degree of that change may be subject to some review as to whether it meets expectations—and the work we present is a new way to rethink how sponsors go about choosing to support local program efforts.

A growing literature relates to the evaluation of community leadership programs, although the growth is slow and the focus is not on community-level or social outcomes. Our research demonstrates one proven approach and we expect that others who might choose it can improve it along the way. Our research also raises issues about the theory of change beneath most of these CLD programs and the importance of examining such theories in preparation for conducting evaluation research.

Some readers will wonder why we include a rather extensive discussion of the two central ideas we identify as important to our empirical results: civic engagement and social cohesion. Practitioners, for example, may ask why they should pay attention to this discussion. We argue that, in order to do the best possible job in implementing CLD programs, they need to understand why certain ideas may be central to their task and affect what they do, how they present the opportunity for leadership development to the community, and how they make the best use of the new capacity these programs engender. Evaluators need to understand these ideas because they suggest some different ways to identify and measure program effects. With program evaluation's current emphasis on "logic models" as a vehicle for identifying program theory and expected outcomes, the introductory thinking we present may provide a good starting point. We agree with Kurt Lewin (quoted in Sandelands 1990), who argues: "There is nothing so practical as good theory." Sponsors, too, need to understand these ideas and how they underlay the program activities they support. Sponsors can help reform CLD efforts by extending support to the sort of approach we anticipate in this volume. We have, however, kept the more conceptual discussion of the central ideas separate from the empirical work we describe so that readers may determine what makes the most sense to read and use.

While social science researchers may find some useful information in this volume, we do not consider them our primary audience. We do not test hypotheses and do not robustly review the cited theoretical literature cited in support of the research design, so many researchers will find the work has many shortcomings and we acknowledge that fact.[2] Nevertheless, we feel we have achieved our limited purpose and have produced useful data that will engender thoughtful responses.

STUDY QUESTIONS

1. What societal changes inhibit the building of civic capacity at the community level?
2. How has the emergence of the global economy affected civic engagement and social cohesion in the community?
3. What are the challenges to the rural community leadership structure/capacity in a globalized economy?
4. How does increasing population diversity impact leadership development in rural communities?
5. How are leadership positions in communities and large organizations the same? How are they different?
6. What are some (new) ways to measure CLD program effects?

Part One

COMMUNITY LEADERSHIP DEVELOPMENT
EFFECTS ON COMMUNITY

1.

Community Leadership

Many rural places struggle to keep young people at home and to give them a reason to stay in the form of economic opportunity. Lafayette County in Missouri is one such locality and has taken a regional approach to the challenge. Corinne Estancia is the community economic development director for Lafayette County and a graduate of the community leadership development (CLD) program there.[1] She credits this program and the people with whom she developed relationships with during it with the idea for the Old Trails Regional Tourism project.

The tourism project is intended to create new economic opportunity and builds on three natural and cultural assets of the region, which now includes part or all of ten counties in west central Missouri. First, historically, the region was the head of the Santa Fe Trail along the Missouri River, which was linked to the Lewis and Clark expedition. Several scenic byways are marked to steer tourist traffic to selected sites in the region. Second, it has a notable regional cuisine. Third, it has financial and technical assistance assets that target entrepreneurial development, especially—to build on the second asset—agritourism enterprises that use labels of origin as a primary marketing tool. In fact, it won a Stronger Economies Together program grant in 2010 from the US Department of Agriculture's Rural Development Administration.

Corinne is quick to point out that the Old Trails Regional Tourism project is fundamentally a regional collaboration success story grounded in the education she and several of her fellow leadership program participants undertook.

They learned not only to identify and use these assets as a foundation for a development program, but also how to attract other partners to their purpose. They built relationships and gained political capital from local mayors, county commissioners, and state and federal elected officials. These relationships led to active support from funding and technical support agencies such as USDA Rural Development, the Missouri Economic Development Commission, and the Extension Community Economic and Entrepreneurial Development program sponsored by University of Missouri Extension. The Old Trails project now boasts a membership base of over one hundred business and local government entities that span the region, including artisans, wineries, hospitality and travel enterprises, and agricultural producers.

The project's success can also be attributed to the partnership established among government agencies and businesses and maintained based on the shared purposes its mission defines and its governing board's leaders (who represent the different interest groups across the region) consistently emphasize. "We just keep at it," says Don Battey, who is president of the board. "Communication to potential partners and to the tourism marketplace is an important part of our strategy. Our speakers' bureau does a terrific job of telling people around the region about this project, its vision for the region and its successes to date." Battey also notes:

> The leadership program in Lafayette County of which I was part gave me the tools, network, and confidence to reach beyond my own community to all those in the region and build relationships from a common point of reference, selling the idea on a sharing of interests that was bigger than any single community. That was not always an easy sell in rural Missouri, but I learned that you can't order people around in community work; instead you have to communicate your common interests and be consistent and enthusiastic about it. You also have to demonstrate that some influential people have committed political capital to the outcomes we want to achieve.

The strength of this partnership group was tested a few years ago when an agricultural producer wanted to establish a concentrated hog feeding operation close to a primary historic community along one a scenic byway. According to members of the partnership, this operation would have seriously affected the area's tourism by damaging the landscape. "The odors would have kept the tourists away, I'm sure," said Battey. The organization rallied other regional groups, the local people, and their elected representatives to pressure the producer to change its plans and to convince the relevant regulating agencies to deny a rezoning permit for property so close to the community.

Corinne and Don's experience demonstrates what we argue for in this volume. That is, de Tocqueville's Mother Science, which focused primarily on Americans' associational tendencies, is only a part of the "science" today. Getting together and convincing individuals and groups to work for a common cause must be coupled with leadership and political (or civic) engagement in order to be successful. Our research will demonstrate the central importance of civic engagement and social cohesion, created in the form of new associations and relationships, for achieving community change.

Increasing Community Capacity and Civic Engagement

The term "community capacity" often refers to the local ability to accomplish local change (Gittell and Vidal 1998). Some authors argue that high capacity means successful community organizing, which results in associational tendencies somewhat similar to those de Tocqueville outlined. Others argue that increasing capacity involves the ability to recognize and mobilize community assets (Kretzmann and McKnight 1993). Still others find that community capacity-building is very similar to community development (Robinson and Green 2011). Regardless of the definition of community capacity-building in concept or operation, all seem to agree that this capacity is important for community change.

Civic (or political) engagement is also implicit in nearly all discussions about how to increase and use community capacity to change communities. Further, the authors above recognize that one of civic engagement's fundamental elements is leadership or leaders' ability to use this capacity for change. Without community leaders' demonstrated ability to mobilize resources, institutional leaders do not recognize citizens involved in change activities as having any influence or power to actually induce change, which neuters their "capacity." Effective community change requires civic engagement—direct involvement in publicly acknowledged work that produces desired community outcomes.

This is the lesson Corrine learned in her leadership development program. By the time the program ended, she felt empowered to act—but she now also knew that acting alone was not the answer. Rather, she had to connect both with others who had similar interests and also those who controlled the resources necessary to achieve her goals. This required engaging in political or civic activity: Corinne and her partners' work was for public rather than private benefit, was transparent to the residents of the communities it would affect, and depended on certain political officials' influence to acquire important material resources.

Many of those in the field use the term civic engagement to describe the nature of the individual's political activity and relationship with political institutions and processes at all levels of society, but especially at the community level (Mathews 1999; Putnam 1993b). We use this term to relate primarily to residents' political engagement in the public life of their community. Our research identifies civic engagement as an outcome of leadership development programs created to increase people's capacity to act as leaders. Such interventions explain program participants' increased civic engagement and, subsequently, the benefits that result from their involvement in community actions. Further, we argue that community leadership is often fundamentally political, involving civic actions or "public work" as Boyte and Kari (1998) describe it, though practitioners and sponsors largely ignore this aspect of CLD activity.

INCREASED COMMUNITY CAPACITY AND CLD

Each year, CLD programs are widely implemented with millions of dollars in support from various sources. In 1995, the National Association for Community Leadership Organizations estimated that close to five million—a conservative guess—was spent annually on an estimated 650 to 750 individual programs (Fredricks 1999). Although there are state-level programs in addition to community-level ones, these tend to have somewhat different objectives with more focus on political agendas. According to a study the National Association for Community Leadership Organizations published in 1988, the first CLD program was in Philadelphia; this program began in 1959 and is still in operation, and its approach has been duplicated in a number of places (Moore 1988). Rural communities have taken note and, facing equally difficult challenges, have developed their own approaches with assistance from local chambers of commerce and non-profits, universities, and foundations such as W. K. Kellogg, the Ford Family Foundation, and the Pew Foundation, among others.

Considerable resources have been expended to document effects of these efforts, with mixed results. While most sponsors, especially external ones, want to evaluate programs and determine results, many programs end without systematic evaluations (Reinelt et al. 2002). The evaluations that do occur rarely assess programs' actual effects on their communities. After all, CLD programs are intended not only to change individuals, but also to produce collective benefits within communities. The only reason to increase citizens' capacity to act as effective community leaders is that there are unmet needs in the community that existing leaders are insufficient or unable to meet. Figure 1.1

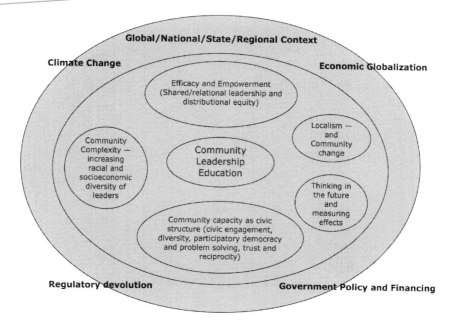

Figure 1.1. Key factors in community leadership education.

summarizes the environmental and social factors CLD must confront. Questions related to how community residents can be empowered to engage in civic activity are central, as this engagement is what produces change and local development. Local leaders must learn how to envision a possible and compelling future by thinking ahead, and how to thoroughly assess the local resources and strengths they can use to produce change. They must also learn to manage and address community complexity; they must understand that communities cannot directly control the complex global factors at play, but can manage the local effects if their leaders recognize and learn to adapt to them (Heifetz and Linsky 2002). In addition, local leaders must learn how to build their systemic civic structure's capacity so that decision-making is effective and efficient, conflicts are resolved in mutually acceptable ways, resources are usefully allocated, and the local community's values and norms are recognized (Couto 1992).

The research we report in this volume directly addresses most of the factors figure 1.1 presents. We demonstrate how CLD efforts can enhance capacity at the individual, organizational, and community levels. We frame our discussion very broadly, incorporating de Tocqueville's ideas from his nineteenth-century visits to America to Margaret Wheatley's ideas from complexity theory, from Robert Dahl's political economy to Ken Wilkinson's sociology. We also draw upon the limited research work done, mostly in the 1980s, by a number of people in agencies and organizations that historically sponsored CLD program efforts.

Our research only initiates what we envision as a long-term effort to better understand community leadership and how it forms and functions most effectively at the local level. We begin the process by linking individual outcomes of what many people will understand as an educational intervention, a programmatic effort organized to improve and increase the local pool of leaders for community betterment, to the community effects these leaders produce based on their experience. We recognize this is but the beginning. We cannot address every factor in the figure 1.1 infogram, the contextual ones, although we speculate about them in logical ways. We wish to engage readers in a more comprehensive consideration of the nature of the intervention as well as its purpose as seen in this broader context. We also wish to challenge readers to consider leadership itself as a social relationship rather than an individual attribute. If you accept such a challenge, read on.

CLD PROGRAMS ARE DIVERSE

Data for the study reported here were drawn from research conducted in six states, from six locations in each state. The data set regarding individual effects came from an online survey conducted in 2008 to determine the effects of participation in CLD programs. The second part of the study to determine community effects involved data from five of the original six states and four locations in each state.

From the beginning, we wanted to demonstrate the impact of CLD programs, and so we devised a way to identify both a treatment and comparison sample to achieve this objective. We also wanted to show that our approach would accommodate at least some variation in program design and implementation. For the six initial states—Illinois, Minnesota, Missouri, South Carolina, Ohio, and West Virginia—we demonstrate that sort of variation with programs devised and sponsored by various educational institutions, nonprofit organizations, foundations, and individuals (including participants). These sponsors include: Cooperative Extension Services; chambers of commerce; local, regional, and national foundations; community colleges; and, often, some combination of these organizations. However, all the programs are community-based. We define a community-based program as: (1) focused on community issues and needs; (2) organized and managed locally by a community group of some sort; and (3) sponsored, wholly or largely, by local resources. Many of these programs also rely on local human resources, such as schools and law enforcement agencies, to deliver content such as that related to local history and local institutions and organizations. In addition, these programs emphasize an educational rather than a training approach; in other words, they introduce and explore ideas about leadership and related concepts using various educational strategies, including self-study, group discussion, role play, and presentations, but do not attempt to turn these ideas into practiced skill sets. Instead, the sponsors recognize the range of applications that will be required and the need for general cognitive and behavioral abilities. While these programs may have opportunities to practice learning and may incorporate some coaching techniques into their curriculums, they do not use more rigorous training models.

Despite these commonalities the available local conditions, sponsorship, and resources lead to many differences. Some CLD programs we studied comprised over 120 hours of contact time, including weekend retreats, tours, and intensive day and evening sessions, while others included half as many hours with a corresponding difference in design elements. Most of the programs generally aimed to increase local leaders' capacity to improve the community's well-being. For some sponsors, this objective translated into support for economic development program efforts; for others, into attempts to redress poverty or improve education or cultural facilities. Where multiple possible sponsors were interested in leadership development efforts but had limited resources, they developed partnerships with resulting compromises in curriculum design. Most of the programs studied operated on "the academy model," enrolling a group of fifteen to thirty participants in a class of three to nine months, complete with a graduation ceremony. Others term this design a "cohort model" (Sandfort and Bloomberg 2012).

Individual sessions may have focused on individual skills development and self-discovery, team building exercises, and diversity, as well as learning sessions that addressed different sectors of the community and the operations, resources, and needs of each. These topical sessions often introduced participants to formal leaders in the community and broke down barriers between residents and institutional authorities. Such sessions also led to the "network effect" that frequent and intense interaction produces among the participants over the course of a CLD program (Rasmussen et al. 2011). The network effect refers to the relationships developed through this interaction and the knowledge about others' interests and skills that may become useful in collaboration later on.

Depending on the sponsoring organization, participant recruitment varied. Some programs welcomed anyone interested who could dedicate the time (and, often, the funds) to take part. Since most programs charged a fee to cover implementation costs, sponsors often raised money for "scholarships" from among community businesses and individuals. Other programs were more selective—for example, chamber programs were typically restricted to chamber of commerce members, and many CLD programs sponsored by external foundations had to include specific target audiences. An exception to this general design can be found in the two sites in Minnesota that participated in the Horizons program, sponsored by the Northwest Area Foundation, in which a broad spectrum of community residents followed a prescribed off-the-shelf curriculum borrowed from external sources and adapted somewhat to local conditions (Allen and Lachapelle 2012).

Despite these differences—and some others that we will discuss in later chapters—our analysis found the twenty-four programs had much in common among their effects. The completed analysis shows the consequences of demographics and curriculum on individual outcomes, the relationship of these outcomes to organizational involvement in the community, and what community effects actually were. While we cannot place a precise economic value on each community effect or estimate the total effect in this manner, it will benefit many sponsors to know that there is, in fact, a positive return-on-investment from these programs.

There are, of course, leader development programs that are not community-based, programs that focus almost entirely on personal development or the enhancement of political skills to affect state and federal public policy. We do not consider these programs unimportant or ineffective, but they differ from CLD programs and their outcomes and should be considered using different criteria. On the other hand, if potential sponsors and community organizers aim to promote change and escalate community well-being by increasing residents' capacity to provide visionary, action-oriented leadership, we prefer a community-based approach. This approach can be extremely empowering at the individual and collective levels (Pigg 2002), while at the same time expanding the base upon which future generations can rely for guidance of community decision-making and governance.

A NEW DIRECTION FOR LEADERSHIP DEVELOPMENT

Notwithstanding our original intent and strategy, we found ourselves rethinking our notions about leadership development, its purpose(s), and its approaches. Empirically, it became clear to us that the goals of the CLD programs we investigated led to collateral outcomes. Perhaps the program sponsors who read this volume will conclude that the outcomes we document were at least implicit in the design of the programs we examine, but we found little evidence of this thinking at the local level. The individual-level outcomes we document are important for undergirding leadership, and there are extensive literatures on each. Furthermore, the finding that these individual outcomes can be empirically linked to organizational and community effect represents a new way of looking at what we do in CLD programs. As we argue in this volume, the sponsors could probably accomplish more, especially in the context of community development, with a shift in focus and implementation.

One new direction for CLD is the use of outcomes as a starting point for evaluation and research on community effects. Drath and associates (2008) make a persuasive case for starting with outcomes (albeit in a somewhat different context) and examining the social and political functions by which those outcomes are produced. We measure outcomes for individual participants, for organizations, and for communities. While we were unable to develop actual measures for the functional relationships involved in producing these outcomes, our data do provide some rough insight into how these outcomes are produced over and above the empirical relationships produced. (In the last chapter of this volume, we discuss this approach at greater length and propose a specific strategy for future research.)

Another new direction is to rethink our understanding of what constitutes leadership in communities. Community residents involved in efforts to improve their communities were often reluctant to acknowledge that they exhibited "leadership." We believe this is the case for two reasons. First, in small communities where relationships are often personal, residents see leaders as different from others, and often do not want to be considered different from their neighbors or fellow residents. Second, a sense of obligation often accompanies local leadership roles: if you have been a successful leader before, you will likely be called upon again and be obligated to step up to the challenge.

If our interpretation of this situation is accurate, we support the proposals of Drath and associates (2008) and of Ospina and Schall (2001) that our basic ideas and ways of talking about leadership must change. This will be difficult and is not likely to happen quickly. However, a functional notion of leadership as a social process that features collaboration and interaction around a shared understanding of the desired outcome and the work necessary to achieve it that is clearly communicated to participants in a CLD experience may lead to new perceptions about what and how leadership emerges in community settings. "Therefore, an important contribution . . . to leadership is to call attention to the implications of the idea that leadership belongs to the community rather than to an individual" (Ospina and Schall 2001, 6). Or, as Drath (2001, 22) notes: "The idea of leadership development has traditionally been concerned with the individual manager who has authority and is held responsible; it has typically aimed to improve his or her ability to direct and influence others." The concept of leadership development changes when leadership is seen as a social concept that emerges from actions of the people in the community engaged in social and political activity. Leadership development must now involve the development of the entire community, not just the individual leader. The community has to recognize that there has been a change from one leadership principle to the next.

Such a view reinterprets the foundational idea of what Drath and associates (2008) call a twentieth century notion of leadership that relies on three principal elements: leaders, followers, and shared goals. Moving our basic idea of leadership from individuals and goals to communities, functions, and outcomes will be a major challenge that sponsors, researchers, and practitioners will have to share in order for change to take place. In place of this former idea, we propose (in part) an approach similar to that of Drath and associates (2008), and suggest that leadership has three important outcomes: direction, alignment, and commitment. Directing community work means articulating a vision and a strategic path to accomplish it, as well as giving it a proper frame of reference: "This task helps people know roughly where they are going, why they are doing it and how it will happen. It also explains and reminds the community of its origin and keeps a sense of purpose alive in the group" (Ospina and Schall 2001, 12). Second, creating and maintaining commitment helps a community develop unity, become more aligned, and overcome obstacles. And finally, being able to effectively deal with adaptive challenges ensures community commitment's long-term sustainability (Heifetz 1994).

As we note in the introduction to this volume, CLD has a long history. We can identify some leadership development initiatives as early as the late 1940s. Most of the content of these early activities drew on newly emerging work in formal organizations, which focused on developing individual skills and knowledge with the assumption that these attributes were general enough to apply successfully in communities as well as in their original organizations. Gradually, some of this content began to include more information about communities themselves, although it did not and has not completely disappeared. In fact, there seems to be considerable inertia in the adoption of new ideas and practices in this important field. We believe our empirical results lay a foundation for overcoming this inertia and introducing some new ideas about community leadership and ways of doing leadership development. With that task in mind, let us begin.

STUDY QUESTIONS

1. Why is leadership the key to linking community capacity resources to civic engagement?
2. What are the differences between community-based leadership development programs and leader development programs?
3. While there are variations in CLD programs, what are the three characteristics they have in common?
4. What constitutes leadership in communities? How does leadership emerge in community settings?

2.

Impact of Leadership Development Programs on Individual Participants

Cary Chan left her meeting with the chamber executive director, the city manager, and the university's community relations director confused and frustrated. They had discussed how to revitalize the community and create a better sense of community identity, but not constructively. Everyone felt some sort of action was needed—something that would help residents take pride in their community and, perhaps, draw tourism or even new businesses into town. However, it seemed that no one had an idea for a practical, effective strategy—except for Cary.

The idea Cary proposed was one she had explored in a leadership development program she had recently finished, which the local extension office and a number of financial supporters in the community had sponsored. Part of the program challenged participants to design a project or activity that might improve the community. Cary and a small group of about six other participants had come up with the idea for a Fourth of July celebration that would feature local performers, community history, local vendors, and artisans. The celebration would last three days and end with the usual fireworks display and some entertainment from a local performer who was beginning to gain recognition nationally, and would ideally attract outsiders as well as remind locals that there was some talent among them.

Cary went home and dug out her participant list from the leadership development program and began to call the people who had been in her group. They had learned some of the same things during the program—surely they would be willing to collaborate in devising a detailed proposal that would benefit the community. As she talked with each person, Cary reminded them of their previous assignment and the project they had envisioned and asked if they still shared her conviction that this Fourth of July event would work. She practiced the communication skills she had learned in the course and emphasized the outcomes they had discussed and the importance of working together. All but one of the former participants seemed enthused by the idea of actually developing a more detailed plan and making it a reality. Individually, they expressed their commitment to the community and its future, as well as their willingness to work together to make the festival a success. Cary invited them to a meeting at her home to begin work.

As they sat down at their first meeting, each member of the group remembered what they had learned in the leadership development course about the community's history and how to approach work like that at hand. They understood who they would need support from, both politically and financially. As they talked and planned, they developed a schedule of events for the weekend festival, a list of the resources they would need, and who had access to those resources. They recognized they would have to convince the city manager that this project would work, because they need city support to use its property, buildings, and security personnel over the festival period. They knew they would have to create some excitement among local businesses that might want to set up food and drink tents during the festival or run shopping promotions. They invited the local community historical society chair and the local performing arts organization director to be part of the festival's planning and execution in a second meeting. Since they had met both of these individuals during several sessions of the leadership development program, they knew them personally and understood that their organizations were an asset and might be very useful in implementing the festival plans.

After several meetings, the group felt it had likely addressed all of the possible questions that might be raised by those from whom they needed political and material support and cooperation. Cary represented the group in presenting the plan to the city manager and director of the Chamber of Commerce. One of the other members who worked at the university took the plan to the community relations director. Two others who worked for local businesses began to canvass community business owners and managers, securing their participation.

Once it secured these core commitments, the group held a larger meeting to finalize the festival planning. Cary's fellow leadership program participants wanted her to chair the meeting. While initially hesitant, Cary thought about what she had learned and practiced during the program and decided that she was able and confident enough to act as chair. The planning session went well, and collaborators grew very enthusiastic for the festival idea and the original group's initial outline of it. Other partners were recruited so there would be enough volunteers to help get the work done. New partners presented ideas for unique contributions not in the initial plan, and the group adopted many for implementation. Together, they developed a full schedule for a festival that collaborators felt would attract the community as well as visitors, and a local advertising firm led a marketing campaign along with the support of the chamber director and her board.

Weeks later, when the festival was over, the subsequent project review was completed with the partners, and the leadership group committed to holding the festival the next year, Cary was relaxing on her porch with some iced tea. She was happy that the project had been so successful that it seemed next year's festival would be even bigger and better. She was also pleased that the chamber director had agreed to assume the organizing role so she would not have to take on the responsibility next year. This year's festival had taken a great deal of time and energy. Cary did not regret that part of the process; in fact, she felt a surge of confidence in her ability to contribute to her community and was excited that there were more resources in the community than most people recognized. The festival had opened a lot of eyes to the rich resource base represented by local residents, and Cary felt confident that future projects would likely be much easier to organize, no matter whose ideas they were.

Community Leadership Development Engenders Benefits

The need to develop leadership in local communities is relatively widely accepted. Just as the sponsors of the community leadership development (CLD) program in which Cary participated recognized, building the capacity to lead activities designed to produce developmental and future-looking changes may require an intervention to empower residents to help make changes happen in their community. Frequently, this intervention takes the form of a program that focuses on the development of leader skills and attitudes toward change that may benefit community residents and strengthen the community overall. In this chapter, we examine CLD programs' effects on individual participants in twenty-four locations in six states. The research we report uses a comparison design, and includes twelve additional locations where no leadership development programs were available. The participant effects are captured in six indices reflecting changes in the participants' self-assessments of changes in their attitudes and skills. Unlike other studies that assess these effects, this research demonstrates that the individual effects are significantly related, suggesting there should be a redesign in CLD programs.

Modern society—afflicted as it is by mobility, complexity, and the effects of technology and globalization—has made historical norms irrelevant. It used to be that community leaders came from either the dominant local business(es) or the highest-status family (Hunter 1953; Moore 1988; Lovell 2009). Today, this influence and power is generally more dispersed or diffused through the social structure of most rural communities (Boyte and Kari 1998). In addition, we frequently find that a large number of individuals periodically leave and re-enter the leadership group as time, interests, and motivation dictate (Israel and Beaulieu 1988; Sandmann and Vandenberg 1995; Day 2011).

For community leaders, or those with aspirations to leadership positions and roles, the situation may be uncomfortable and unintelligible. The conventional leadership models adapted from the military and businesses (in the 1950s), based on command and control, simply do not work well in a community setting (Leighninger 2006). The position and authority as leader is relative rather than absolute and transitory rather than continuous. Effective group leadership now depends on willingness to exert influence and be influenced by others (Vandenberg, Fear, and Thullen 1988; Sandmann and Vandenberg 1995; Rost 1991; Northouse 2004). It also means that association with specific community issues or functions often circumscribes the scope of leadership. Thus, it may be difficult for the school superintendent or the local hospital's clinical director to help implement an effective community economic development plan. In this context, better understanding of civic engagement and civic structure is critical.

However, much of the work on civic engagement treats the citizen in ways that do not support a role as leader role in the community. Leighninger (2006) observes that the current literature treats "citizen" in one of six different ways. Arguing that the literature often stereotypes citizens in ways that sees their participation in political processes as limited by various norms, each of these six stereotypical images circumscribes the role of citizen to such roles as "voter" or "consumer" or "volunteer."

None of Leighninger's citizen stereotypes is that of the civically engaged, publicly minded individual who assumes the role of leader in partnership with other citizens.[1] None captures what Boyte and Kari (1998, 16) call "public work: work by ordinary people that builds and sustains our basic public goods and resources—what used to be called 'our commonwealth.'" Public work "solves common problems and creates common things." This public work results from civic engagement and the sense of social cohesion that is built from either a feeling of solidarity in opposition to something or inclusionary behavior that welcomes diversity as a source of strength and innovation (Leighninger 2006). As others argue (Bryson and Crosby 1992), and as we demonstrate in this chapter, civic engagement and social cohesion are important outcomes of current CLD efforts to support citizens who attempt to increase their leadership capacity.

Effects Can Be Diverse

The work of many people in the field of leadership development is a response to the recognition that the skills and aptitudes citizens need to be successful civic leaders are often missing or underdeveloped, especially in smaller rural communities and disadvantaged neighborhoods (Wituk et al. 2005). A small number of studies demonstrate that participants in CLD programs acquire and develop new skills, knowledge, and attitudes (Bolton 1991; Cook 1985; Earnest 1996; Ehmke and Shipp 2007; Emery et al. 2007; Hughes 1998; Michael et al. 1990; Pigg 2001; Schauber and Kirk 2001; Langone and Rohs 1992; Wituk et al. 2005). For example, Rohs and Langone (1993) show significant gains in CLD participants' self-rated ability to motivate people, make informed decisions on public issues, work with others, and lead a group. They also report anecdotal evidence of community impacts, such as self-reports of increased involvement in local organizations, and partnerships with local leaders to resolve local problems, obtain infrastructure grants, and make other community improvements. However, no attempt was made to link the individual-level effects to the community effect and the individual effects are treated as separate leader attributes. The small number of research subjects in many of these studies makes them difficult to use for comparison even though many of their individual indicators are very similar to our own.

Another weakness of much of the existing research on CLD programs is that the effects on participants are treated in isolation. In other words, previous research on effects like "leadership skills," often self-defined, might be examined as a function of demographics (Schauber and Kirk 2001; Earnest 1996; Bolton 1991) or time spent participating in organized programs (Ohnoutka et al. 2005) rather than combined effects.

These studies are not comparable as the populations studied are much different, the samples often very small, and the intervention designs substantially varied. For example, Wituk and associates (2005) used a "train the trainer" approach to reach seventeen rural community program sponsors' boards of directors in Kansas. Others, like Bolton (1991), specifically target community organization, rather than civic, leaders.

One of the most important findings we report here is that respondents who participated in CLD programs had significant learning when compared to respondents who lived in counties without programs. Very few other studies of CLD effects—with Rohs and Langone (1993) an exception—can claim this effect. The participants in the programs we studied had more learning and attitude changes than those who did not have a leadership development program in their community. This result was true for all six of the indices we used to measure individual-level effects or program impacts. In addition, in this chapter we reveal that the participant outcomes from CLD program involvement form a structural model. That is, the outcomes relate to each other systematically rather than idiosyncratically.

The Effects of CLD in Six States

Leadership in the community is individual and collective behavior that is intended to keep the community viable. Following Rost (1991), community leadership is an emergent property of shared purpose among community residents who take action to achieve such purpose. What role does the CLD intervention play in the six states selected for study? These programs not only create or increase leadership capacity but also empower individuals to behave as leaders. As noted above, we identify this capacity in the context of six characteristics or attributes of individuals that may result from participation in CLD programs. As we will show, these attributes are interrelated and sequenced; together they tend to especially influence civic engagement. We conclude from this research that empowering community residents—supported by networks of bridging social capital (social cohesion)—to become civically engaged is what provides the connecting link between individual attributes and the immediate effects of CLD programs on individuals and the more distal effects on communities.

FORMS OF SOCIAL CAPITAL

A useful way to look at leadership behaviors for community improvement is through the lens of social capital, with a special focus on bridging social capital

(Putnam 2000), especially since it forms one of the important individual effects of CLD participation: social cohesion. Putnam (1993b) defines social capital as the features of social organization such as networks, norms, and trust that facilitate coordination and cooperation for mutual benefit. Clearly, Putnam's focus is on the benefits to members of society that accrue by working together. As such, his work is essential for CLD studies. He suggests that a community can have a stock of social capital; the more it has, the easier it may be to address challenges. One of the main (although usually implicit) goals of CLD efforts is just that: to increase the capacity for community development or to grow the community's stock of social capital so that it can be leveraged to improve other community assets.

For Putnam, social capital is embodied in norms and networks of civic engagement. Networks of civic engagement embody past success and previous relationships that can serve as a template for future collaboration. People who have worked together to complete a project, for instance in finding new resources for addressing mental illness among children, will find it easier to collaborate in future related projects, for example when challenged to develop a local safe house for abused children. The former relationships of trust and information sharing that provide access to resources supports any new activity this same group may initiate. Putman asserts that successful collaboration in one endeavor builds connections and trust that facilitate future collaboration in unrelated areas. Sometimes these norms and networks are embodied in temporary organizations or informal groups with limited objectives that accomplish a specific task and disband. At other times, the embodiment takes the form of a more institutionalized or formal organization, constituted by its membership for long-term general purposes. These purposes may be civic, cultural, religious, economic, or recreational, but they typically have a formal structure that includes clear roles for leaders.

Putnam defines two types of social capital: bonding and bridging. Bonding social capital is found in homogenous groups and is used to reinforce identities and values (Putnam 2000). It is, by nature, exclusive. Bridging social capital ties people in dissimilar networks together, often across some kind of social cleavage such as differences in race, class, gender, religion, age, or tenure in the community (Putnam 2000). There is some debate in the existing literature on whether bonding and bridging social capital are mutually beneficial or not (Agnitsch et al. 2006; Gittell and Vidal 1998). Some research demonstrates that they are (Agnitsch et al. 2006), while other research finds more mixed results (Besser 2009). It is generally argued that without the sort of bridging social capital created by interactions across these kinds of differences, the community would likely be fractured and have different sectors working toward different goals. That is, the more bridging the relationships, the more resources will be available to support development. This is because the different groups possess mutually exclusive resources and information that they can mobilize for mutual benefit in the presence of a shared vision of community betterment and a shared sense of the importance of the public good. This creates a different sense of cohesiveness than that created among those groups with bonding social capital where the norm is internally focused on maintaining boundaries that may be established on the basis of familial ties, religion, culture, or other attributes. However, bonding social capital can help create a sense of commitment to the community if leaders are able to manage it well. Put in more general terms, the more inclusive and cohesive the social networks in a community, the more balance there is between bridging and bonding social capital (Agnitsch et al. 2006), and the more effective is the leadership.[2]

Further, bridging social capital may link people and groups to other groups outside the community. Such links result in access to external assets and facilitates information diffusion and diversity of ideas, and are important for breaking down power and access inequalities (Flora and Flora 2008; Gittell and Vidal 1998). As noted above, Putnam (2000) points out that bonding and bridging are not mutually exclusive categories into which social networks can be divided. Rather, they are relative—dimensions along which different forms of social capital can be compared.

STUDY METHODS

Data for the study of individual effects were drawn from research conducted in six states—Illinois, Minnesota, Missouri, South Carolina, Ohio, and West Virginia—and in six locations in each state. We chose these six states because each had CLD programs in place from 2000 to 2006 (table 2.1 and figure 2.1). In each, we selected four "treatment" communities, for a total of twenty-four sites. The treatment communities were matched on social, economic, and demographic data from the 1990 population census and all had populations of less than 20,000. They were typical of non-metropolitan communities, and selected because they were located in counties that fit in either the rural county or the mixed rural county classification of Isserman's (2005, 475) urban-rural density typology based on 1990 census information. A "rural" county is one with a population density of less than 500 people per square mile, with at least 90 percent of the population in rural areas (meaning the county has no jurisdiction that has a population of 10,000 or more). A "mixed rural" county is one with a population density of less than 320 people per square mile that meets neither the rural

Table 2.1
List of treatment and comparison counties in study population

Map No.	State	Treatment Counties	Map No.	Comparison Counties
1	Illinois	Christian	5	Bond
2		Crawford	6	White
3		Edgar		
4		Jo Daviess		
7	Minnesota	Douglas	11	Pine
8		Isanti	12	Swift
9		Jackson		
10		Stevens		
13	Missouri	Adair	17	Lewis
14		Camden	18	Webster
15		Lafayette		
16		Randolph		
19	Ohio	Hardin	23	Morgan
20		Henry	24	Harrison
21		Highland		
22		Holmes		
25	South Carolina	Clarendon	29	Barnwell
26		Edgefield	30	Calhoun
27		Jasper		
28		Lancaster		
31	West Virginia	Marion	35	Morgan
32		Monongalia	36	Wetzel
33		Summers		
34		Monroe		

nor urban criterion. An "urban" county is one with a density of 500 people per square mile, with 90 percent of the population in urban areas that have a population of at least 50,000. In addition, two "comparison" sites were also chosen in each state and matched in the same fashion; these sites had no CLD program in place during the study period.

In addition to the longevity of their CLD programs, we selected the six states for study primarily on a convenience basis. Each of the three primary researchers involved had prior relationships with colleagues in five of the states involved,

Figure 2.1. Map of treatment and comparison counties in study population.

which we deemed important in the conduct of the research. These relationships provided useful insights and sources of information about leadership program activities and participants in each state, which helped the research team get access to individuals and information more easily.

These six states each had different approaches to their CLD education activities. For example, Missouri had consistently used two approaches: one was Experiment in Community Enterprise and Leadership (Cook 1985) developed by Cooperative Extension, while the other was a chamber of commerce model, which typically includes a heavy social networking emphasis. Illinois also featured the chamber model, along with a Cooperative Extension model and a community college model. Ohio's leadership programs were sponsored by chambers, extension, universities, and chamber/extension combined. Both Minnesota and West Virginia featured multiple approaches sponsored by chambers, extension, foundations, and other organizations interested in leadership development. South Carolina used a chamber model alongside a variety of extension models. All states had active programs since at least the year 2000, with some more involved in offering programs than others.

We selected each locality based on its relative score on a viability index created by summing the ratios of per capita income and population growth for the locality and the state as a whole from among the rural and mixed rural counties in each state. We achieved a balance by selecting half the cases from the upper quartile and half from the lower quartile, so long as other criteria were met, such as the operation of a leadership development program in the past five years. Similarly, the group of twelve comparison localities was selected where no leadership development program had been held to further demonstrate the effects of such programs.

Once we selected study sites, we had to identify CLD participants for our planned survey of participation outcomes. We contacted program sponsors and asked each to provide a list of and contact information for participants in all the CLD programs held between 2000 and 2006. We had planned an electronic survey, so access to accurate email addresses was important.

The online survey we administered to program participants relied on previously developed instrumentation that had proven reliable in several applications (Pigg 2001). We tested each email address with a preliminary invitational and explanatory message, eliminating those that were not current and, where possible, updating them. In all, 637 people responded to the survey with an overall response rate of 62 percent; some cases involve a lower number of respondents due to missing data.

No participant lists were available for comparison sites, so we used a reputational snowball procedure (Bonjean 1963) to identify "community leaders." We contacted three individuals in each site—the cooperative extension agent for that location, the mayor or city/county administrator, and a chamber of commerce director or other economic development organization representative—and asked them to each identify three individuals that they considered community leaders. In turn, we contacted each of these nine individuals and requested similar referrals. We eliminated duplicates, verified email information, and invited these individuals, now numbering as many as twenty-seven, to participate in the survey. In most cases, this process occurred by phone, except in South Carolina where a member of the research team secured names, contact information, and statements of willingness to participate from identified community leaders face to face. In the comparison counties, we did not know the number of respondents in the population, so we could not compute the response rate. The total number of respondents was over 150.

The measurement technique employed a discrepancy analysis (Provus 1971) in that we asked participants to rate themselves on the same questions twice—both before starting and after finishing the educational program. We used the same approach for the comparison locations, except the framework shifted to reflect a time "five years ago" versus "today." From this data, we subtracted the pre-program scores from the post-program scores and computed "discrepancy" or "impact" scores. We then organized the individual indicators into six indices, based on previous studies, for summarizing the impacts experienced (see table 2.2). We computed reliability coefficients for each of these indices and generally produced high coefficients, meaning these are very reliable.

We developed these indices using an exploratory approach in which we asked former participants and sponsors about the kinds of effects they observed among CLD program alumni (Pigg 2001). We developed five of the indices using exploratory factor analysis and one using confirmatory factor analysis from the initial set of over seventy indicators of program effects. The current set of indicators numbers less than forty to make the survey more manageable for respondents. Each index consists of four to six individual indicators. The indices are labeled: Personal Growth and Efficacy, Community Knowledge, Community Commitment, Shared Future and Purpose, Social Cohesion, and Civic Engagement. The actual scores we discuss below are the differences between how individuals rated themselves on each indicator before and after the CLD experience. Each indicator has a maximum score of four and a minimum score of one.

It is useful to understand more fully the substance implied by the indicators for each of these composite indices that we used. Personal Growth and Efficacy represents the leadership skills that participants learn in the CLD experience, some of which are technical (such as analytical skills) and some of which are attitudinal (feeling more confident in providing a role model for others with leadership responsibilities). Community Knowledge, rather straightforwardly, accounts for the knowledge gained about how the community works, what its major institutional leaders think about the future and how to achieve institutional goals, and its needs. Shared Future and Purpose consists of indicators that reflect the understanding of how important it is for a community to have direction and to believe it can achieve the desired future. Community Commitment captures each participant's sense of the importance of their civic involvement in the community and dedication to a shared ownership of what happens in the community, as well as a belief that they can personally have an effect on how the community develops. Civic Engagement, as a composite indicator, represents the participant's sense of potential involvement in the community's political life of the community and their confidence that they will be able to affect change. In addition, this index represents their willingness to acknowledge the importance of working with and appreciating the contributions of others. Social Cohesion includes elements of knowledge of the diverse

Table 2.2
Impact indices components from factor analysis

Impact Factor	Indicator	Factor Score	Factor Score	Factor Score	Factor Score	Factor Score	Factor Score
Personal Growth and Efficacy (= .9006)	I know the difference between management and leadership	.718					
	I know how to assess and tackle problems in systematic ways	.748					
	I try to increase analysis and reasoning skills	.687					
	I move out of my comfort zone and learn to grow	.660					
	I aim to improve consensus building skills	.530					
	I provide a leadership role model for others in community	.516					
Community Commitment (= .9174)	I strive to improve quality of life in the community		.741				
	I Strive to make this community a better place for everyone		.593				
	I value the contributions others make		.604				
	I am involved in the community		.741				
	I have a sense of community ownership		.626		.355		
	I appreciate local businesses		.528				
Shared Future and Purpose (= .8771)	I talk optimistically about the future			.813			
	I can articulate a convincing vision			.796			
	I envision new possibilities			.787			
	I have confidence that we can achieve goals			.772			

resources represented by individuals and sectors in—as well as external to—the community. This index also represents the importance of building working relationships with the diverse set of actors and institutions that make up the community.

Table 2.2 continued

Impact Factor	Indicator	Factor Score	Factor Score	Factor Score	Factor Score	Factor Score	Factor Score
Community Knowledge (= .8536)	I understand the community's structure and dynamics				.744		
	I have knowledge of local, county and state resources				.673		
	I am aware of all the needs in my community				.589		
	I understand the implications of local issues				.517	.377	
	I know how to change things in my community				.435		
Civic Engagement (= .8739)	I could do a good job in public office					.756	
	I am well qualified to participate in public issues					.661	
	I seek to forge new connections					.471	
	I am confident of my ability to work with others					.425	
	I have a good understanding of public issues in the community					.617	

In this chapter, we provide the results of this research effort and conclude that there is a measurable difference between the treatment and comparison groups. That is, those who participated in the leadership development programs showed higher gain scores on the impact measures than those in the comparison counties where no leadership development programs had been offered in recent years.

IMPACT SCORES DEMONSTRATE EFFICACY OF LEADERSHIP DEVELOPMENT

Those study sites that had CLD programs are called treatment sites. Those without CLD programs are called comparison sites—they cannot be called control sites because there was no random assignment to one site or another, which is impossible to accomplish in community studies.

There are significant differences in the scores on the six outcome indices between the treatment and comparison counties as shown in tables 2.3 and 2.4. Table 2.3 shows the raw scores; for example, the score on the index of Personal

Table 2.3

Mean values of the post- and pre-program impact scores for treatment counties and mean values of present and five years ago for comparison counties

Outcome Indices	Treatment Counties			Comparison Counties		
	Post-program	Pre-program	N	Present	Five Years ago	N
Personal Growth and Efficacy	20.0120	17.1355	502	20.5828	18.7219	151
Community Commitment	21.3241	18.0278	503	22.5325	20.5260	154
Shared Future and Purpose	12.6713	10.4724	508	13.2179	11.9744	156
Community Knowledge	15.4783	12.1542	506	16.1871	14.1806	155
Civic Engagement	16.0611	13.0059	507	17.1429	15.1364	154
Social Cohesion	19.8103	17.3281	506	20.2500	18.5461	152

Community Leadership is measured in six dimensions. Each dimension includes four to six questions from the survey (see table 2.1).(1) Personal Growth and Efficacy; (2) Community Commitment; (3) Shared Future and Purpose; (4) Community Knowledge; (5) Civic Engagement; (6) Social Cohesion

Growth and Efficacy shows a pre-program score of 17.14 and a post-program score of 20.01 for an impact (outcome) score of 2.88, which is statistically significant (as table 2.4 shows). Similar results can be found by examining the remaining results in these two tables. The scores for the treatment county participants and the comparison county participants in the survey were significantly different (statistically—see table 2.4). Those individuals in leadership programs participated in the program either to become leaders or to improve their existing leadership skills. Thus, they wanted to accomplish individual goals through participating. The programs helped them achieve these goals, as the greater increases in their impact scores compared to those in the comparison counties show.

Interestingly, in many cases, respondents in the comparison counties rated themselves higher in the present (and past) in absolute terms than did those in the treatment counties, even though the actual differences over time were not as large. This suggests some learning that took place just based on experience in the comparison county group, but a larger amount of learning took place with those in the treatment counties who participated in the educational programs. We return to this finding later in our discussion.

Table 2.4

Paired mean analysis for six impact measures of CLD

Outcome Indices	Treatment Counties			Comparison Counties		
	Mean Differences between the Post- and Pre-program	N	Sig (2-tailed)	Mean Differences between Now and Five Years Ago	N	Sig. (2-tailed)
Personal Growth and Efficacy	2.87649 (1)	502(2)	.000 (3)	1.86093	151	.000
Community Commitment	3.29622	503	.000	2.00649	154	.000
Shared Future and Purpose	2.19882	508	.000	1.24359	156	.000
Community Knowledge	3.32411	506	.000	2.00645	155	.000
Civic Engagement	3.05523	507	.000	2.00649	154	.000
Social Cohesion	2.48221	506	.000	1.70395	152	.000

(1) 2.87649 is the difference between the mean of the post-personal growth index (20.0120) and the pre-personal growth index (17.1355). Mean differences between the post- and pre-program is the impact score.
(2) 502 is the total number of cases that contributed to the paired mean analysis for the personal growth dimension.
(3) A low significance value for the *t*-test (typically less than 0.05) indicates that there is a significant difference between the two indices, post- and pre-program, for the treatment counties and the comparison counties.

THE SIMILAR CHARACTERISTICS OF THESE RESPONDENTS

The median age of the respondents in *all* counties was just over forty-five years (table 2.5). Of the respondents in treatment counties, 67 percent were female and 33 percent were male. However, this ratio was reversed in comparison counties, where about 35 percent were female and 65 percent were male. Over 90 percent of respondents were white and about 4 percent were African American with the balance from several other minority groups in comparison counties, while almost 97 percent of respondents in treatment counties were white and 3 percent were minorities. While there was some evidence of increasing diversity in the treatment counties, there were still few non-white respondents. US Census data for 2000 shows that the rural minority population for the states in our sample ranged from 32 percent in South Carolina to 2.9 percent in Ohio and West Virginia, with Missouri and Minnesota having about 4 percent rural minority population and Illinois about 9 percent.[3] Over half of all the respondents had lived in the community for about twenty-five years and almost 80 percent of both treatment and comparison county respondents had family living in the same community. For the respondents in treatment counties, there is some evidence in the overall distribution that the leadership education programs attracted relative newcomers as participants. Most of the respondents in treatment and comparison counties were employed full-time, but there were greater numbers of respondents working part-time and retired in the comparison counties. Comparing respondents' educational levels reveals some interesting differences, but overall respondents in both treatment and comparison counties were very well educated, with over 80 percent having completed at least some college and almost equal proportions having completed high school. US Census data for these six states in 2000 shows that participants' median age was generally higher than for the states as a whole (38.9 to 34.7) and the respondents' gender was skewed toward women. The ratio of men to women in the general population in these six states was generally in the range of 48.6 percent male to 51.4 percent female or less.

Income levels were also similar between the respondents in treatment and comparison counties. About 27 percent of respondents in treatment counties earned $50,000 to $75,000, while only about 15 percent of respondents in comparison counties were in this category. On the other hand, over 32 percent of respondents in comparison counties reported earning over $100,000 annually, compared with 23 percent of respondents in treatment counties. Other income categories were rather similar in comparison. Hardly any respondents reported making under $20,000 annually and only a few respondents reported making $20,000 to $30,000. As rural counties go, these numbers suggest that respondents in both types of counties were relatively well-off financially. Again, US Census figures reports for median household income (not the same measure as personal income used in this study) in 1999 shows a range of $27,130 in West Virginia to $42,078 in Illinois, which suggests that our study group is over-represented by individuals in higher income categories.

Nearly 87 percent of respondents in comparison counties reported they were married. About twice as many respondents in treatment counties reported they were single or never married as in comparison counties. These results indicate that the respondents to this study were more likely to be married than individuals in the general population as the US Census reports for 2000 indicates that the percentage of the married population over age fifteen ranged from 57.2 to 53.6 percent, which are much smaller proportions than in our study group.

It is worth noting what this profile suggests about the participants in these CLD programs as it may relate to the existing leadership core in these communities. The sponsors did not reach many minorities, even though minority populations are growing in many rural communities; also left out were those of

Table 2.5

Demographic characteristics of respondents in treatment and comparison counties

Variable	Treatment	Comparison
Age	45.6 years	50.7 years
Years in Community	24.2 years	30.3 years
Gender		
Female	67%	35%
Male	33%	65%
Education		
College Grad	37%	30%
Post College	29%	39%
Other	34%	31%
Marital Status		
Married/Sig. Other	81%	87%
Never Married	9%	5%
Others	10%	8%
Race		
White	97%	94%
Other	3%	6%
Employment Status		
Full-Time	84%	71%
Part-Time	6%	8%
Self-Employed	8%	17%
Unemployed	2%	4%
Income		
$0–$49,999	18%	20%
$50,000–$74,999	27%	15%
$75,000–$99,999	23%	24%
$100,000 and more	23%	32%
Missing/Refused	9%	9%

lower income and education. Further, the participant base often did not include many newcomers to the community, suggesting that there is an "orientation" or adjustment period that in-migrants typically face before they decide they might be in a position to enter local leadership. This participant profile raises questions that need further consideration in program design and participant recruitment.

Of interest in this sort of research is whether the participants' demographic attributes affect the participation outcomes that we have measured and shown to be significant. In most sociological studies, demographic attributes contribute significantly to explaining these kinds of results. To do this analysis, we relied on hierarchical linear modeling or multiple level regression analysis, a technique that permits the control the effects of different variables, as we discuss in the following section.

MULTIPLE LEVEL ANALYSIS OF PARTICIPANT EFFECTS

Our data violates some assumptions underlying the typical methods of statistical analysis we might use (e.g., ANOVA, linear regression) as recommended by Rencher (2002). For example, it would be obvious to most readers that the responses to the questions about the participants' status before the CLD experience would highly correlate with their responses afterward. Such correlations significantly bias the result of any analysis using these typical techniques.

Therefore, we conducted our analysis using a multi-level approach to better account for such bias. In fact, our chosen methods were designed to permit us to account for these sources of bias by comparing effects at different times as well as at different levels, in this case individual and site. This multi-level approach is known as hierarchical linear modeling or generalized linear mixed modeling (Raudenbush et al. 2002). This approach preserves the assumptions of linearity and normality found in traditional linear models, but does not preserve the assumptions of randomness and independence among indicators modifying these latter factors so that they can better be accounted for in the analysis by using the variance generally found there.

We specifically intended our analysis to explore the impact of demographic variables on the participant effects such as Community Knowledge, Civic Engagement, Personal Growth and Efficacy, and so forth as compared to the treatment effect. It would be generally assumed in the social sciences that such variables would be important predictors of such outcomes, especially gender, education and other socio-economic indicators as well as the length of time one has lived in a community. While other studies had investigated these factors using standard linear regression techniques, we knew the basic assumptions above would not hold, so we chose this alternative to better represent any existing relationships.

Table 2.6 shows the results of the analysis of multiple levels, in this case time, treatment, and participant attributes. The figures in this table demonstrate the effects of the demographic variables as well as the effects of the differentials of time and treatment (coded as 0 = time1 and 1 = time2, and 0 = treatment group versus 1 = comparison group). The time factor is the distinction between pre- and post-data collection. The treatment factor represents the difference between treatment and comparison group membership. As this table shows, only time and treatment are consistently significant in their fixed effects on the outcome indices. The results of the multi-level analysis indicate that the difference between pre- and post-index scores, as measured, is significant for all indices. In other words, the time factor does make a difference in that learning has definitely occurred. The results also indicate there is a difference in the rate of learning that takes place (i.e., the slope of the fitted distribution line) between the CLD participants and the comparison group of community leaders surveyed. Finally, in the fixed effect section of table 2.6, the interaction effect of time x treatment shows that the coefficients are all negative (likely due to the way in which these binary factors were coded) but still significant.Education is a significant factor in four of the models; however, its estimated effect is rather small though still statistically noteworthy. Income is significant in only one model—for Personal Growth and Efficacy—and its effect is similarly small. Although it is not shown here, the income indicator often becomes insignificant when the effect of education is also considered; these indicators appear to have very similar effects on the indices. Age has fixed effects on Civic Engagement (0.0064), Personal Growth and Efficacy (0.0065), and Community Commitment (0.0067), but the estimates are again very small. Family living in the community is a significant, although negative factor in the analysis of Community Commitment (−0.098) and its estimated effect is small as well. Gender has a significant effect on Civic Engagement and this finding shows the largest statistical result of any of the demographic attributes, but only for this one outcome index. Further, none of the interaction effects measured are significant. No other demographic variable affects these outcome indices, either fixed or random, although time has only a random, negative effect on Shared Future and Purpose (−0.272). One additional observation could be made from this table: randomness in the intercept is diminished for all models, except for Shared Future and Purpose where the estimated random effects are fairly large (0.8335). Clearly there are other factors affecting this index the analysis does not include. (We will return to this finding in our discussion of community effects.) The important conclusion here is that personal

Table 2.6
Fixed effect estimates (top) and variance-covariance/random estimates (bottom) of models of the predictors of CLD participant outcomes

Parameter	Civic Engagement	Personal Growth and Efficacy	Community Knowledge	Community Commitment	Social Cohesion	Shared Future and Purpose
Fixed Effects						
Intercept	1.3356 (.16)***	1.8732 (.019)***	1.5468 (.11)***	2.7453 (.13)***	2.6802 (.11)***	1.7227 (.06)***
Level 1 (time)						
Time	0.6350 (.03)***	0.5699 (.03)***	0.6880 (.03)***	0.5017 (.02)***	0.5017 (.02)***	0.6799 (.03)***
Treatment	0.2337 (.06)***	0.2247 (.06)***	0.2854 (.06)***	0.2028 (.06)***	0.2028 (.06)***	0.3045 (.05)***
Time* Treatment	−0.1781 (.06)*	−0.1616 (.07)*	−.2719 (.06)***	−0.1703 (.06)**	−0.1703 (.06)**	−0.2736 (.06)***
Level 2 (participant)						
Gender	0.1629 (.05)***					
Time* Gender						
Family in Community				−0.09823 (.05)*		
Time* Family						
Years Lived in Community						
Time*Years Lived						
Education	0.04743 (.02)*	0.06637 (.02)***	0.04982 (.05)*		0.05105 (.02)**	
Time* Education						
Income		0.05141 (.02)**				
Time* Income						
Age	0.006362 (.002)**	0.006509 (.002)*		0.00666 (.002)**		
Time*Age						

Table 2.6 continued

Parameter	Civic Engagement	Personal Growth and Efficacy	Community Knowledge	Community Commitment	Social Cohesion	Shared Future and Purpose
Fixed Effects						
Level 2						
Intercept(0,0)	0.2019***	0.2214***	0.1737 (.02)***	0.1619 (.02)***	0.2288 (.02)***	0.8335 (.12)***
Time (1,1)						−0.2719 (.06)***
Intercept*Rate of Change CoVariance (0,1)						0.08668 (.04)***
Level 1						
Intercept (2)	0.1572***	0.1773***	0.2119 (.01)***	0.2119 (.01)***	0.1316 (.008)***	0.1346 (.02)***
−2Log Likelihood	1686.3	1757.0	1873.2	1811.2	1760.6	1995.3

Note: Levels of significance are represented as follows: *** = Pr value is greater than 0.0001; where ** = Pr value is greater than 0.001, and where * = Pr value is greater than 0.01. Standard errors are in parentheses. Family in community is the number of family members living in the community; education is a categorical variable as is income. Gender is coded 0 = male and 1 = female.

characteristics have little effect on the outcomes, especially when controlling for the treatment and time effects. The small effects that do exist are inconsistent across the outcomes measured. This analysis can be used to derive a mathematical expression to determine the estimated score on any one of the indices for an individual participant or any that shared certain characteristics using their estimated scores. For example:

Civic Engagement (est'd) = 1.3356 + 0.64 (time) + 0.23 (treatment) − 0.18 (time*treatment) + 0.16 (gender) + 0.047 (education) + 0.006 (age).

For example, a female participant in a CLD program with four years of college education and aged forty-five would have an initial score (estimated value) on the Civic Engagement index of 2.18 (where time = 0, treatment = 1, gender = 1, education = 4, and time*treatment = 0). Similar mathematical equations could be established for any participant and any of the six outcome indices measured.

A Model for CLD Effects on Participants

The research team was interested in constructing a more complete model of the CLD effects on individual participants from this data. Figure 2.2 shows the results of the path analysis (or the structured equation model result) conducted from the relationships shown in the previous multi-level analysis. In other words, the team took the significant relationships shown in this analysis between the demographic variables and the individual outcome indices as well as the results of a regression analysis using the outcome indices, and formulated a theoretical model to test using this path analysis technique (SPSS/Amos). The theoretical model was quite simple: Civic Engagement was considered the dependent variable, as it was considered the possible link between individual and community effects. The other variables comprised a set of independent predictor variables using the hypothesis that each contributed to the dependent variable in similar fashion.

In fact, what we found in "fitting" the path analysis results to the data and their relationships was that Civic Engagement was, in fact, a useful dependent variable for this data set. However, there was another useful dependent variable, Social Cohesion, which did not contribute much to the explained variation in Civic Engagement but rather stood on its own. To derive this path analysis model we used our own understanding of relevant theoretical perspectives as well as the statistical tools provided in the software to make sure the final model that resulted from several trials was a valid model (RSEA < 0.08). The resulting model is the one shown in figure 2.2.

This model of CLD effects on individuals shows that about 80 percent of the variation in the Civic Engagement index and 73 percent of the variation in the Social Cohesion index is explained by a combination of other indices measured and several demographic factors as well as time and CLD program participation. Specifically, Civic Engagement is a function of Community Commitment, which in turn is a function of Personal Growth and Efficacy and Community Knowledge as well as time and treatment effects, along with the participant's age. Shared Future and Purpose also affects Community Commitment; this means that the effect of Shared Future and Purpose on Civic Engagement is mediated by Community Commitment. Personal Growth and Efficacy and Community Knowledge directly affect Civic Engagement as does gender. Except for gender,

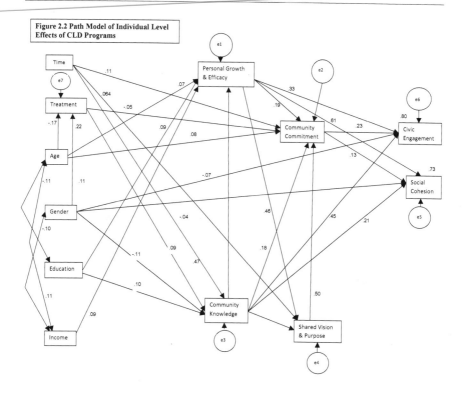

Figure 2.2. Path Model of Individual Level Effects of CLD Programs.

the other demographic attributes of participants only affect Civic Engagement as they are mediated by Personal Growth and Efficacy and Community Knowledge and Commitment.

To sum up this part of the model, we argue that Civic Engagement is an outcome produced by CLD participation and its variation is highly correlated with the variation of gender, Community Commitment, Personal Growth and Efficacy, and Community Knowledge. Shared Future and Purpose plays a role, but only indirectly. The same is true for the demographic effects that are mediated by these composite measures. Notice that none of the demographic attributes strongly affect any of the outcome indices; neither do the time and treatment variables. Comparing this result with that shown in table 2.5, it is likely that the interaction effects play a role in enhancing the role of the demographic effects shown in the model, even though they remain small. There are much stronger relationships among the composite indices, with the results suggesting a very central role for Community Commitment—and Shared Future and Purpose explains much of the variation in Community Commitment. As for Civic Engagement, the variation in this index is largely explained by the direct and indirect effects of three composite indices with gender having a very minor role but reflecting a positive effect for men as opposed to women.

As it regards the Social Cohesion outcome, the model is equally complex. The major explanatory effect is from Personal Growth and Efficacy, directly and indirectly, with lesser correlations made by Community Knowledge, directly and indirectly, and Community Commitment directly. A small effect by gender also indicates that Social Cohesion is more positively related to being a female than male. An important indirect factor is the correlation of time and Social Cohesion primarily through the Community Knowledge index; this relationship indicates the positive effect the difference between the initial measurement and the end measurement has on Social Cohesion. Except indirectly through Community Commitment, Shared Future and Purpose does not have any relationship with Social Cohesion. The effects of age, income, and education are all indirect and small, as are the correlations between them.

Overall, we may conclude that the demographic indicators' impact on CLD effects is not particularly important and that the outcomes experienced are important. The central focus on Civic Engagement theoretically holds in the analysis, and further research is necessary to determine how it helps to account for community effects. The Social Cohesion elements, on the other hand, produced a result that requires some further consideration for unmeasured factors such as the nature of social networks resulting from program participation in CLD programs.

Community Commitment has a central role in both Civic Engagement and Social Cohesion. Of course, arguably the recruitment process alone attracts individuals already committed to the community—commitment that participation clearly increases. It appears that whatever else a CLD program accomplishes, a focus on increasing Community Commitment is important to achieving other outcomes. In turn, this indicator is affected by the increase in Personal Growth and Efficacy and Community Knowledge, and, to a smaller extent, by the time factor of participation. Community Commitment is often considered to be related to having relatives and close friends who live in the community and to the length of time one has lived there, but in this research, those factors did not have any significant effect.

Of the People, by the People, for the People

There are some interesting observations to be made as the result of this analysis. First, the significant difference between groups demonstrates the effect of the treatment (educational program). Those in leadership programs want either to become leaders or to improve their skills as leaders. Thus, they have individual goals to accomplish through their participation. Based on our results, the programs we examined effectively helped them achieve these goals, as the greater increases in their impact scores compared to those in the comparison counties shows. However, the fact that some of the effects of CLD programs on participants extend beyond expectations offers possibilities for communities that sponsors may not anticipate. Further testing of this notion is necessary, but if our evidence is accurate, these programs may intend to increase capacity for community development, but in fact could lead to something different—enhanced self-confidence for effective political engagement through the primary outcome of civic engagement as supported by the effect of social cohesion.

Second, the fact that comparison group participants' assessment of their knowledge and skills was higher than that of those in the treatment group raises some interesting questions. It appears that there is a secondary, contextualized effect. Those who participated in educational programs finished with a new framework to assess what they know and what they can do while those in the comparison group had a different framework. Programs caused participants to recalibrate their thinking about effective leadership in the community. So, because they now have a new framework for thinking about community leadership, the treatment participants understand their strengths and weaknesses differently than do those in the comparison counties. Those in the comparison group were typically recognized as community leaders by contemporaries and so likely had considerable prior experience as leaders to draw from in responding to the survey. (We did not have a way to control for this experiential effect in this study.) This effect could also be related to the fact that the survey participants in the comparison counties were given a five-year framework to assess their individual attributes while those in the treatment counties were more diverse in terms of the length of time since they had completed their educational program experience.

However, we should not disregard the finding that experience is a good teacher. Members of the comparison group also felt they had learned things during the five-year period they used as a reference frame for this study. This suggests that community leadership education efforts should make more effective use of experience and experiential learning activities in their overall program design. Sponsoring agencies and organizations may want to find local resources as active mentors for the new leaders developed in these programs. Such strategies may also ease the transition from one generation to another, although they could also perpetuate existing power structures (Drath et al. 2008).

We expended considerable effort to determine the effects of program participants' and community leaders' demographic attributes. A great deal of previous research in sociology would suggest that various demographic indicators should have an effect on these outcomes. For example, educational attainment is often highly correlated with leadership skills and holding official positions (Rost 1991). However, we found little effect. Our multi-level analysis showed inconsistent and tiny though significant effects related to these attributes on the composite indices used as outcome indicators for the CLD programs.[4] Our path analysis further explored the effects of the demographics on Civic Engagement and Social Cohesion and found small and mostly indirect effects from these attributes. While some of this lack of effect may be due to being an artifact of measurement, the measures we used were similar to those used in a great deal of other social research. (Rost [1991] provides an extensive review of literature that includes the sort of demographic variables often used in leadership research). We expected these indicators would have shown a somewhat greater effect. The effects of gender on Civic Engagement and Social Cohesion—the only direct effects found in the path model between any demographic attribute and the outcomes of interest—need further empirical exploration and deserve more attention.

Returning to our opening discussion in this chapter and Leighninger's (2006) six stereotypical images of the citizen, it is apparent that participants finish their CLD experiences with a variety of perspectives on what it means to be a community leader, some of which may be consistent with the listed stereotypes. As we show in the next chapter, some participants return to community organizations as more active and empowered leaders. We also have limited anecdotal evidence that some participants become actively involved in political affairs and holding elective offices, at the local level especially. More important is the fact that participants think they leave CLD programs with a better sense of what it means to be civically engaged and of the importance of social cohesion despite different perspective, as Cary did in the beginning of this chapter. We have not been able to trace the community involvement of every participant in any of these programs, but we do have a large respondent group that we feel is representative of the total population of CLD participants in these states. We recognize these respondents may represent those who feel they benefitted the most from their experiences and therefore are biased in a positive manner. Nevertheless, CLD program sponsors should be aware that the outcome model we present in this chapter strongly suggests that more is happening, that sponsors' efforts produce unintended outcomes in addition to increasing community development capacity. Civic work is often similar to community development work and produces tangible benefits for the community, but citizens who feel empowered to act in public venues are also a political force that, when working together and guided by a shared vision, can become a strong and powerful agent for other kinds of community change (Drath and Paulus 1994). As such, these civic actors can be seen as threats to or as protectors of the status quo and the existing power structure in the community will not always react predictably. CLD sponsors should take heed and be prepared to teach participants how to make change take place, if that is what is desired, in ways that will not be perceived as threats to the status quo but as collaborative efforts to work toward common ends (Boyte and Kari 1998; Bryson and Crosby 1992). It is clear from our results that community capacity is politically grounded.

In summary, one of the most important findings of this research are that the treatment—being a participant in a community-based CLD program—makes a difference in the perceived creation and expansion of participants' capabilities in important areas related to leader development. These areas include: Civic Engagement, Social Cohesion, Personal Growth and Efficacy, Community Knowledge and Commitment, and Shared Future and Purpose. Further, the increased capacity in these areas is demonstrably statistically significant. A model showing how these CLD outcomes are related to each other in a statistical and logical sense demonstrates the role each outcome may play in explaining a large portion of the variation in civic engagement and social cohesion. Determining how these two factors affect community-level outcomes is the next challenge facing this research activity.

STUDY QUESTIONS

1. In community leadership, a leader's position and authority is relative rather than absolute, and transitory rather than continuing. Do you agree or disagree with this statement and why?
2. What is social capital? How it has been viewed in the literature on community leadership as a useful resource for community improvement initiatives?

3. Describe the two types of social capital (bonding and bridging) and why/how each contributes to community development.

4. Why are civic engagement and social cohesion important outcomes of CLD efforts?

5. Why is building local capacity important for community development purposes? How is local capacity linked to civic engagement and social cohesion?

3.

Program Outcomes in Organizational Behavior

Cathy Ernst had only lived in town a couple of years. She had moved to the small, Midwestern city to take a job as the director of human resources for the local medical center. Cathy and her family joined a church to meet people, and she soon became an active member. Between her career, raising two daughters, and some church activities, she was busy. But she still felt like somewhat of an outsider in a community that offered so many opportunities.

The medical center CEO recommended that Cathy participate in the local community leadership development (CLD) program, which was sponsored by the chamber of commerce and supported by the area branch of the state's land grant university. The program was entering its fourteenth year and many in the community, including her CEO, who was a graduate, touted it as a success. The CEO offered to sponsor Cathy's participation in the program.

The community leadership program was eight months long and included leadership skill development, networking, and educational "issue" tours of area businesses and organizations. Cathy was particularly interested in Social Services Day, wherein her leadership class listened to panel discussions with local government, school, and non-profit leaders on the topic of early childhood mental health status. Cathy learned that, in her seemingly idyllic community, there were disconnects in service delivery for the county's most vulnerable population. Cathy learned that her county was part of a nine-county coalition of organizations that aimed to address regional mental health concerns. In addition to learning about the challenges facing her community, she also built ties with her fellow participants and to the business and organizational leaders that presented data over the course of the program.

Just before the program ended, Cathy began to ask her church friends about the preschool program that was housed in the church. She wanted to know if the preschool leaders were aware of the issues in early childhood illness and treatment. As often happens in small towns, church board members noticed Cathy's enthusiasm and nominated her for a board position to represent the preschool. She was elected, and immediately began to use some of the teamwork and project management skills she learned in her CLD program. But those weren't the only skills she used. About one year into her appointment, Cathy began to reach out to the friends she made in the leadership program. She felt that the preschool program had untapped potential to serve area children. So she contacted area business leaders and the folks she met in county government. She asked her boss if she could start to represent the medical center at chamber of commerce functions, and he agreed. After several lunchtime discussions with new friends at the county's human services division, Cathy was asked to serve on the county's steering committee for the county's Early Childhood Initiative—the organization administering regional grant funding for a host of birth to five programs, including mental health service delivery. Cathy collaborated with her chamber colleagues to raise private funds to complement the grant funding for the early childhood initiatives. Eighteen months into her involvement in these organizations, she saw increased funding for early childhood initiatives locally, the creation of an association of local preschool providers, and the production of free health workshops for families with young children held at the medical center where she worked.

Within three years of graduating from her CLD program, newcomer Cathy went from being a member of to playing a leadership role within her church, networked as a chamber member in the business community, and served as an important link to the county's mental health delivery system. In essence, her organizational behavior changed dramatically after her participation in the leadership program. Before it, her organizational behavior was one-dimensional: she was bonded with like-minded church members and enjoyed the social capital that builds in such settings. After learning that community leadership is essentially about forging relationships of trust in pursuit of mutual goals, Cathy began to identify herself as a leader and saw how she could make a difference in the community on issues she cared about. She just needed to align with others who also cared. As a graduate of the leadership program, Cathy not only deepened her organizational involvement individually by taking on a leadership position in her church, but also broadened it by knitting together people and resources from multiple asset areas in the community to address the rather silent issue of early childhood mental health. As we show in the chapter ahead, Cathy went from involvement in primarily social capital aspects of her community to extending her networks across sectors to practice leadership in financial aspects of the community through the chamber and ultimately in human capital areas with her work on the early childhood coalition.

Cathy's example is one of hundreds that we found in our data. We discovered that (1) getting more deeply involved within a community organization and (2) reaching out to become involved across multiple types of organizations are behaviors that are more likely to occur among people who have participated in CLD programs. Cathy's story is important for communities, especially rural communities that need to look inside their borders for problem-solving. To the extent that people like Cathy can serve as social network bridges across different types of organizations—social, political, financial, and others—the likelihood of survival and positive outcomes improve.

Leader Development and Organizational Engagement

Ideally, leader development produces not only growth and change in participants' knowledge, skills, and attitudes, but also enhanced community leadership behaviors. Community leadership behaviors are viewed as actions that help increase community capacity for change and civic engagement. Often this capacity comes from community associations or organizations that comprise the voluntary sector. In this chapter, we address the effects of CLD programs on the voluntary sector, and examine whether the participants in these programs become more involved in these associations as leaders as a result of their participation.

Our research determined that some programs for leader development focused primarily on training community residents to take on more effective roles in community organizations (Etuk et al. 2013; Moore 1988) and viewed these organizations as the primary vehicles for mobilizing resources for community change. As such, the curriculum in such programs was more often akin to that in training programs focused on learning how to run meetings, manage agendas, organize and manage task groups, manage financial affairs, communicate effectively, and other specific organizational leadership related skills (Black and Earnest 2009; Reinelt et al. 2002). Most of the programs in our study did not take this approach, although they did spend differing amounts of time on topics related to these kinds of skills by each of the programs examined. (We explore this aspect in more depth in a later chapter.)

To fully examine the effect of CLD on organizational involvement, we introduced the community capitals framework (CCF) (Flora and Flora 2008) as a tool in the analysis. This framework is comprised of seven elements or capital assets of a community: social, human, political, cultural, financial, natural, and built capitals. Each of these works in relationship with one another to produce community development in a broader sense. That is, human capital in the form of well-educated workers is required to create the sort of successful businesses that will provide for the community's long-term economic viability. Financial capital to support those businesses may also require political capital to secure the administrative permits necessary to locate a business in a community. This process is akin to what Briggs (1998) calls "leveraging." Investing in one form of capital to increase the stock of another is a basic development strategy. The community capitals approach is also similar to Green and Haines's (2002) "asset building" approach.

USING THE COMMUNITY CAPITALS FRAMEWORK

The CCF as developed by Flora and Flora (2008) is a highly useful extension of the capitals approach to community and is an effective rubric for designing, analyzing, and evaluating community development efforts. According to the CCF, capital includes resources used to create new resources. Small rural communities must turn resources into different forms of capital by first identifying and then investing in them. For example, making a unique natural area a local wildlife preserve might require the use of some political capital to secure the necessary permits, some financial capital to secure access to the land area itself in perpetuity, and some social capital to organize the effort to raise the money necessary to purchase the land. The community identifies the existing capital resources, mobilizes available assets, and leverages those to create a new resource or capital—the nature preserve.

Emery and Flora (2006) and Gutierrez-Montes and associates (2009) provide straightforward definitions for the components of the framework. Natural capital refers to the local area's geophysical attributes, including its flora and fauna. Cultural capital typically refers to resources related to the arts and historical heritage. Human capital refers to the talents and expertise of the community's population. Social capital, as noted above, includes the norms of trust and reciprocity as well as the networks of social relations that exist in the community.

For our purposes in this analysis, social capital includes both bonding and bridging types of organizations in accord with the definitions Flora and Flora (2008) and Emery and Flora (2006) offer. Political capital relates to the ability to influence decision-making in the community; it is often closely related to social capital. Financial capital represents the economic structures and fiscal wealth of the community, the actual money that circulates in the local economy. Built capital refers to the community's infrastructure, namely its housing, institutional structures, business facilities, recreational facilities, and so on. The research we present here uses the CCF to analyze data about the types of community organizations in which community leaders engage.

Rasmussen and associates (2011) demonstrate the CCF's utility. They interviewed twenty CLD alumni in a rural county in Minnesota and found that, post-program, participants engaged in community activities representing each of the community capitals, but especially in the social capital area. Participants typically reported on the benefits of their personal relationships with people from other parts of the county because of their participation in the program. These researchers argue that CLD studies should focus on outcomes related to bridging social capital. They illustrate the kind of analysis incorporated into this research although they did not involve a comparison group to isolate program effects. Similarly, Emery and Flora (2006) use the CCF to assess the effects of a more comprehensive rural development program that included leadership development as one component. They find examples of effects in each of the CCF categories, although the leadership development component seemed to produce more social capital effects than other capital effects. Neither did this study use a comparison group in its methodology.

SOCIAL CAPITAL AND COMMUNITY ORGANIZATIONS

Organizations may simultaneously foster bonding and bridging. Some organizations are known for establishing and maintaining boundaries between themselves and their environment. Some have membership criteria. Such groups sustain themselves by their internal bonds and the distinctions they maintain between themselves and outsiders. Many religious groups fit this category. In some instances, local groups are formed that serve to consolidate political power and are instrumental in the election of candidates for local office (Flora and Flora 2008; Lovell 2009). Organizations that only want to maintain this sort of boundary between themselves and the rest of the community, generally speaking, have little interest in broader community development goals or activities—unfortunately, since the bonds that hold people to a specific organization could be a significant resource in collective activities, as disaster responses or community responses to external threats show (Hawkins and Maurer 2009; Elliott and Pais 2006). Even organizations with an identity bound up with specific attributes, such as religion, race, or culture, may have dimensions of that identity that can be drawn upon to engage them and their resources for broader community contributions. For example, Cathy's church members were convinced that their identity included outreach efforts to assist the community's mentally ill youth, and the strength of their bonds meant that the church as an organization could contribute to outreach and partner with mental health professionals and the school system.

Bridging social capital is found in social networks that are inclusive and reach outward. Chaskin and associates (2001) argue that the concept of social capital serves as a key idea in conceptualizing community capacity, and suggest that it is a "resource potential of personal and organizational networks" (Sampson 1999 quoted in Chaskin et al. 2001). Further, in a study linking social capital to civic structure, Morton (2003) suggests that it is not enough for leader development practitioners to focus on building individual and organizational skills. Instead, she argues that building civic structure requires space and resources for multiple groups to cooperate in solving community problems (Morton 2003, 117). The bridging form of social capital is central to the research proposed here.

Richard Couto (1999) links organizations and social capital directly, and treats the organization as a "mediating institution" and a form of social capital. His studies of the dynamics of Appalachian communities lead him to conclude that the social capital community organizations represent is more than just a network of trust and reciprocal relations, but reflect a set of mediating organizations that serve as links among different groups, as a resource for member benefit, and as the community's civic structure. This conclusion also appears in our work—for example, we found several examples of CLD participants like Cary and Cathy organizing cultural events or human service activities after their CLD experience. To be successful, they usually determined that they needed to collaborate with existing groups such as the local historical society, a local arts or actors group, the chamber of commerce or other business group in town, local government agencies, the county fair board, and other organizations that might be interested in their broad purpose or have resources that might make their venture more successful. In Cary's case, a local high school drama class chose historical figures from the community's cemetery. The students then wrote short skits about their ancestors' lives based on research they did with the historical society and performed them in period costume as one of the attractions during a weekend event for tourists. In the broad sense, each of these organizations performed a civic function that benefitted the community by acting as a mediating institution. Putnam's (1993b, 185) words are prescient: "Those concerned with democracy and development . . . should be building a more civic community . . . [and aiming for] local transformation of local structures rather than reliance upon national initiatives."

LEADERSHIP AND COMMUNITY ORGANIZATIONS

The notion of mediating institutions and the central importance of social capital in them brings us to the connection between leaders and community organizations. While de Tocqueville (2000) notes Americans' propensity to come together and form associations to address community problems of every type, Couto (1999) frames this situation as a more updated and nuanced connection sociologically. As Couto notes, Putnam's (1993b) research in Italy tends to show that involvement in local organizations led to greater community and political involvement because of the social capital that was formed among the participants. Their participation gave them opportunities to share information about civic affairs, debate issues, arrive at common views on local matters of shared interest, decide upon courses of action, and follow through as appropriate. In later work, Putnam (2000) shows that bridging social capital led to greater community prosperity. This finding was replicated in a study in rural Canada (Tiepoh and Reimer 2004).

Israel and Beaulieu (1988) also address community leadership with a focus on organizational involvement. They contend that three elements comprise community leadership behavior: (1) the degree to which an individual is involved in various phases of local action such as initiating activity and implementation of plans; (2) the span of an individual's participation in interest areas such as economic development, environment, education, and so forth; and (3) the extent to which an individual participates in actions that involve a common set of actors (a network) who work for the concerns of the community, usually represented by membership in an organization (Israel and Beaulieu 1988). These elements often manifest in a person's involvement in organizations. As different organizations may represent different interests and resources, such as information and members' political influence, leaders' involvement in diverse organizations and the nature of that involvement can be useful in organizing activities that lead to community benefit. These elements seem to describe bridging social capital. Putnam and Feldstein (2003) describe a similar dynamic as the creation of federations of organizations and groups where mutual purposes are similar and there is access to diverse resources.

Granted, sometimes federations and individuals with similar interests can organize to try to improve the community, but in ways that may undermine other developmental change efforts. For example, a group of individuals who belong to different organizations but share a common interest in reducing local property taxes may organize to take political action that would reduce the resources of local governments to respond to community needs. These leaders represent a capacity to initiate change and a network of (somewhat) diverse resources; they can become a mediating institution or a form of bridging social capital. Obviously, the values within different social networks and how they relate to the desired future of the community can be very important.

We would like to know from this research whether community leadership programs enhance the civic structure in communities. Civic structure is viewed as the social relations within and across different institutions that produce community benefit (Morton 2003). The primary benefit that accrues is the capacity to solve collective problems in the broad community interest. Morton (2003, 105) suggests that civic structure features a high degree of social capital, namely bridging social capital, as it is inclusive, respects minority group perspectives, and involves active participation in public problem solving. Civic organizations make up this structure and may represent economic, cultural, religious, or other interests. Civic organizations differ from non-civic ones by the nature of their goals. Organizations focused on maintaining identity tend not to be very civic-minded or engaged. They mostly pay attention to internal affairs and boundary maintenance. Organizations that are part of the civic structure have goals and activities that are externally focused and generally align with the broader community's shared interests. As indicators of civic structure, we can examine participants' involvement within and across community organizations. We can determine if CLD program interventions have an effect on the nature of this involvement, and thus on civic structure.

Organizational Involvement Broadens and Intensifies

Our survey data tell us about three elements of organizational leadership related to individuals' actions in community organizations that potentially build civic structure: (1) membership or participation in organizations, (2) level of involvement in organizations, and (3) number of community capitals represented by all organizations. We chose each of these variables for the analysis as corresponding to some of the basic ideas that Putnam (1993b), Couto (1999), and Morton (2003) discuss. Membership in community organizations may be important as an initial entry point into the civic structure network that begins the process

Table 3.1

Examples of community organizations coded using the community capitals framework

Built Capital	Cultural Capital	Financial Capital	Human Capital	Natural Capital	Political Capital	Social Capital
Housing authority	Arts council	Chamber of commerce	School-related organization	Parks committee	Elected official	Church or church-related organization member
Electric utility co-op	Local festival committee	Economic/industrial development council	Health-related organization	Clean up/beautification committee	Appointed public official	Service club (Rotary, Lions, Jr. League, Sertoma)
Highway commission	Community visioning organization	Local foundation	Safety-related organization (includes police and fire)	Land conservation organization	Political party member	Adult athletic league
Water and sewer board	Historical society	United Way	Youth development organization	Water quality organization	Lobbying organization	Senior citizen organization
Habitat for Humanity	Ethnic organization	Friends of or Boosters organization	Food security initiative	Wildlife organization	Tax/levy committee	Local informal club (e.g., moms club)

of developing linkages of trust and reciprocity. As a member becomes more involved in an organization, she acquires skills that make her participation more meaningful; she becomes more influential and begins to develop a sense of efficacy and empowerment. Eventually, she may even take on a formal leader role in the organization and may use the influence she has acquired through her network of resources to assist her in getting things done. She may even become involved in other community organizations with different interests. The number of capitals indicated in the types of organizations in which she is involved represents the diversity of organizations and is a surrogate for the kinds of bridging social capital Putnam (1993b, 2000) and Couto (1999) deem important. Of course, some of this bridging capital may develop in a single organization, but it is more obvious when an individual is active in organizations that represent different fields of interest.

In our research, we coded each of these three elements as a binary outcome of whether there was a differential increase in a specific organizational behavior after the CLD experience compared to before it. Membership was coded "1" if the respondent reported belonging to more total organizations in the post-condition compared to the pre-condition. Involvement was coded "1" if the respondent's total organizational involvement was higher after the program than before (we first created an involvement index by summing scores across all organizations in the pre- and post-conditions where for each organization "1" equals an inactive member, "2" equals an active member, and "3" equals a leadership position). In addition, each respondent listed the names or types of organizations in which they participated before and after the program. We divided these organizations into categories to represent each of the community capitals according to their primary purpose as indicated by their names. For example, a business organization would be categorized as financial capital; a local arts group would be categorized as cultural capital (see table 3.1). We used a multiple rater process to increase reliability. In addition, we conducted online searches where it was not clear what category the named organization might fall into. The diversity of community capitals reflects the scope of participants' organizational affiliations across different types of asset areas in the community and was coded "1" if the total number of unique capital asset areas of involvement was higher in the post- than the pre-condition. (We chose this binary coding procedure as the most conservative approach available given that we coded the dependent variable in this fashion.) Table 3.2 presents the results of binary logistic regression analysis of factors that may predict changes in behavioral leadership development. Next, we describe each of the models for membership, involvement, and capitals.

CLD SUPPORTS DIVERSE NETWORKS

Survey respondents were asked about their involvement before and after their CLD participation in community organizations. They could also indicate the organization(s) in which they were involved at both times, as well as the level of that involvement (whether they were a member, a board/committee member, or an officer of the organization). We determined the number of unique community capital asset areas in which the respondent participated by assigning each named organization to a community capital category and a capitals code for that category. We summed the unique number of capitals. If the number of unique capitals was greater in the post-CLD period, the participant's score was "1." Otherwise, it was "0." This was done because the CCF categories do not represent continuous variables and we were determining whether or not there was any change at all in these categories.

Similarly, if the participant belonged to more organizations in total after the CLD program, their score was "1"; otherwise, it was "0." However, the nature or degree of involvement was handled differently. In the pre- and

Table 3.2

Results from binary logistic regression analyses predicting behavioral leadership outcomes in community organizations

	Change in Behavioral Leadership Development		
	Membership	Involvement	Capitals
Independent Variables	Model 1 Exp(B)	Model 2 Exp(B)	Model 3 Exp(B)
Community Leadership			
Program Participation	2.795*** (0.398)	2.823*** (0.731)	1.478* (0.268)
Individual Characteristics			
Age	0.958*** (0.008)	0.950*** (0.009)	0.979* (0.010)
Gender (Female)	1.001 (0.198)	1.169 (0.213)	0.877 (0.153)
Income Level	0.871* (0.059)	0.904 (0.081)	0.948 (0.082)
Education Level	0.836** (0.051)	0.923 (0.067)	0.909 (0.074)
Residential Tenure	0.993 (0.006)	0.987* (0.006)	0.994 (0.006)
Pseudo R2	0.090	0.120	0.025

* $p < 0.05$ ** $p < 0.01$ *** $p < 0.001$ (two-tailed tests)
Coefficients presented are odds ratios. Robust standard errors (adjusted for clustering in thirty-six counties) are in parentheses.

post-CLD periods, the responses were coded such that inactive membership was "1," active membership, such as taking a leader role as a volunteer or as a board or committee member, was "2," and being an officer was "3." We then summed the totals for each participant for each period and compared. If the post-period score was higher, the participant score was "1"; otherwise, it was "0." For the logistic analysis, this seemed like a more direct comparison than any alternative we might have used.

Logistic regression analysis was used to determine effects of each of the following variables on changes in the three dimensions of organizational leadership for CLD participants compared to the non-participants.

Membership. Model 1 in table 3.2 shows that CLD program participation is associated with joining more community organizations over time. The odds of joining more community organizations over time are 2.8 times higher for participants in CLD programs compared to non-participants with similar years of education, residential tenure, age, sex, and income. In addition, the odds of joining more community organizations over time are significantly lower for older people and for people with higher education and income levels.

Involvement. In table 3.2, model 2 shows that, controlling for individual characteristics, participation in a CLD program is associated with higher involvement in community organizations over time. Specifically, individuals who participate in a community leadership program are 2.8 times more likely to increase their involvement in organizations versus those who do not. The results also show that older people and people who have lived in a community longer are less likely to become more involved in community organizations, controlling for all other variables including the program intervention.

Capitals. Model 3 shows that people who participate in CLD programs are more likely to get involved in a greater number of capital asset areas over time net of other variables in the equation. The model shows that individuals who have participated in a community leadership program are 1.5 times more likely, over time, to increase the number of capital asset areas of involvement compared to leaders who do not participate in community leadership programs. Age is again negatively associated with adding capitals in this model.

Results summary. Results from binary logistic regression analysis show that participation in CLD programs—versus non-participation—is associated with significantly higher odds of all three community leadership behaviors: increased organizational membership, increased organizational involvement, and an expanded reach into multiple capital asset areas in the community. Regardless of training, age remains a robust variable. As age increases, the odds of joining more organizations, of becoming more deeply involved, and of reaching out to multiple asset areas decreases, a concern Besser (2009) expresses. Further, leaders with higher education and those with higher incomes are less likely to increase their total number of organizational memberships over time, even when controlling for participation in CLD programs. Taken together, the change in these organizational behaviors establishes opportunities to create and access bridging social capital in the community. As residents become more deeply engaged in a wider array of organizations, the potential for making meaningful social connections across different capital asset areas in the community grows.

Why Does Increased Organizational Involvement Matter?

Community development occurs when people work together to solve problems, purposively expanding the focus of their civic networks beyond limited special interests and toward generalized community interests (Wilkinson 1991). This expansion and elaboration is akin to bridging social capital (Putnam 2000; Flora and Flora 2008). Thus, program interventions that claim to promote community leadership may do well to focus on the potential for this network expansion.

This study supports the notion that participation in CLD programs is associated with increases in community leadership behaviors at the organizational level (Black and Earnest 2009, 2009; Bono et al. 2010; Fredricks 2003; Rohs and Langone 1993; Scheffert 2007). Though other research draws the same connection between program participation and increased organizational engagement in the community, this study makes a more definitive case in that it uses a comparison group design and controls for individual characteristics and group-level variation. Specifically, data from this study show that participation in CLD programs is uniquely associated with joining more community organizations, increasing overall organizational involvement, and getting involved in more diverse capital asset areas in the community. We briefly discuss each of these behaviors next.

From our research, we conclude that people who participate in CLD programs are far more likely to add to their total number of community organization memberships than comparable peers who do not. That is, program participants are more likely to join more community organizations after the program. These findings might reflect the changes across all the program outcomes. Perhaps attitudes and intentions about getting involved in the community that develop during program participation actually come to fruition through organizational behavior. For example, there is a significant positive relationship between gains in the outcome measure of civic engagement and behavioral gains in organizational membership among leadership program participants ($r = 0.18, p < 0.001$). There is also a significant positive relationship between changes in community commitment and behavioral gains in organizational membership ($r = 0.19, p < 0.001$).

Though organizational membership itself is important, practicing leadership in the community often requires deeper engagement within community organizations—being an active member or taking a leadership role. This study shows that participants in CLD programs are much more likely to change their level of involvement across all the organizations they belong to compared to peers in other rural communities who have not participated in such a program. That is, participation in CLD programs is associated with a behavioral trajectory that goes from relatively low activity to high activity to assuming leader roles within community organizations. This trajectory is important in terms of opportunities for bridging social capital, as the more centralized a person becomes in their organization or social network, the more chances they may have to link to other organizations or social networks (Burt 2002). Here again, there may be a connection between community leadership outcomes from CLD participation and community leadership behaviors; there are significant positive relationships between increased organizational involvement and increases in the individual-level outcomes we demonstrated in the previous chapter.

One of the most important contributions this study makes to the literature on CLD programs comes from the analysis of program effects on organizational involvement across multiple capital asset areas in a community. Our research shows that people who participate in CLD programs are more likely to become involved in more capital asset areas across the community over time versus comparable peers in other communities who do not. The CCF recognizes that investment in one capital asset area can be transformed to benefit other capital asset areas (Flora and Flora 2008). Thus, when all capital asset areas are supported, together they can create sustainable communities with healthy ecosystems, vital economies, and social empowerment. No other study of CLD program outcomes of this scope specifically examines participants' behaviors with regard to the expansion of their community capital areas of involvement. Moreover, we likely underestimated the effects for program participation, since respondents could report only three or fewer organizations in which they were involved.

The importance of community leaders' involvement in multiple capital asset areas may be appreciated from the perspective of the "strength of weak ties" phenomenon (Granovetter 1973). According to this idea, open social networks among people who interact relatively infrequently are more likely to introduce their members to new ideas and opportunities compared to closed networks. Further, individuals with many weak ties can exercise influence or act as brokers within their social networks by bridging two networks that are not directly linked—an activity called filling structural holes (Burt 2002). We can link this notion back to the idea of civic structure. That is, the more that people and groups collaborate across institutional boundaries, the stronger and more vital the civic structure. When people engage in the community across multiple asset areas (versus one specialized interest area), the likelihood is greater that they will forge connections among diverse networks to enhance civic structure (Marwell et al. 1988).

Moreover, data from this study show that gains in the number of capitals do not seem to be directly tied to gains in organizational membership overall, since there is not a high correlation between the two outcomes. It is not that leadership program participants join more organizations and therefore become more involved in more capitals. Instead, it seems that they expand their "capitals reach" irrespective of the total number of organizations. For example, a participant might be involved in three human capital organizations before the program and shift their involvement to one human capital organization, one financial capital organization, and one cultural capital organization after the program. In this example, there would be zero change in total memberships but an overall increase in the number of capitals represented. This is the type of behavior that is uniquely associated with CLD program participants (versus non-participants) and that establishes the potential to increase bridging social capital in a community. In support of this notion, data from both the individual level analysis of CLD outcomes and the behavioral studies show significant positive relationship between gains in the number of capitals (behavior) and gains in Community Commitment and Shared Future and Purpose. One interpretation could be that CLD programs' main value is the exposure to a wider array of community needs as well as assets and resources, and a more diverse set of community social networks than a person might otherwise experience on their own.

Taken together, these organizational behaviors represent opportunities to develop bridging social capital in communities and thereby strengthen civic infrastructure (Morton 2003). In the community, people often act with mutual purpose through organizations. Joining more organizations and becoming more involved in them enhances one's social network and adds to the potential for social bridging. Importantly, when those organizational areas of involvement are across multiple capital asset areas in the community, then those bridging opportunities become even more powerful as the potential for linking asset areas is established and social bridges between, possibly, cultural and financial areas or political and natural areas emerge. Residents who have participated in a CLD program enter into these potentials with greater bridging attitudes, as evidenced by the programs' cognitive effects. So by building leader capacity, we set people on a course not only to have improved attitudes about building bridges in the community, but also to actualize bridge-building through their boundary-crossing organizational behaviors.

BEHAVIORAL OUTCOMES AND INDIVIDUAL CHARACTERISTICS

Program effects for all three behavioral outcomes—more organizational membership, greater organizational involvement, and involvement across more capital asset areas—were maintained even after controls for age, sex, education, income, and number of years in the community. Results also showed that, similar to changes in attitudes, older community leaders experienced less gain in organizational leadership behaviors over time. Perhaps older community residents do not perceive as much value in growing their organizational involvement versus younger residents who may be more likely to be motivated by its economic and social benefits. Or, perhaps older individuals were more involved before their program, so their post-program involvement did not show much change (especially since the number of experiences that could be listed was limited to three).

In addition, we found that higher levels of education were negatively related to growth in community organization membership despite program participation. This finding is counter-intuitive and may be partially explained by how we measured membership growth. Descriptive data show that a high percentage of people at the top levels of education (college degree and graduate school) were already involved in three organizations before they participated in a CLD experience. Because of this, they may not have experienced as much change or growth in organizational membership. Clearly, more investigation is warranted to better understand the relationship between education, age, and organizational behaviors at the community level. Indeed, future evaluation tools should be constructed to capture a fuller range of organizational participation in order to avoid a ceiling effect.

THE IMPORTANCE OF BRIDGING SOCIAL CAPITAL FOR CIVIC ENGAGEMENT

Results from our investigation suggest that participation in CLD programs has a beneficial effect on community through the participant's involvement in local organizations. By accepting greater responsibilities in these organizations as leaders and extending their involvement over a broader range of organization types, they expand their reach, expand their impact, and, perhaps, begin to create the sort of networking among organizations that could create important synergistic results for the complex problems local communities face. Traditionally, organizational participation has been considered synonymous with civic engagement. In recent decades, some scholars have warned that the United States is seeing a dangerous decline in local organizational participation, that is to say, low civic engagement. Skocpol (2003) points out that, historically, local organizations such as parent-teacher associations, church groups, and business leagues were training grounds for democratic civic practice. Now that communities are seeing more special interest and advocacy organizations spring up that are managed by professionals (versus volunteers) and non-local in origin, Skocpol warns that the valuable democracy-training aspects of local organizations may be lost, and calls this trend "diminished democracy." Results from our study give hope. Indeed, it appears that the participants in CLD programs in rural communities tend to join more community organizations over time and also get involved in more leadership roles in those organizations over time. Moreover, residents who participate in CLD programs not only become more deeply involved, but also engage across a wider breadth of local organizational types.

In this sense, CLD participants help to build organizational density and diversity, which are some of the structural components of civic infrastructure (Morton 2003). Organizational diversity becomes important when we consider its potential to link disparate networks together. Indeed, this link can be made deliberate in community leadership programming. For example, we found some CLD program coordinators who made their alumni lists available to local volunteer organizations so that they might more effectively recruit new board members for leader positions. Educational programmers would do well to put equal, or more, resources into building bridging social capital. Chaskin et al. (2001) agree, and find that it is possible to strengthen associational networks and interlocking board memberships that, based on the networks formed in CLD programs, interconnect organizations and expand civic capacity through these associational networks. Further, arguably network size contributes to access to more and more diverse resources that can be mobilized for change—with reciprocity implications—thus enhancing the empowerment effects. Making this sort of connection between bridging social capital (our definition of social cohesion) then better connects us to the leadership discussion extant in the literature cited above.

The analysis we present in this chapter suggests a new theoretical lens through which to evaluate programs, namely as opportunities to develop bridging social capital or social cohesion—a social asset seen as a requisite for enhancing civic structure and collaborative civic engagement. In terms of methodological contributions, this research represents a novel way to use the community capitals framework for analysis of data on community organizations and organizational behavior change. Finally, this research provides direction to CLD program administrators and funders, particularly with regard to program design and development. In rural places where social diversity is rising, collaborative, do-it-yourself solutions are often the only answer to community problems. The more abundant and well-supported the social bridges, the greater the likelihood of success.

STUDY QUESTIONS

1. How do community organizations benefit from CLD programs?
2. What are some examples of how CLD contributes to enhancing the seven community capitals (social, human, political, cultural, financial, natural, and built) as they relate to community organizations?
3. Why is bridging social capital important for connecting community organizations to community development initiatives?
4. If membership in more diverse organizations builds and leverages bridging social capital or social cohesiveness, how can a CLD program pay more explicit attention to building an appreciation for this outcome and the skills to make it happen effectively?
5. What attributes of organizations that feature bonding social capital as a primary structural norm could be identified as having links to external interests and assets that might be useful in attracting such organizations to engage in collaborative efforts to benefit themselves as well as the rest of the community?

4.

Community Leadership Development's Effects on Community

The courtroom was bustling after the proceeding; people were crying, loudly protesting, and lamenting the judge's lack of empathy for the plaintiff and her situation. Law enforcement officials were trying to establish some degree of order so the next proceeding could begin. Charles Rios was frustrated. As prosecutor, he had tried to accomplish two things in this proceeding: keep a former husband in jail or otherwise separated from his former wife, and find a safe place for the wife and kids to stay until they could find a place to live where the former husband would be unlikely to find them. But there was no place available in the community to support his second objective and the judge did not find sufficient cause to keep the husband locked up. She did issue a restraining order, for the second time, with a stern warning to the husband to keep his distance from his former family or he would be, if caught, declared in contempt and locked up for a longer period of time.

Later that day, Charles ran into the judge, a long-time friend, as he was leaving the courthouse, and decided to discuss his frustrations: "Hi Verna. Were you as frustrated as I was with this morning's proceedings? I think we have to do something other than what we are now doing to make this town safer for abused families. These abusive husbands make a mockery of our legal system and, more importantly, create very unsafe conditions for spouses and children."

"Yes I was," said Verna. "I regret I could not support your intentions in there to keep the husband in jail. I know there are communities in the state where there are safe houses that could really be useful here. I don't think we're going to change very quickly. The laws did not give me much leeway for putting this guy behind bars for a good long while, and the county does not have much money these days for supporting the development of a decent shelter of some sort. Instead, all we can do is hope someone doesn't get killed and that the hospital will keep treating these folks for any injuries they sustain and not charging them for the service."

Charles shrugged and nodded. He understood the funding limitations faced by the county commissioners, but he had recognized the need for a shelter for abused women and children many years ago when he was on the police force. In fact, one of the reasons he had decided to go to law school was so he could help find better ways to deal with problems like this, yet the legal system had its own limitations. He was convinced someone had to do something to change the situation regardless of the limitations the community faced. Family issues were always complicated, and he knew he could not resolve all of them with the same course of action. He would have to think about what to do.

Later that week, Charles was at the weekly Rotary Club meeting and ran into Debbie Raymond and Bud Roark, who he knew from a leadership class that the Chamber had sponsored a couple years before. He was still frustrated and worried about the domestic abuse problems in the community, and shared his concerns with his two colleagues. Debbie listened thoughtfully and told him that one of her neighbors had also been subjected to this sort of domestic abuse and finally just ran away with her children. "I guess she depends on her parents for financial support as she is unlikely to get anything from him to support the two kids," Debbie said. Bud, who was the former president of the Rotary Club, raised his eyebrows and observed that the club was always looking for new projects to support and in the past had been successful in raising substantial sums of money for projects that would benefit the community. He still had a couple good friends on the club board that he thought would be sympathetic to this kind of proposal, and mentioned "they both just completed the same leadership program we participated in."

"What do we need to do?" said Charles. "Well," said Bud, "let's see if we can find Carlotta and Jim and see what they think about this." Debbie said, "I might know a few other people who might be interested in this sort of project and could be really helpful."

The three of them circulated through the room after the Rotary Club program was over that day and finally cornered Carlotta and Jim. After a lengthy discussion about the need in the community that Charles had witnessed and that Debbie's neighbor was a recent example of, both Carlotta and Jim said they would take a proposal to the club board to support a fundraising effort to build or lease a facility where people subjected to domestic abuse could find safety in the community. Bud indicated he thought they might be able to access some state or federal grant funds for sustaining a staff member or two; he would explore this possibility with the local legislator, who was one of his business associates. Charles indicated he would draft a more detailed plan to outline the facility's needs for space and staffing. He said he would talk with the sheriff to see if he had some flexibility in his staffing to handle security concerns. Charles knew that the most powerful way to gain political and financial support would be to convince others that, without such a facility, the legal system's ability to effectively prosecute offenders and protect women and children was severely restricted. He decided he would find other avenues to deal with the legal stric- tures he and Verna faced in addressing this problem. Maybe Bud's legislative friend would be the one to talk to—but after they got this safe house project underway. That seemed like enough work right now.

Projected to cost about $300,000, the safe house facility project was well underway in just a couple months and the Rotary Club had helped raise almost half the money already. Bud's legislative friend was working with a US senator he knew pretty well from the region to get access to a matching grant program. The grant came through within a few months, just as the large old Victorian home Debbie had found through a real estate agent friend of a friend became avail- able for the same amount, and the Rotary Club purchased it for the safe house. Charles helped the group secure a charter as a non-profit service organization to operate the facility. The sheriff said his staff could provide some limited on-site security and make sure they cruised the neighborhood frequently day and night. All that remained was to find suitable staff and the money to support them. Nadia, a friend of Carlotta's who had been in the chamber's leadership program with her, stepped up late in the process and asked if she could help, as her sister had been through an ugly divorce and been abused several times before deciding a shelter was her only refuge. Charles and Debbie welcomed the extra help as Nadia had excellent contacts through her business with some of the "old money" families in the community. A few months later, Nadia called Debbie to tell her that she had a commitment from two anonymous donors to establish a working endowment that would provide most of the support necessary for staffing. Debbie said, "That's wonderful news. The safe house is almost refurbished and ready for hiring staff. We'll get to work on that right away." In six more months, the rest of the operating budget had been underwritten with a fundraising campaign among the local churches and some regional foundations. Staff had been identified and were ready to go to work. Charles wondered at how everything had seemed to come together so effortlessly, yet he knew everyone involved had spent a lot of time, just as he had, in working toward achieving this end. The chamber's leadership course instructors were right, he thought—getting people together around a common goal, when they had confidence in their leadership abilities and the networks of resources they could identify and use, could really make a difference in the community. I can hardly wait, he thought. There are so many other things we need to do to make our community better for everyone.

Leaders Make a Difference

In this chapter, we examine the effects of community leadership development (CLD) programs on the communities in which participants live. In particular, we investigate what these effects may be and characterize them in a manner that can be easily interpreted as or related to community improvement in some fashion. Improving community residents' well-being is usually called "community development," and we use that term extensively in this chapter. However, we do not assess the effects of CLD in the context of community development theory, as the literature usually fails to connect leadership and community change. So, there is little prior research to guide our endeavor. Nevertheless, we are interested in how the participants, individually and collectively, practice what they feel they have learned and apply new skills they feel they have acquired to improve their communities.

Community change can occur in many ways and many forms. Some of these changes can be termed "development," as the changes increase or enhance residents' well-being. So long as residents consider this state of well-being satisfactory, they will remain in the community, their institutions will continue to function, and the community can be termed "viable." Identifying instances of intentional and purposeful community change that is intended to keep the community viable is one of the data sources we use in this research to address the broader question of whether and how CLD programs affect communities.

Further, we posit that any changes these participants pursue can be more fully understood by using some sort of systematic approach to interpret these actions. We again apply the community capitals framework (CCF) as a way to organize our information and ideas about how community development takes place as the result of CLD participation. Flora, Flora, and Fey (2003) have proposed the

CCF as a way to understand the nature of and process(es) beneath community development. The elements of this framework are described as seven forms of capital existing in communities that can be used individually and in combination to produce local change.[1] While there is a growing literature on the community capitals by many of the proponents of this perspective (Green and Haines 2012), there is little published empirical work that details the interaction of the capitals as community residents may deploy them. One of the questions we seek to answer is whether the CLD experience teaches participants about these capitals and how to mobilize the resources the capitals represent to achieve changes in their communities.

Obviously, community change or development can result from many sources. Often, local agencies or organizations employ professionals trained in community development or community organizing to assist citizens in this process. Much of the actual work may fall upon the shoulders of the professional even as she may strive to promote broad community participation. State and federal agencies may also employ professionals to serve in community consultation roles who take broad proposals to community residents and work to develop a systematic assessment of the desirability and details of the proposal for implementation by the agency. Boyte and Kari (1998) describe the process used by the Highlander Research and Education Center in Tennessee in its citizenship schools to teach citizens how to be community organizers and affect community change in ways that professionals had ignored for many decades. Kirk and Shutte (2004) describe a different sort of process in which action research is used in a consultative process with local community organizations to empower leaders to act on agendas they create through dialogue and connective leadership.

Our data provide a somewhat different perspective, as they show little evidence that these kinds of interventions are common in smaller, rural communities. Residents can and do act without professional assistance or guidance when they feel empowered to become civically engaged and believe they can be effective (see chapter 2 in this volume).

Since the early years of the American democracy, civic engagement has been considered instrumental in community affairs and development (de Tocqueville 2000; Putnam 1993b, 2000). In a vibrant democracy, it is a given that people will be informed about and engaged in a variety of issues and activities that are intended to improve all residents' well-being. As Marquart-Pyatt and Petrzelka (2009) note, there is little in the literature on local-level civic engagement or community politics that guides researchers investigating how this process actually works and what role interventions such as CLD might play. Nevertheless, the literature broadly agrees that civic engagement is key to any progress communities make toward resolving issues (Israel and Beaulieu 1988; Morton 2003). Coupling civic engagement with social cohesion (or forms of bridging social capital), as we do, may increase citizens' capacity to affect community change (O'Brien et al. 1991).

Few other studies even tackle the task of determining community-level effects of leadership or leadership development. Rasmussen and associates (2011) address this deficit in a study of a Minnesota program in one county and find change in social and human capital, especially in the nature of networking among the participants. Ricketts and Ladewig (2008), in a study of two Florida counties, show how important empowered community leaders who displayed trust in others in the community were to the future of community change. Scheffert (2007) surveyed over 200 participants of CLD programs in Minnesota and determined that their participation led to greater involvement in various kinds of community leadership positions (ostensibly in organizations and agencies). Earnest (1995) reports anecdotal evidence showing that participants in a statewide leadership development program became involved in local activities upon their re-engagement in their home communities. These few studies do not constitute very convincing empirical evidence of a direct link between the individual effects of the CLD program from which participants graduated and material community effects.

By comparison, our research demonstrates valid and reliable linkages between the individual effects of CLD programs from a variety of sites and the material effects in communities in which participants reside. More importantly, it shows that links exist between specific individual effects—civic engagement and social cohesion—and community action. As we demonstrated in chapter 3, our analysis provides an understanding of the manner in which CLD programs prepare participants for public work. Should these individuals later choose to become active in civic affairs, it is important to understand the nature of the issues they choose to tackle and the effectiveness of their actions in community leader roles, with special attention to the nature of the resources they mobilize to support their goals. This is our task in the current chapter.

Using the CCF to Measure Community Effect

In this research, we use the CCF from Flora, Flora, and Fey (2003) to sort out the community effects. As mentioned above, CCF represents the diversity of community resources as capitals in a manner similar to that economists use to describe capital assets. However, the CCF extends the notion of capital to include non-financial and non-material forms. Though each of these capital categories is distinct, they have a symbiotic relationship in that leveraging one (or more) form of capital can be instrumental in increasing the stock of another. We do not present the CCF as a theory of community development, although it certainly has implications for theory development. Rather, we use it as a guide to organize information gathered about the nature of collective actions taken, the shared goals, and the process of change followed.

This measurement became a bigger challenge than we expected, because it is often difficult to sort out which capital is actually being measured as so many of them appear to be closely linked operationally. That is not to say this difficulty cannot be managed. For example, in a piece of work on sustainable forestry and community resiliency, there is an extensive set of indicators for the community capitals listed (Magis 2010).[2] This document provided a basic starting point for accomplishing what we set out to do. In other words, this framework provided an initial set of indicators from which we could create an index for each of the community capitals. We incorporated additional items to reflect the writings in the literature (Flora, Flora, and Fey 2003; Flora and Flora 2008). Using additional sources such as this, which often dealt with only one or two of the capitals (e.g., Crowe 2006), we developed indicators for each capital. We used these indicators, usually ten to twelve for each capital, to develop indices to measure the basic concepts associated with the capitals (see appendix B). The information regarding these indices primarily came from key informants in the communities. In most cases, the indicators are either presence or absence data and therefore suitable for confirming from key informants or from secondary data. This approach let us test the original question posed in the research, namely whether or not CLD produces community effects.

However, we determined that this approach was too restrictive, as it required a lengthy, structured instrument that would be difficult to administer with community informants, especially via phone as planned. An alternative was to use the CCF more heuristically and develop a semi-structured interview schedule. We would use the schedule with key informants to elicit a broad picture of the community and derive the events that have shaped it in recent years. We would need to identify specific individuals involved in activities/episodes of community change/development. We would then match these individuals to our list of CLD participants so that we could pair their outcome scores with this involvement. We would gather sufficient information to describe in some depth the events of community change identified so that we could apply the CCF in the analysis. If we interviewed enough key informants, we could construct a reasonably reliable community-level index for the capitals from this data. This sort of approach suggested the possibility of using the "instrument" as more of a checklist and using key informant responses to fill in information in cumulative fashion rather than using it as a questionnaire. This approach, we determined, might produce information we might not otherwise obtain with a more structured and focused instrument, and so we adopted it in the final stage of data collection.

MEASURING COMMUNITY EFFECTS

Members of the research team traveled to each locality and assembled a focus group of about five key informants, identified with program sponsors' assistance. Researchers conducted the focus group interview and identified community projects that had benefitted the community in some fashion in the past two to three years, initially completing the community capitals checklist (appendix B) for each project or activity, gathering initial information about them, and learning the names of individuals involved as project leaders. We arranged focus groups via phone in advance of travel with the local contact person's assistance (with participants, location, food service, etc.) as necessary. Two people were required to conduct each focus group: one concentrated on soliciting information about the local projects and the other took notes and recorded the focus group session.

Following the focus group session, researchers compared the list of project leaders key informants named with the individuals in the survey respondent population. Those projects and activities in which the leaders could be identified as CLD program participants became the focus of further investigation.

We conducted follow-up interviews with the identified individuals by phone (or personal interview if resources permitted) to confirm whether they were involved in any of the local CLD programs, what their roles were in the relevant project(s), and how they linked their learning to their leadership involvement in these projects. We also intended to further our understanding of how the community capitals may have been affected as well. (If these individuals participated in a leadership education program before 2000, we included them as a previous study [Pigg 2001] demonstrates the stability of the individual outcome measures we used.)

We either recorded or took extensive notes during each telephone interview with one of these community project leaders. Once we obtained a relatively complete description of each project or activity, we reviewed items on the CCF checklist and marked those present. This approach confirmed the initial information collected in the focus groups and/or expanded the available information permitting additional items on the checklist to be included in the analysis. In about half the cases, we conducted two interviews; in the remainder, we conducted three or more interviews. From these project-specific checklists we constructed a set of indices for each of the community capitals. These indices were simply additive in nature.

Do CLD Participants Engage in Civic Affairs?

To recall briefly, this research focused on twenty sites in five states where at least one CLD program between 2002 and 2006 had been implemented.[3] We invited a small group of key informants to share with us a list of projects and activities undertaken in their communities during the previous two to three years and to identify individuals who had led these activities. We then matched the names of these individuals with the list of CLD participants the program sponsors provided. Matching individuals were interviewed to gather details of each activity—what took place, who was involved, goals, obstacles, resources, and their overall assessment of their CLD experience and its applicability to these activities.

For these twenty sites during the period of time covered by the research, we identified 212 projects and activities for which former CLD participants had served as leaders, or about eleven examples for each locality. For each of these projects or activities we constructed a set of indices using our CCF checklist. We analyzed the resulting indices to determine whether the items in the indices were likely measuring one concept, but they were all multi-dimensional in nature according to our factor analyses. We determined this to mean that the capitals, as operational constructs, were also multidimensional; this means, for example, that natural capital could take many forms in a single community, and across several communities might encompass even more forms—a complexity we could not effectively capture in our index. The same was likely true for the other capitals; this area clearly deserves more research.

Some of these activities involved recurring events, such as holiday festivals. Some involved the construction of new community facilities or the improvement of existing facilities. Some involved remediation or protection of natural resources for the betterment of the community and others involved projects to improve the health and/or safety of disadvantaged residents or youth. In short, the specific nature of these projects and activities was diverse across the twenty sites we studied. The number of individuals named as associated with these projects and activities included well over 400 former CLD participants.

We also coded each of these projects or activities based on our judgment using the CCF framework. Each activity was assigned as many as four types of capital using the definitions Flora, Flora, and Fey (2003) provide. The first type of capital

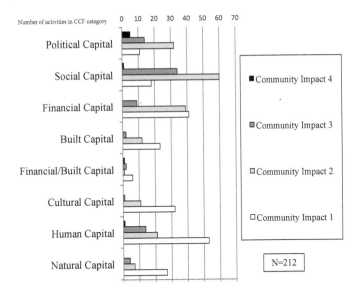

Figure 4.1 Type and frequency of community capitals reflected in community projects and activities.

assigned identified what the respondents indicated as the activity's primary goal or purpose. So, a project to create a shelter for abused children was categorized as a human capital project as it addressed residents' health and safety. A project intended to develop a community center was coded as a built capital project first, even if it required raising financial capital and using some political capital to access these financial resources. Additional CCF categories were assigned based on the respondents' description of the project's activities and implementation. So, as we note above, if the shelter project required raising money to purchase or build a facility, the category for financial capital was assigned to the project as a secondary capital represented. If the shelter project required some sort of agency support or local government approval, the category for political capital was also assigned. Finally, if the respondents described the process as involving people from other community sectors or counterparts from the CLD program, the category of social capital was assigned. Likewise, if a project involved a special holiday celebration that was designed to promote community solidarity and attract tourism as well as emphasize the community's cultural heritage, the project would likely have been assigned a first category of cultural capital, a second category of social capital, and a third category of financial capital, with no fourth

Table 4.1

Mean values of community capital for community projects, by type of primary capital represented

	SOCAP-SUM	POLCAP-SUM	HUCAP-SUM	CUL-CAPSUM	FINCAP-SUM	BILT-CAPSUM	NATCAP-SUM
HUCAP Projects	1.5472	1.6226	3.1887	.377	1.0189	.3019	.0943
FINCAP Projects	1.4634	.8049	1.4878	.4390	1.6829	.2683	.0732
NATCAP Projects	2.4444	3.0741	1.8519	1.4074	.8148	.6667	3.3333
CULCAP Projects	2.2813	1.1563	1.2500	3.5938	.7813	.5000	.7813

category unless—and this often occurred—local government approvals were necessary; then the fourth category of political capital was assigned.

As figure 4.1 shows, for all cases we studied, human capital projects were implemented most frequently, followed by financial capital and cultural capital projects. Especially as it deals with the first two of these capital categories, the frequency of their appearance should be of little surprise given the needs often identified in small, rural communities for retaining young people and skilled workforces and for finding the necessary financial resources to support efforts to meet community needs. As for the frequency with which cultural capital appears, recall that many rural communities use their cultural heritage as the basis for tourism development efforts and identity preservation. The second most frequently mentioned type of community capital employed in these projects and activities was social capital, followed by financial capital and political capital. Clearly, to get things done in their communities, CLD participants drew heavily on their networks of like-minded citizens and had to raise funds and find political support for their efforts in order to achieve their goals. While this sort of interpretation is quite simplistic, it does give us a sense of the interrelatedness of the community capitals in these twenty places.[4]

We entered the completed checklists into the database and used summative indices to further measure the nature and amount of each capital used in each project or activity. As table 4.1 shows, if a project or activity was considered primarily focused on a human capital outcome, the score on the human capital

Table 4.2

Logistic regression analysis of community projects classified by CCF (odds ratio estimates)

CCF Index	Community Activities and Projects						
	Natural Capital	Human Capital	Cultural Capital	Built Capital	Financial Capital	Social Capital	Political Capital
Natural Capital	17.236***	0.612**	0.415***				0.700*
Human Capital		2.906***	0.394***	0.248*	0.481***		
Cultural Capital	0.494**	0.396***	5.996***		0.600*	0.650***	
Built Capital					7.733***		0.525**
Financial Capital			0.369**			4.787***	
Social Capital	0.350***		1.652**				3.363***
Political Capital							0.741**
Percent Concordant	97.7	86.8	93.0	69.0	90.1	82.2	82.7

Note: Levels of significance are represented as follows: *** = significance greater than 0.0001; ** = significance greater than 0.001; and * = significance greater than 0.01.

index used in the research was higher than for any other index. However, it is important to note the second and third highest index scores for each type of project listed; these were often social, human, and/or political capital. This result again demonstrates the community capitals' interrelatedness.

As we note above, the research team collected information on recent community projects and activities from key informants in focus group interviews and follow-up interviews with leaders involved with each project or activity. We coded these projects according to the community capitals represented (by interviewees) in each project. We tried to capture each project's primary capital and as many as three additional capitals that may have been involved in its success. For table 4.2, we considered each of the four possible classifications of the community capitals represented such that, if one of the impacts was mentioned among the four, the score for that capital was "1," and if it was not mentioned, the score for that capital was "0." We then performed logistic regression for each capital as the dependent variable, as this is the most appropriate form of analysis when the dependent variable is dichotomous.

The independent variables we used in the regression represent the scores on the particular indicators used for each of the community capitals from the CCF checklist devised for this research. We summed the number of indicators present according to the interviewees for all the CCF capitals.[5] In other words, we examine the relationship between our classification of each project or event against the individual project scores on each of the CCF indices as recorded from the interviews. This provides yet another test of the relationship between the two measures.

The results in table 4.2 represent the odds ratio estimates for each of the community capitals represented in the various projects and activities and per-cent concordant measure for each index score from the SAS routine for logistic regression. Concordance is defined as "a pair of observations with different observed responses is said to be concordant if the observation with the lower ordered response value (human capital = 0 or "not human capital") has a lower predicted mean score than the observation with the higher ordered response value (human capital = 1 or "human capital")."[6] The concordance measure indicates the percentage of cases in which the independent variables accurately predicted the result represented by the dichotomous dependent variable.

As this table indicates, the odds of a project being classified as addressing natural capital in some fashion grew by a factor of seventeen through the use of the natural capital index in the research. The same analysis shows that the odds of a project being classified as addressing natural capital fell by a factor of 0.49 through the inclusion of the cultural capital index score and by a factor of 0.35 through the inclusion of the social capital index score. Another way to interpret this result is that the natural capital index validates the project's classification as having a natural capital component with cultural capital and social capital also involved, although in a different fashion, or that the significant effects of cul-tural capital and social capital mean that the lower the value in these indexes, the lower the odds that a project will be classified as natural capital, holding the natural capital index constant (because the odds are less than one). Almost 98 percent of all the projects are consistent with this result.

Similarly, the odds of a project being classified as having a human capital component rise by a factor of 2.90 by the human capital index score, fall by 0.6 when including the natural capital index, and fall by 0.40 when including the cultural capital index score. About 87 percent of the projects are consistent with this result.

The odds of projects being classified as having a cultural capital component rise by a factor of nearly six when considering the score on the cultural capital index. The odds of a project being so classified also rise by the social capital index score in these cases by a factor of 1.65. The odds of being classified as a cultural capital project fall by the natural capital, human capital, and financial capital indices (0.42, 0.39, and 0.37 respectively).

The results shown for the remaining community capital designations of projects are more complicated. For example, the odds of a project being classified as having a built capital component fall about 0.25 by the human capital index score. None of the other indices played a significant part in this logistic regression analysis, and only about 69 percent of the analyses are consistent with this result. It is possible that, since there are so few projects/activities designated as having a built capital component, this result does not tell us very much about the relationship. The result for the financial capital classification of projects also omits the financial capital index as having any significant effect. Instead, the built capital index increases the odds of being classified as having a financial capital component by 7.73, while the human capital index decreases the odds of being so classified by nearly 0.50 and the cultural capital index decreases the odds by 0.60. In other words, knowing the score on the built capital index increases the odds of a project being classified as having a financial capital component, and this relationship makes sense because most building projects would require finding substantial financial capital. This analysis shows a 90 percent concordance rate.

The result for social capital as a component of a community project or activity is also complex. The odds of a project being classified as having social capital involved are increased by the financial capital index (over 4.70) and reduced by the cultural capital index (by 0.65). In other words, to know whether a project or activity would be classified as a social capital project, it is better to examine the score on the financial capital index than to look at the actual score on the social capital index. Another way to see this result, assuming the measurement was good, is that people involved in activities in a small town see that financial capital can be a substitute for social capital; it may be easier to raise the funds necessary to hire the work done than to frequently need to call in favors and ask for volunteers. The odds of a project being classified as having a political capital component are increased by the social capital index (by over 3.30) but reduced by the natural capital, built capital, and political capital indices (0.70, 0.52, and 0.74 respectively). This result may reflect the likely close relationship between social and political capital (when viewed as the attribute of networks).

In summary, the indicators we used to measure the degree of natural, human, and cultural capital appear to be discriminating as intended, while those for the other capitals are not. There may be some problem with the indicators used to separately identify built and financial capital, and indeed some of the literature on community capitals does not separate these categories. In addition, the indicators we used in the indices for social and political capital appear to be off target, although there is some evidence in the literature (Woolcock and Narayan 2000; Putnam 1993a) of very close links between social and political capital. The fact that interviewees' discussions of the various community projects often included social and political capital indicates that these components are generally recognized as present and separable conceptually. Another element this analysis shows is the dynamic nature of the relationship among the community capitals. Emery and Flora (2006) and Stofferahn (2012) note this sort of relationship in their characterization of the capitals' "spiraling up." While we may not agree with the specific imagery Emery and Flora or Stofferahn use, this analysis appears to demonstrate that different community capitals are often involved in community projects in different ways. Logically, this seems appropriate as the status of any of the community capitals at any given time differ within and among communities. How they may be employed may also differ according to local conditions and the nature of the collective actions and interactions among the project leaders. Sturtevant (2006), Gittell and Vidal (1998), Putnam and Feldstein (2003), and Putnam (1993b) all demonstrate how social capital supports and is enhanced by collective civic action. Similar demonstrations could likely be developed for the other community capitals with sufficient research such as that by Gasteyer and Araj (2009). These dynamics are important elements of civic engagement and collective action for improving community well-being.

Community Effects Model

Proceeding with the analysis to identify community outcomes of CLD program participation produced a structured equation (path) model, as figure 4.2 shows. This model is similar in its elements to figure 2.2, but it omits demographic variables and uses the community mean scores on cognitive leadership indices. In addition, we used the CCF index scores for the dependent variables. Figure 4.2 shows only the results for only those relationships that are statistically significant at the 0.01 level or above.

As shown, the model relates the individual-level outcomes (converted to community mean scores for each of the twenty communities remaining in the analysis) to the CCF index scores to determine whether or not there is a community

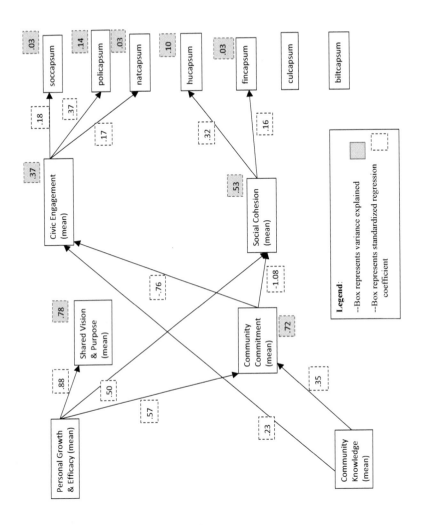

Figure 4.2. Structural Equation Model of Selected Community Effects of CLD Programs.

effect. This structured equation model is basically a set of regression models, produced simultaneously, that take into account the effects of each of the variables on each other as well as the dependent variable(s).

Likely because of the way in which the independent variables have been modified to produce a community-level analysis, the relationships this model shows differ somewhat from those in the previous model of individual-level effects of the educational intervention (CLD program). For example, the relationships between Personal Growth and Efficacy (now a community mean) and Shared Future and Purpose (0.88), and Personal Growth and Efficacy and Community Commitment (0.57) have both increased. The effect of Community Knowledge on Community Commitment has also increased (0.35). Shared Future and Purpose still has no direct effect on either Civic Engagement or Social Cohesion; its effect is only apparent through its relationship with Community Commitment, as in the previous model. Further, the relationship between Personal Growth and Efficacy and Civic Engagement has disappeared in this model, and the relationship of Personal Growth and Efficacy with Social Cohesion has shrunk (0.61 to 0.50). The relationship between Community Knowledge and Civic Engagement has shrunk (0.45 to 0.23), and its relationship with Social Cohesion has disappeared. Again, these reductions may be the effect of the reduced variation resulting from the use of the mean scores to represent community level indicators rather than individual level scores (see chapter 2).

More importantly, the overall variation explained by the model fell for Civic Engagement (0.80 to 0.37) and for Social Cohesion (0.60 to 0.53). Once again, the reduced variance resulting in this model may be an artifact of our transforming the values to represent the community means, thus attenuating the overall variation.[7] Finally, even though the amount of variation explained in the model for the dependent variables—the CCF index scores (summative)—is statistically significant, these values are rather small. Further, the relationships show some additional evidence of differences among the community capitals, with Civic Engagement affecting Social, Political and Natural Capital, and Social Cohesion affecting Human and Financial Capital. Cultural and Built Capital show no relationship with the individual level variables. The RMSEA (root mean square error of approximation) for this model is 0.122, which indicates the fit of the model is not very good despite its statistical significance.

This problem of fit might be the result of the sign of the coefficient for the relationship between Community Commitment and both Civic Engagement and Social Cohesion being negative in this model. In other words, the data analysis in the model indicates that an increase in the Community Commitment index is associated with a decrease in both Civic Engagement (−0.76) and Social Cohesion (−1.08). We do not have an explanation for this change in the sign of the coefficients at this point. The Community Commitment index clearly has a mollifying influence since both the Community Knowledge and Personal Growth and Efficacy have direct positive effects on Civic Engagement (Community Knowledge only) and Social Cohesion (Personal Growth and Efficacy only). However, this is conjecture on our part at present.

We see even more clearly the lack of effect of participant characteristics in the community level model. None of the demographic attributes remained in this model. We feel this speaks well of community residents' opportunity to assume roles as leaders in public work and to engage in leadership relationships without regard for their status in the community. Since we do not measure the effect of contextual factors, this conclusion should be taken with care as many factors enter into an individual's decision to engage in community affairs (Grint 2005).

More importantly, this analysis demonstrates that it is possible to link CLD participation's individual effects to community effects as changes in the levels of community capitals as measured indicate. While the amount of change explained is small in this study, the model is statistically significant and the size of the coefficients of change may be partially explained by the small number of cases we deal with for each of the capitals and communities. Certainly, further research would be helpful.

It is interesting to speculate about the different and independent effects of civic engagement and social cohesion with regard to the community capitals. The interaction effects of the individual level effects clearly make a difference in how the capitals relate to each other in the multivariate case. It is still somewhat of a mystery why the social capital index we used would be explained by Civic Engagement rather than by Social Cohesion, since the index is composed of many bridging elements. However, the index is also composed of quite a few "organizational participation" items (following Putnam 1993b, 2000), which may explain part of this differential effect, as may the fact that social cohesion is an index made up of individual level knowledge and behaviors while the social capital index is composed of community level measures.

For community developers, it is likely a surprise that the Shared Future and Purpose indicator does not affect the community capitals. Most CLD programs would likely spend some time dealing with this topic, at least trying to convince participants of its importance to the community's future. However, if that is all that a program addresses due to limitations on time and resources, this may explain the lack of community effect. Perhaps such programs should expend additional efforts to teach participants how to actually work with other community residents to develop a shared vision and, from that vision, develop an action plan for community improvement. This kind of activity requires significant engagement from community residents and demands CLD program sponsors try to include it in their curricula designs. However, there is a large and growing resource base that can be used for this purpose so improvements in this area can be made with a bit of research on the part of sponsors (Gershon 2009; Walzer 1996).

Summary of Community Effects Analysis

Our initial supposition that CLD programs have a concrete, positive effect on the community that sponsors them has been demonstrated as valid. The data collected in this project show that CLD participants take on and complete a variety of projects and activities they feel will benefit the material lives in their community. They employ a variety of community resources to achieve their goals. These activities appear to be self-organizing, in that individuals who feel empowered as the result of their CLD experience are brought together through interactions that focus on a shared purpose or objective without any apparent intervention, encouragement, or approval by formal authorities in the local community.[8] These newly empowered citizens may take on problems that range from conserving natural resources and green spaces for environmental reasons or leisure activities to raising money to support health objectives to creating spaces in which the arts can flourish to organizing community events that may attract tourists and supplement the local economy and more. While these community activists undoubtedly faced obstacles and other activities organized to preserve the status quo, these sorts of obstacles were not mentioned in any of our key informant interviews. The fact that our selection process included what we had defined as high and low viability communities (based on quantitative, time series data) may indicate that such external classifications are inaccurate and unwarranted. What matters is how local people feel about themselves and their neighbors, how they assess their personal and collective leadership efficacy, and their commitment to the place they live. Add a bit of knowledge about how to get things done in their community and some network connections, and you have the basis for forms of public work that can benefit all community residents.

We attempted to understand the nature of the changes these CLD participants achieved using the CCF by examining the relationships among the seven capitals

others identified and posited as reflecting a way to analyze community development efforts from a structural perspective (Emery and Flora 2006). Our research
supports this basic proposition. Community leaders exhibit an understanding of
the variety of resources present in the community and how to mobilize and deploy
those resources (in the form of capitals) to produce desired change. Interesting is
the fact that few of the CLD curricula from the sites selected actually contained
any discussion of the CCF or the ideas about how to produce changes in the
community based on the CCF rationale.[9] Rather, community leaders appear to
generally recognize and broadly understand the ideas related to this framework.
What matters most is their willingness to engage in civic affairs and whether
they feel they can be successful in what they want to achieve. Independent of
this willingness is their sense of social cohesion existing in the community and
their understanding of the benefits of cohesiveness in situations where there are
increasing ways to achieve social, political, and economic change. This willingness to interact to achieve some sort of change provides the basis for action. Our
research demonstrates that the CCF elements are quite useful for understanding
the nature and scope of community development efforts. It demonstrates that
most community development activities deployed multiple capitals that appear
to interact in mutually beneficial ways. The term "leveraging" describes how the
deployment of one capital appears to influence the deployment of another.

We have an additional caveat related to the research results presented here.
We have noted that the structural model in figure 4.2 uses community-level
indicators that have limited variation, which probably limits the ability of the
statistical methods used to produce more robust results. The amount of variation in the dependent variables explained by the individual outcomes that
were converted to community indicators in the form of mean scores is considerably reduced. In addition, the amount of variation explained in the community capital indices themselves was also very small, which may be an artifact of
how we measured these factors. While our approach may be justifiable, there
are undoubtedly different ways to approach this task that might produce more
robust results. The fact that the model in figure 4.2 is statistically significant
suggests that this research is on the right track and future efforts may be able to
improve the measurements used and produce a more robust model.

On a concluding note, we wish to question whether the purposes of CLD
programs truly align with their outcomes. If, at the individual level, the primary
effects are increased knowledge, capacity for civic engagement, and appreciation
for social cohesion, shouldn't the desired outcome reflect something more akin
to enhanced civic infrastructure (Morton 2003; Marquart-Pyatt and Petrzelka

2009; Mathews 1999) rather than community development? Such an outcome would lead to greater participation in decision-making, public officials' greater appreciation for local citizens' ideas and contributions, less dependence on outside experts, more open and inclusive dialogue about the complex problems facing the community, and greater involvement in governance overall (Boyte and Kari 1998). Is it not possible that such an outcome might itself produce community development outcomes, including improvements in local education and health care systems, economic well-being, infrastructure, and so on? Too many times, decisions about these things are contested locally as different interest groups battle over priorities. Losing once too often leads to apathy and non-participation (Mills 2005; Hartley and Benington 2011).

If development *of* the community were the real intended outcome, it would seem reasonable to conclude that something different than numerous unrelated, idiosyncratic projects would be the outcome of CLD programs' efforts (Wilkinson 1991). This is, in fact, what we found in our identification of projects and activities in which participants in CLD programs engaged following their learning experience. Small groups of these participants, each with their own vision in regards to what would benefit the community, recruited like-minded people—some from prior CLD classes—and proceeded to plan and execute projects that they felt would be helpful. We are not critical of this activity, as many of these projects were likely of substantial benefit to their communities. However, these are typically one-off projects that occur in the community but do not necessarily contribute to building a stronger community overall—in Wilkinson's (1991) terms, they do not contribute to building the community field. This may be explained by the lack of effect of the Shared Future and Purpose indicator in figure 4.2. A more explicit focus on "civic leadership development" (Azzam and Riggio 2003) and the goal of building a stronger civic infrastructure might help overcome this tendency toward isolated and uncoordinated community projects that provide some benefit but do not create stronger a community in the long term.

STUDY QUESTIONS

1. How are community development initiatives promoted and supported in smaller rural communities compared to larger communities?
2. Discuss the importance of trust, networking, social capital, and human capital for facilitating civic engagement and building social cohesion. If these are important elements for leadership, how does a CLD produce/ affect change in these elements?

3. Why are human capital, financial capital, and cultural capital frequently referenced as primary community capitals for rural community development projects and activities?

4. How could CLD programs be better focused to build civic infrastructure?

5.

Participant Diversity, Curriculum Design, and Community Effects

Joyce Sanders ran into her longtime friend Britney Koslowski for the first time in twelve years at their high school reunion. They decided to have lunch the following day before departing for their homes, which were far away from each other. During lunch, Britney introduced Joyce to her husband Dan, who had accompanied Britney to her high school reunion but did not attend the event itself. Dan and Britney had met at a local community leadership forum where they had both spoken fervently in support of a proposed ballot levy to finance the construction of a community swimming pool. After the meeting, they introduced themselves and later shared their experiences of community leadership development (CLD) programs they had participated in at different locations and sponsored by different agencies. Subsequently, they became friends, got engaged, and married.

After lunch, Britney and Joyce continued to reminisce about the past. They recalled the good times they had together at their high school cheerleading practices and football games. Joyce told Britney about her recent move to Wellsville in Morgan County and the many challenges facing the community. A coworker in her local government department had invited her several times to community meetings, but she never attended because she was new to the community and thought she would be unable to contribute. She also felt she didn't know the community well enough to know its movers and shakers and didn't have the skills to speak in public.

Dan, who until then had been quietly bored by Joyce and Britney's high school stories, suddenly joined the conversation. Dan is a small business entrepreneur who owns an antique store in the downtown area where he and Britney live. Dan told Joyce that she should consider participating in a CLD program, which could be organized by the local chamber of commerce, extension, or another entity such as a university or not-for-profit organization. He noted that Britney had completed an extension-sponsored CLD program and he had completed a chamber-of-commerce-sponsored one. Since the end of their respective programs, they had both attended and engaged in community meetings, and had been involved in organizing and implementing local projects that had gone a long way toward improving community well-being. These wonderful experiences helped them become local celebrities, and they were proud of it!

Dan also told Joyce that leadership development programs could help to develop her leadership skills and knowledge, thereby empowering her to support her community. For instance, Dan mentioned that she would be able to learn about the community's strengths, weaknesses, opportunities, and threats, and about how to use that information to help bring about meaningful change. He added that leadership development programs could help her become a successful candidate for local office: "You may be able to run for local office and win if you are involved in community issues. The topics they teach are very elementary and easy to follow. You will also get to experience tours and visits to important community sites and businesses. You'll love it. These topics will help build your leadership skills, including public speaking."

Britney talked about how proud she was of her leadership roles. Her extension-sponsored leadership development program had been a good fit and matched her interests in building social networks in the community and working to improve the well-being of the less fortunate. She has since become known for her work in those areas. She said that Joyce had the potential to do the same in Wellsville if she participated in a CLD program: "Look, I got involved in building a five-mile bike trail for our city, a fundraising program to support the school library, and an expansion of the local food pantry," Dan offered that he helped to raise funds for the renovation of the museum and historical buildings in the community, and for a new dog park. He also mentioned that, as a businessman and entrepreneur, his participation in the chamber-of-commerce-sponsored program really helped him strengthen the fundraising skills needed for his involvement in capital-intensive community improvement projects. Joyce was convinced.

The Importance of Program Design

In this chapter, we take a critical look at the content and design of these leadership programs. In chapter 2, we demonstrated that CLD programs are linked to increased self-efficacy and civic engagement by individual participants. In chapters 3 and 4, we demonstrated that CLD programs overall have also created community level benefits in terms of greater engagement in community activities and engagement by participants in different kinds of organizations. In this chapter, we tease apart the mechanisms of this process by investigating two key aspects of the CLD program process related to how the programs themselves are organized: the demographics of the participants in the CLD programs we analyzed, and the content of the programs themselves.

We do this through two phases of analysis. First, we investigate who participates, specifically looking at the relationship between the types of participants and the sponsoring organizations. Second, we analyze the content and topics used to develop community leaders related to the six leadership outcome variables measured at the individual level in chapter 2: Personal Growth and Efficacy, Community Commitment, Shared Future and Purpose, Community Knowledge, Civic Engagement, and Social Cohesion. The relationships between the content and CLD program outcomes provide convincing evidence that CLD programs build citizen leaders' capacities to improve rural community quality of life.

In explaining why there has been a growth in CLD programs, Fear and his colleagues (1985) note that CLD programs help to guarantee an adequate supply of effective leaders who are vital to the success of community development activities because they provide the basis for improving the well-being of people in rural communities. In building on this analysis, others focus on these programs' role in increasing the diversity of those prepared to take on community leadership roles as part of the goal of stimulating social change and improving rural people's quality of life (Summers 1986; Williams and Wade 2002; Kirk and Shutte 2004). Wituk and associates (2005) argue that if the pool of people who are involved in leadership is to increase, then leadership programming must aim to train a more diverse set of people who can take on leadership roles.

There is some evidence that is happening already. Langone (1994) reports that CLD programs have expanded the pool of emerging leaders who are increasingly involved in local issues. Allen and Lachapelle (2012) used a comparative case study approach to document the role CLD programs in community action to alleviate poverty. Participants' diversity in ethnicity, gender, employment, educational background as well as other factors was a key component of the programs.

Still, few studies document the demographic makeup of CLD programs as related to sponsorship. Some concerns have been raised that leadership programming still caters too much to the categories of people who have traditionally occupied leadership positions (Vandenberg et al. 1988). Below, we discuss the differences in CLD programs by sponsoring organization.

Program design is a topic that includes such elements of how participants are selected from the community population, how the program (intervention via education elements) is assembled and implemented, and how the intervention functions cognitively and behaviorally to produce the outcomes intended to benefit individuals and the community. Over and above our analysis of the effects of these elements of program design is our observation that the designs in place today do not differ much from those Fear and associates analyzed in the 1980s, which—given what we have learned over this period about improving educational interventions and the new ideas that are being implemented in leadership development efforts in other contexts—represents a remarkable stagnation in efforts that might improve the outcomes and the overall effectiveness of these programs.

EXTENSION AND OTHER LEADERSHIP PROGRAMS

Dating back to the 1970s and 1980s, studies identified the role of CLD programs in improving community capacity for collaboration and accessing information. For instance, in a summary of findings from assessments of extension leadership development programs, Fear and associates (1987) argue that extension-sponsored programs could significantly improve civic engagement and community capacity through (a) engaging a diverse set of stakeholders as participants; and (b) education and practice not only in skills, but also in relationship-building and joint project development. These scholars, however, criticize some of the early CLD programs for serving upper middle class rural residents. They argue that the programs were not diverse enough to solve pressing long-term problems in rural communities, but also likely trained those who were most likely to go elsewhere during economic downturns.

Leadership programs are sponsored by multiple types of organizations with different stated missions—specifically the chamber of commerce, state university extension, foundations/non-profits, and others, including non-land grant educational institutions (e.g., community colleges). Studies have looked at the impact of each of these sponsors individually on community leadership programs, but have not looked at comparative effects. Some of these studies pose concerns about lack of diversity. For instance, one notes that chamber of commerce programs were more likely than other types of programs to include upper middle class residents—specifically those associated with the economic sector (Fear et al. 1987).

THE SPONSORING ORGANIZATION'S ROLE IN PROGRAM DESIGN AND IMPLEMENTATION

There are surprisingly few systematic studies on the role of sponsoring organizations in determining the possible benefits of CLD programs (Williams and Wade 2002). Further, some community development literature highlights tension over changing leadership structure (Dillon 2012), and the tendency of community development initiatives to reproduce cultural practices and existing leadership structures in small towns (Zacharakis and Flora 2005). Other literature expresses concerns that business-led leadership efforts that result in new community brands or similar outcomes may have insufficient buy-in by local residents to lead to either positive economic impacts or broader positive community change (Swinney et al. 2012).

Below, we ask whether different sponsors of leadership programs may lead to different participant demographics. We also examine whether the content of CLD programs affects the outcomes for the individual participants and the community.

Data Sources

We use three data sets for the analyses we report in this chapter. For the first level of analysis (CLD programs' role in improving the diversity of participants), we simply disaggregated the data from the online survey of participants by program type and used a difference-of-means test to examine the extent to which different program sponsors produced different participant diversity profiles. We then used a second data set to analyze the structure and content of these programs. We obtained the data from phone interviews with the leadership program coordinators and program websites from our initial study group, and collected them in only five states—Minnesota, Illinois, Missouri, Ohio, and West Virginia—due to difficulties in operationalizing our procedures in South Carolina. We gathered the third data set through focus group and phone interviews involving program graduates and persons knowledgeable about the type of projects and activities that leadership-program graduates participated in and/or organized in their respective communities, such as program organizers (as described in chapter 4).

To obtain data on the CLD programs' content and design, we conducted

Table 5.1

Significance levels for differences among attendees

		Sum of Squares	df	Mean Square	F	Sig.
Gender	Between Groups	0.881	4	0.220	0.972	0.423
	Within Groups	103.827	458	0.227		
	Total	104.708	462			
Age	Between Groups	1921.555	4	480.389	4.562	0.001
	Within Groups	46435.676	441	105.296		
	Total	48357.231	445			
Employment Status	Between Groups	5.014	4	1.254	2.529	0.040
	Within Groups	226.538	457	0.496		
	Total	231.552	461			
Education Level	Between Groups	6.219	4	1.555	1.052	0.380
	Within Groups	677.000	458	1.478		
	Total	683.218	462			
Income	Between Groups	13.038	4	3.260	2.265	0.061
	Within Groups	592.775	412	1.439		
	Total	605.813	416			
Years Living in Community	Between Groups	5328.737	4	1332.184	5.245	0.000
	Within Groups	116068.084	457	253.978		
	Total	121396.821	461			
Voting	Between Groups	0.929	4	0.232	2.296	0.058
	Within Groups	46.051	455	0.101		
	Total	46.980	459			

phone interviews with twenty community leadership program coordinators about their leadership program design, including structure and content. We asked them about the organization of the programs, the number of sessions, and the duration/length of the sessions. We coded the length of sessions in contact hours by topical content. We also asked them about the nature of the content and sponsorship organizations, and the intended audience. We identified the content using a typology described in previous studies, discussed below. We also collected supplemental data about content and design from the websites of these leadership development programs, where available.

Determining the Effects on Participants

The participants in this study were graduates of CLD programs from twenty rural communities in the five states listed above. They were citizens who lived and worked in the rural communities where the CLD program operated. Background information variables for the analysis included age, gender, education, and income.[1] For descriptive purposes, we also collected information on marital status, employment status, and years living in the community. For the first part of our analysis, we looked at the mean scores for the attributes listed above (age, gender, etc.), and grouped respondents according to the sponsors of the program with which they were affiliated. We ran a statistical difference of means or analysis of variance (ANOVA) test to see if there were statistically significant average differences in the attributes among those who participated in different leadership programs. Figure 5.1 demonstrates the findings for those attributes for which there was a significant difference (in the average age, income, employment, and years living in the community) based on who sponsored the program. The sponsor is listed on the x-axis across the bottom of the charts within the figure. The scale of measurement for each attribute is listed on the y-axis. These scales of measurement change based on what is being measured. For instance, for "age" and "years living in the community," the numbers on the y-axis represent the actual average ages and years in the community of program participants (from forty-three to forty-nine years, and twenty to thirty years, respectively). Obviously, a program where the average duration in the community is twenty years implies that a number of participants had been in the community for substantially less time as well as more time. The survey asked that respondents check a category to indicate employment (where 1 was fully employed and 5 was unemployed). Likewise, they selected a category to indicate annual income (where 1 was <$20,000 per year and 7 was >$100,000 per year). These are reflected on the y-axis of the charts for employment and income.

Two community level variables—community viability and Appalachian residence—were added to the analysis models. This was to determine whether there would be fixed effects on participants' ability to develop leadership skills and knowledge and improve their leadership outcomes in communities. Six out of the twenty counties in the study represent Appalachian communities—Monongalia, Marion, Monroe, and Summers counties in West Virginia, and Highland and Holmes counties in Ohio. We measured community viability by community viability index scores ranging from 1.742 (highest) to 0.968 (lowest), computed as ratios of population change and income change (local versus statewide rates) over the decade from 1990 to 2000 and across the types of study sites (see Higgins and McCorkle 2006).

SPONSORSHIP AND ATTENDEES

Using existing stereotypes, we assumed the following:

- The chamber-of-commerce-sponsored programs would be most likely to have participants who were male, younger (new business managers being groomed for leadership), fully employed, highly educated, newer to the community, and more likely to vote. In sum, the stereotypical assumption would be that chamber-of-commerce-sponsored programs would be populated by the rising business elite (mostly male in rural areas) of the community.
- Extension programs would be more interested in increasing diversity, and thus would have more women who were more likely slightly older, less than fully employed, less educated, longer-term residents, and less likely to vote.
- Extension-chamber-partnership programs would include more non-elite participants, but would otherwise maintain many of the same qualities as chamber programs.
- The private-foundation-sponsored programs, and those with other sponsors often leadership programs dedicated to poverty alleviation, would include more women who were on average older, less likely to be fully employed, longer-term community residents, and less likely to vote. These programs often targeted those who did not represent the "usual suspects."

The findings from this research did, in fact, support some of these assumptions. As table 5.1 demonstrates, there were no significant differences in gender and educational attainment. All leadership programs had more female than male participants. This should not be surprising. Since CLD programs aim

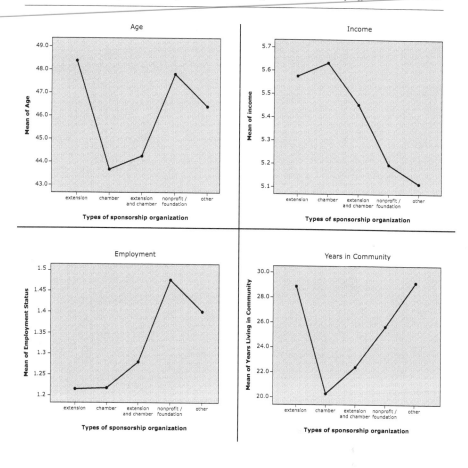

Figure 5.1. Sponsors of CLD Programs Recruit Different Participants.

to empower non-positional leaders, all of the leadership programs, regardless of sponsor, would have been likely to recruit women as participants. Women are increasingly important actors in economic and other areas of public life. According to the US Economic Statistics Administration, women own just over 30 percent of all firms in the United States, and the percentage is higher for small firms. Further, women often play important roles as non-positional community leaders, especially in activities to provide services in the community.

Likewise, in small communities, high educational attainment is less important for taking on leadership positions then it might be in an urban context—though even in urban contexts, non-positional leaders are often not highly educated professionals. In the rural context, leaders may be farmers or other people who work with their hands, rather than doctors or lawyers (Flora and Flora 2008).

As figure 5.1 demonstrates, we see sponsorship differences in age, income, employment status, and time lived in the community. As expected, participants' average age is lowest in the chamber programs and second lowest in the chamber-extension partnerships. We expected this, as chamber programs are frequently designed to provide skills and create networks for young managers on the executive track. Since this was not a goal in programs with other sponsors, it is not surprising that the other programs' participants were on average older.

It is somewhat surprising that there was a significant difference in employment status. While we expected that chamber-of-commerce-sponsored programs would have a high proportion of participants who were fully employed, our data indicated this was true of extension-sponsored programs as well (see figure 5.1). Extension-chamber partnerships had a higher percentage of participants who were employed less than full time. For extension-sponsored programs, this may have been due to county extension offices' dependence on county government and other local elites to fund both the leadership initiative and the county extension office. The programs non-profits, foundations, and other organizations sponsored indeed included a higher percentage of people who were part-time employed or unemployed.

In keeping with the pattern for employment, chamber-sponsored programs had the highest average income, followed by extension-sponsored programs. Interestingly, the average income was lower in leadership development programs sponsored by the extension-chamber partnership in comparison with extension-sponsored or chamber-sponsored programs alone. The other programs sponsored by non-profits, foundations, and a community college had much lower average income—again not surprising, as these programs were designed to serve lower income populations.

As we might expect given the conventional wisdom about voting trends, participants in chamber-of-commerce-sponsored programs were the most likely to have voted in recent elections, followed by those in chamber-extension partnerships, and then in extension-sponsored programs, with participants in foundation-, non-profit-, and community-college-sponsored programs the least likely to have voted in local elections. This matches the national data on voting—where the better educated and more economically well-off are more likely to vote and to have well-formed opinions about public policy (e.g., Bartels 2005).

These findings are only surprising in that extension programs do not include more lower income and more disadvantaged participants in leadership programs. The reason for this is likely because extension-sponsored leadership programs, while developed through an ethos of public participation and inclusiveness, are also intended (in part) to improve economic development capacity—which implies a need to include those perceived as existing community leaders. Another possible explanation is that the Cooperative Extension "institution" does not often represent a very diverse audience and is perceived as serving primarily the agricultural population in rural areas. On the other hand, extension-chamber partnerships did seem to consistently include participants with diverse backgrounds.

Non-profit, foundation, and community college-sponsored programs consistently had a greater percentage of participants who had lower incomes, inconsistent employment status, higher ages, and longer tenure in the community, but who were less civically engaged, as indicated by voting. We expected that these participants would show the greatest gains between pre- and post-program individual outcomes.

In the next section, we review previous research on CLD programs' content by looking at its identification, categorization, and emphasis, and the research questions.

CLD Program Content

Surveys of existing community leadership programs provide insights on the scope of potential leadership development content. Thullen and colleagues (1981) find that many different topics contribute to the education of potential leaders. For example, a national survey of Cooperative Extension CLD programs cataloged content information into four areas: personal leadership skills and knowledge, organizational skills and knowledge, process skills and knowledge, and specific community issues (North Central Regional Interest Network on Community Leadership Programs 1984).

Similarly, a review of four rural leadership programs identifies several common content characteristics considered essential to the programs' success (Howell et al. 1979). The topics addressed included government structures, public policy processes, action strategies, and personal improvement. All were selected to expose rural participants to broader learning experiences.

Fear and associates (1985) also contribute to the knowledge of CLD programs' content. They create a content categorization based on theoretical literature and program development criteria and argue that a comprehensive set of necessary knowledge and skills for effective community leadership can be classified into five categories of knowledge and skills applicable to CLD: human behavior, leadership dynamics, community leadership contexts (e.g., small groups, organizations, communities, and legislative process), community development process, and issue-specific concerns (e.g., economic development, tourism, etc.). For most leadership development programs, content's substance and difficulty are contingent on the expertise and confidence of participants, the demands of leadership roles, local community development experiences, and the importance of the community leadership role vis-à-vis other roles of participants (Fear et al. 1985).

Vandenberg and associates (1988) summarize four content areas identifiable in a number of CLD programs. These areas are: personal leadership skills and resources, working with groups and organizations, understanding communities and community development processes, and understanding public policy processes. We will use these four content areas in the analysis below to look at the relationship of CLD program content and program outcomes.

Rossing and Heasley (1987) note that CLD programs focus heavily on areas that reflect societal trends and issues affecting rural life, including the analysis of problems, developing and implementing policy changes, human relations, and leadership and organizational skills. They detail key research areas for further exploration that would demonstrate the effects of different content patterns and content decisions that community development practitioners may need. They propose the following research questions for future studies: (1) What content elements, if any, are critical in achieving different program objectives?; (2) How do various content elements interact in achieving program objectives?; and (3) What are important individual variations in the response to various content elements?

The content across rural leadership development programs displays some consistency at a very general level, but becomes extremely diverse at a specific topical level. Furthermore, we can note a distinction between programs that emphasize issue content and those that emphasize leadership and public policy process content. Often, it is difficult to determine whether the variety of content reflects careful and appropriate tailoring to local circumstances and to the needs of clientele (or of the practitioner), or whether it reflects the lack of a clear consensus on the most important content for leadership development.

The broad literature on community leadership comes from applied journals, such as the *Journal of the Community Development Society* and the *Journal of Extension*, and focuses mostly on evaluating individual participants in leadership programs. The literature on leadership does not satisfactorily address many of the questions noted above. Although published quite some time ago, the questions Rossing and Heasley pose for further study have not been addressed. Our analysis addresses these research questions by determining the effects of CLD program curriculum design (content) on participants' leadership skills development, as measured by six expected outcomes variables of community leadership, and by exploring the effects of CLD programs' curriculum design (content) on the development of community capitals.

PROGRAM VARIABLES

The program variables for this study included four community leadership program content areas, all based on the number of hours spent on each:

- Personal leadership skills and resources—measured by the number of program hours devoted to topics such as problem-solving techniques, motivating people, decision-making techniques, developing listening skills, managing interpersonal conflict, creative thinking, public speaking, and managing stress.
- Community and community-development processes—measured by the number of program hours devoted to topics such as conducting a community needs assessment, mobilizing community resources, increasing citizen participation, increasing minority participation, planning and implementing community development programs, evaluating community development programs, and social action processes.
- Public policy processes—measured by the number of program hours devoted to topics such as local government decision-making processes, local, state and federal government structures and functions, the citizen's role in public policy, and state legislative processes.
- Working with groups and organizations—measured by the number of program hours devoted to topics such as networking and coalition-building, understanding organizations, membership roles, why people join groups and organizations, understanding small groups, and increasing membership participation.

An additional program variable to consider is that sponsorship was included as a fixed effect variable based on the presumption that sponsorship influences the goals and implementation of CLD programs. In addition, since leadership development programs were offered at multiple times in the same locale, sponsorship adds a different dimension than the fixed-effect variables of community vitality and Appalachian residence.

THE EFFECTS ON PARTICIPANT OUTCOMES

The six individual-level outcome indices of CLD we use in this study as the dependent variables were Personal Growth and Efficacy, Community

Table 5.2. Effects of Participant Characteristics, Sponsorship, and Program Content on CLD Outcome Indices

Independent Variables	Dependent Variables											
	Personal Growth & Efficacy		Community Commitment		Shared Future and Purpose		Community Knowledge		Civic Engagement		Social Cohesion	
	Model 1	Model 2	Model 1	Model 2	Model 1	Model 2	Model 1	Model 2	Model 1	Model 2	Model 1	Model 2
College & Beyond	-.89*	-.95*	-.80*	-.89**	-0.33	-0.39	-0.02	-0.18	-0.31	-0.36	-.68*	-.72**
Female	.62*	0.6	0.32	0.28	0.27	0.24	0.24	0.19	.59*	0.55	0.18	0.17
Age	-0.01	-0.01	0	0.01	0	0	0.02	0.03	0	0	-0.02	-0.02
Married	0	0.05	0.43	0.45	0.04	0.07	0.33	0.32	0.2	0.23	0.26	0.31
Employed	-0.35	-0.26	-0.69	-0.71	-0.58	-0.49	-0.55	-0.44	-0.45	-0.37	-0.58	-0.53
Income > $100,000	-0.44	-0.53	-0.63	-.75*	-0.16	-0.26	-.67*	-.75*	-0.32	-0.4	-0.4	-0.5
Years in living in Community	0.01	0.01	-.04***	-.03**	-.02*	-0.01	-.04***	-.03***	-.03**	-.02*	-0.01	0
Community Level												
Community Viability	0.76	-0.04	0.34	-0.52	0.19	-0.5	-0.09	-0.8	0.45	-0.16	0.47	-0.18
Appalachian Residence	-0.23	0.53	-0.47	0.68	-0.27	0.64	-0.4	0.44	-0.57	0.2	0.11	.95*
Sponsor												
Chamber of Commerce	-0.33	-0.18	-0.1	-0.84	0.02	-0.47	0.1	-0.61	-0.26	-0.68	-0.11	-0.5
Chamber of Commerce & Extension	-0.22	-0.58	0	-0.92	-0.13	-1.14	0.27	-0.79	-0.09	-0.92	-0.27	-1.03
Others	-0.03	-1.11	-0.65	-2.12***	-0.31*	-1.62***	0.05	-1.36*	-0.21	-1.34*	0.5	-0.63

Hours of Training On:											
Personal leadership skills & resources		.12**		.12**		.12***		.14***		.11**	.10**
Community & community development processes		-0.02		0.01		-0.12		-0.02		-0.01	0
Public policy processes		0.02		0.06		.08*		.09*		0.06	0.06
Working with groups & organizations		-0.03		-0.06		-.06*		-.09**		-0.05	-0.05
Constant	3.02	3.24	1.36	4.93	3.07	3.17	3.73	4.01	3.45	3.58	3.69
Changed R2	0.01	0.02	0.01	0.04	0.01	0.03	0	0.04	0.02	0.03	0.03
ANOVA Sig F	0.06	0.02	0.02	0	0.38	0	0.04	0	0.11	0.02	0.01

Commitment, Shared Future and Purpose, Community Knowledge, Civic Engagement, and Social Cohesion. The indices were those we outline in chapter 2. We used two different statistical analyses in this study. We used a hierarchical linear regression to look at the relative importance of the predictor variables. The steps involved in the hierarchical regression are as follows: (1) each of the dependent variables was first regressed on the control variables (e.g., Personal Growth and Efficacy was regressed on age, education, gender, marital status, employment status, years of living in the community, and annual income); and (2) based on the findings of the partial correlation analysis, the content variables, such as personal skills and resources, community and community development processes, public policy processes, and working with groups and organizations, were then added to the model as a block. We used the regression result to generate table 5.2 (see following pages).

The important common results of this regression analysis were the negative effects of education and number of years living in the community, and the positive effect of the number of contact hours sponsors devoted to personal growth and development in the curriculum. These results are detailed in the following discussion.

PERSONAL GROWTH AND EFFICACY

For the dependent variable Personal Growth and Efficacy, model 1 shows two statistically significant relationships. Participants with college degrees (–0.89) had smaller change scores in Personal Growth and Efficacy than those without. Being female (0.62) was associated with higher gains in Personal Growth and Efficacy while holding other variables constant.

In model 2, we examined the number of hours for the content area variables—personal leadership skills and resources, community and community development processes, public policy processes, and working with groups and organizations—for effects on the dependent variables. Again, participants with college degrees (–0.95) had smaller change scores in Personal Growth and Efficacy, and the number of hours spent in developing personal leadership skills and resources was significantly and positively correlated (0.12) to Personal Growth and Efficacy.

COMMUNITY COMMITMENT

Model 1 shows that education (–0.80) and years living in the community (–0.04) were significantly and negatively associated with Community Commitment. In model 2, education (–0.89), annual income (–0.75), and years of living in the community (–0.03) were significantly and negatively associated with Community Commitment. These negative relationships indicate that a college degree, annual income over $100,000, and longer time in the community resulted in smaller increases in Community Commitment scores. The number of hours the various CLD programs spent developing personal leadership skills and resources was significantly and positively correlated (0.12) to Community Commitment. Model 2 also reveals a significant negative association (–2.12) with leadership program sponsorship. Extension programs significantly improve Community Commitment scores as compared to other sponsors, namely universities and community foundations.

SHARED FUTURE AND PURPOSE

In model 1, years living in the community (–0.02) was significantly and negatively associated with Shared Future and Purpose. Those living in the community for more time had smaller increases in Shared Future and Purpose scores. There is also a significant negative relationship with leadership program sponsorship (–0.31). Extension programs significantly improve Shared Future and Purpose scores compared to other sponsors (universities and foundations). With the addition of the content variables in model 2, sponsorship remained significant and negative (–1.62), but the number of years living in the community was no longer significant.

Of the four key content areas in the model, the number of hours spent developing personal leadership skills and resources and learning about public policy processes was found to be significantly and positively (0.12 and 0.08 respectively) correlated to Shared Future and Purpose. In other words, more time devoted to these topics resulted in significant gains or improvements in related scores. Time spent working with groups and organizations significantly correlated with Shared Future and Purpose, but the sign of the coefficient was negative (–0.06). This indicates that more time spent on working with groups and organizations only marginally improved Shared Future and Purpose index scores.

COMMUNITY KNOWLEDGE

Model 1 shows a significant negative relationship with annual income (–0.67) and the number of years of living in the community (–0.04). Participants with higher annual incomes (≥ $100,000) had lower improvements in their Community Knowledge scores than those with annual incomes less than $100,000. Participants living in the community longer had smaller increases in Community Knowledge scores. These results are probably associated with the likelihood

Table 5.3

Multinomial logit model: how individual community impact (capitals)-dependent variables fared verses independent variables

Independent Variables	Community Capital Category						
	Natural Capital	Human Capital	Cultural Capital	Built Capital	Financial Capital	Social Capital	Political Capital
Content/Topic Areas							
Personal Leadership Skills and Resources	1.07 (0.06)	0.98 (0.05)	0.91 (0.07)	1.03 (0.05)	1.01 (0.05)	1.01 (0.06)	1.08 (0.05)
Community and Community Development Processes	0.96 (0.04)	1.05* (0.03)	1.07***(0.03)	0.99 (0.03)	1.00 (0.02)	1.01 (0.03)	1.00 (0.03)
Public Policy Processes	0.99 (0.06)	1.02 (0.05)	1.00 (0.06)	0.98 (0.05)	0.98 (0.05)	0.96 (0.05)	1.10* (0.06)
Working with Groups and Organizations	1.03 (0.04)	0.96 (0.03)	1.00 (0.04)	1.01 (0.04)	1.04 (0.03)	1.02 (0.04)	0.98 (0.04)
Learning Style							
Active Learning	0.97 (0.79)	0.68 (0.57)	0.51 (0.68)	1.75 (0.72)	2.46 (0.61)	0.64 (0.65)	7.56* (1.13)
Active and Passive Combined	0.54 (0.92)	1.66 (0.70)	3.82 (0.83)	1.24 (0.81)	0.36 (0.75)	0.74 (0.74)	8.03* (1.16)
Program Sponsor							
Chamber of Commerce	2.68 (1.20)	0.17** (0.90)	0.15* (1.06)	2.74 (0.99)	7.54** (0.94)	1.05 (0.99)	0.90 (1.02)
Extension and Chamber of Commerce	1.38 (0.58)	0.70 (0.45)	1.04 (0.72)	1.81 (0.71)	0.93 (0.63)	2.63 (0.67)	0.57 (0.71)
Non-profit/ Other	0.12 (0.83)	1.02 (0.64)	0.85 (0.56)	1.39 (0.53)	0.72 (0.46)	2.00 (0.51)	0.93 (0.52)
N	222	222	222	222	222	222	222
Hosmer and Lemeshow Test	0.72	0.09 (*)	0.21	0.57	0.96	1.00	0.02 (**)

that long-term residents who are more highly educated (a likely correlation with income) are already pretty-well informed about the community before they join a CLD program.

In model 2, the relationships found in model 1 remained the same for annual income and years living in the community (−0.75 and −0.03 respectively). In addition, as with the Community Commitment and Shared Future and Purpose analyses, extension programs significantly improved Community Knowledge scores compared to other sponsors (universities and foundations). With the addition of the content variables in model 2, sponsorship remained significant and negative (−1.36). Annual income and years of living in the community remained significantly and negatively related to the dependent variable Community Knowledge. The negative effect shows that participants with higher annual incomes had smaller improvements in their Community Knowledge scores than their lower-income counterparts. Also, the longer they had lived in the community, the lower the increase in Community Knowledge scores when compared to participants who had lived there a shorter period of time.

The model 2 analysis again shows a significant and positive effect (0.14) of the number of hours spent on the content area of personal leadership skills and resources on Community Knowledge scores. In addition, time spent on content related to public policy processes was significantly and positively related to increases in Community Knowledge scores (0.09), but the degree of improvement was small. Time spent on content related to working with groups and organizations was significantly correlated with Community Knowledge, but the sign of the coefficient was again negative (−0.09). This indicates that more time spent working with groups and organizations resulted in smaller improvements in Community Knowledge.

CIVIC ENGAGEMENT

For the Civic Engagement dependent variable, model 1 shows that both gender (0.59) and years of living in the community (−0.03) were significantly related to Civic Engagement, although in different directions. Women had greater increases in Civic Engagement scores than men. Years of living in the community was negatively related to Civic Engagement; participants who had lived longer in their communities had smaller increases in their Civic Engagement scores than those who had lived in their communities for a shorter period of time.

In model 2, gender was not significant while years of living in the community remained significantly and negatively (−0.02) related to changes in Civic Engagement scores. With the addition of content variables in model 2, program sponsorship was significant and negative for other sponsors (−1.34), indicating that extension programs significantly improved Civic Engagement scores compared to programs with other sponsors, namely universities and foundations.

Of the four key content areas in model 2, only the number of hours spent in developing personal leadership skills and resources was significantly and positively associated with gains in Civic Engagement (0.11).

SOCIAL COHESION

For Social Cohesion, model 1 documented a significant negative relationship with level of education (–0.72). Participants with college degrees and beyond were associated with lower change scores in improvements on Social Cohesion scores than those with no college education, indicating that those without a college degree had greater improvements in Social Cohesion than those with a college degree. In model 2, the negative relationship between education and Social Cohesion remained significant. In addition, Appalachian residence had a significant positive relationship (0.95) with Social Cohesion, indicating that participants from Appalachian communities had greater increases in social cohesion scores than those from non-Appalachian communities, which in turn suggests the CLD programs increase local diversity. As with the five dependent variables discussed above, the number of hours spent on content related to personal leadership skills and resources was significantly and positively related to Social Cohesion (0.10), resulting in greater increases in Social Cohesion scores.

From this analysis, we can conclude that that content and design of community leadership education programs makes a difference. Community leadership education programs that offered more contact hours resulted in improvements for leadership outcomes for participants in all six outcome indices. However, the content variables differed in their impact. More contact hours focusing on the content area of developing personal leadership skills and resources resulted in significant improvements in outcomes for participants in all leadership outcome indices (Personal Growth and Efficacy, Community Commitment, Shared Future and Purpose, Community Knowledge, Civic Engagement, and Social Cohesion). The impact was not as pronounced for the other three content areas. More contact hours devoted to content associated with public policy processes improved participants' leadership outcomes in two of the six outcome indices. Specifically, significant improvements were indicated for Community Knowledge and for Shared Future and Purpose, respectively. However, providing more contact hours that focused on understanding community and community development processes did not have any significant impact on the six outcome variables. For the fourth content area of working with groups and organizations, more contact hours resulted in a significant negative effect on both Community Knowledge and Shared Future and Purpose outcome indices.

The Impact of CLD Program Content on Community Capitals

To address the second objective, we used the community capital information assigned to projects and activities identified through focus groups and key informant interviews. By combining this information with CLD program data, it is possible to examine how program content, design, and sponsorship contribute to various community capitals. If the ultimate goal of CLD programs is to help broaden participants' knowledge and skills, improve their capacities to act, and empower them to engage in activities and projects that lead to an overall improvement in the quality of life for the citizenry, then it will be helpful to understand how CLD program characteristics contribute to the various community capitals. To conduct this analysis, we used a multinomial logit model, also known as multinomial logistic regression, to determine how program content impacted the various community capitals. The goal of such a model is to predict categorical data. We used it because the dependent variables—Natural Capital, Human Capital, Cultural Capital, Built Capital, Financial Capital, Social Capital, and Political Capital—are nominal variables (a set of categories that cannot be ordered in any meaningful way, also known as categorical variables) and consist of more than two categories. We use the model in this analysis to predict the probabilities of the different possible outcomes of a categorically distributed dependent variable, given a set of independent variables—in this case community capital variables, which are categorical in nature, and the independent variables of curriculum content, learning styles, and sponsor.

In table 5.3, the amount of teaching time focused on community and community development processes in the rural communities that offered CLD programs is significantly and positively related to the initiation of Human and Cultural Capital projects and activities. For example, the odds ratios for the four content areas indicate that more time spent in teaching community and community development processes increases the likelihood that Human and Cultural Capital projects and activities will be initiated (1.05 and 1.07 respectively). The data in table 5.3 also shows that the more time spent in teaching public policy processes content significantly increases the likelihood (1.10

odds ratio) that Political Capital related projects would be initiated. (Level of significance is represented by asterisks where *** = Pr value is greater than 0.0001; where ** = Pr value is greater than 0.001, and where * = Pr value is greater than 0.01.)

In terms of learning style, that is, active and passive learning, the odds ratios are significant and indicate that active learning styles and a combination of active and passive learning styles are more likely to result in the initiation of Political Capital related projects in communities than passive learning approaches alone (odds ratios of 7.56 and 8.03 respectively). For program sponsorship, our data shows that chamber of commerce-sponsored programs differed significantly from extension-sponsored programs (the reference category) in terms of the initiation of activities and projects. Chamber of commerce sponsorship significantly decreased the probability that Human and Cultural projects would be initiated (odds ratios of 0.17 and 0.15 respectively). In contrast, it increased the chance that activities and programs focused on benefitting Financial Capital would be initiated (odds ratio of 7.54).

Effects of Program Content and Design

Our results show that there are significant relationships between the program design and structure and the six outcome indices of community leadership. First, more contact hours used in educational content related to developing personal leadership skills and resources leads to improved outcomes for participants in all leadership outcome indices for individuals—Personal Growth and Efficacy, Community Commitment, Shared Future and Purpose, Community Knowledge, Civic Engagement, and Social Cohesion.

Second, more hours spent in helping participants to understand community and community development processes and in working with groups and organizations do not improve all outcome indices of community leadership. These results were unexpected because we assumed these topic areas would be critical in helping to build participant skills and knowledge to effectively address issues of community development.

Third, more hours spent teaching participants about community and community development processes results in a greater likelihood of their involvement in activities and projects benefiting Human Capital and Cultural Capital. Similarly, more hours spent on teaching public policy processes result in a greater chance that participants will engage in Political Capital activities and projects.

Fourth, curriculum design that stresses active learning, or a combination of active and passive learning, results in a greater likelihood of involvement in activities and projects benefitting Political Capital. Similarly, extension programs are more likely to lead to the initiation of Human and Cultural Capital projects, while chamber of commerce programs are more likely to initiate Financial Capital activities and projects.

Implications for Rural Community Development Practice and Policy

In the past, various rural community development strategies have been used as vehicles for solving social and economic problems and promoting community well-being and decision-making. However, many problems remain formidable for many rural communities. The findings we report above suggest that CLD initiatives can help to improve individuals' capacity to engage in leadership roles in their communities. The CLD programs we studied demonstrate that program content stressing personal leadership skills and resources result in significant and positive perceived impacts on all six key community leadership indicators: Personal Growth and Efficacy, Community Commitment, Shared Future and Purpose, Community Knowledge, Civic Engagement, and Social Cohesion. This suggests that these outcomes help increase participants' leadership capacity. In looking at activities and projects that participants got involved in through leadership roles that benefitted the seven community capitals, the findings document that more program content focused on community and community development processes led to positive impacts on Human Capital and Cultural Capital.

Similarly, more program content focused on public policy processes led to participant leadership roles in activities and projects that has a positive impact on Political Capital. The findings also indicate that active learning approaches result in positive impacts through participant involvement in activities and projects that benefitted Political Capital.

Finally, program sponsorship also impacted community capitals. Chamber of commerce programs had positive impacts through participant involvement in activities and projects that benefitted Political Capital. Similarly, extension programs resulted in positive impacts through participant involvement in activities and projects that benefitted Human Capital and Cultural Capital.

This suggests that program content in three of the four areas produced positive outcomes. More content focused on personal leadership skills and resources benefitted individual respondents by improving their perceived leadership capacity. More content focused on community and community development processes benefitted projects and activities that benefitted Human Capital and Cultural Capital in the community. More content focused on public policy processes benefitted projects and activities that built Political Capital in the community. More content in which participants worked with groups and organizations did not have any impact. Practitioners who design curricula for CLD programs can use these findings. Program content focusing on developing personal leadership skills and resources will contribute positively to the six desired leadership indices.

Questions remain as to whether program content focused on community and community development processes, public policy processes, and working with groups and organizations can contribute to positive outcomes for the six leadership indices. However, program content focused on community and community development processes may work in combination with content that stresses personal leadership skills and resources to encourage participants to engage in projects and activities that enhance and build the community's Human and Cultural Capital. Similarly, program content focused on public policy processes may prepare participants to develop the Political Capital skills necessary to initiate community projects and activities.

More detailed analysis of the program curricula in these three areas is needed. While there was some evidence that various community capitals were positively affected depending on content areas, program sponsorship, and learning styles, working with groups and organizations did not show any impacts on the community capitals. One strategy to explore the potential benefits of program content focused on working with groups and organizations would be to assign participants a community project to work on as a class during their time in the program. A group assignment might lead to greater improvements in one or more of the community capitals impacted by the community and community development program content mentioned above.

We also wonder what content elements would be critical to achieving different program objectives. Our findings support additional review of CLD program curricula to determine what curriculum components are best for building individual leadership capacity and what program components, structure, and sponsorship are best for positively impacting the various community capitals.

6.

Designing More Effective Community Leadership Development Programs

A large number of volumes already in print address leaders and leadership development and we do not intend to review all that literature here again. The literature also documents that a large number of leadership development programs on the landscape purport to develop leaders or leadership or both. As we noted in chapter 1, this literature too often fails to pay attention to the connections between leadership and community as would be required for a community leadership development (CLD) program effort.

A core idea in this volume is that community leadership is about community change. We acknowledge that community leaders may work to stifle change and protect the status quo, but would argue that form of leadership is often not intended to benefit the community but specific individuals or limited interests. There are, of course, situations such as siting a hazardous waste facility near the community that even progressive leaders may want to try to avoid. But the kind of community leadership we are most interested in is about change in the community that is intended to create new conditions that will benefit community residents and set the community on a course toward a viable future. In its best forms, this change is forward looking, progressive, inclusive, and democratic. It is often political in nature, being a process that involves the public in decision-making. The sort of changes that are today most likely to maintain community viability are also what Heifetz (1994) calls "adaptive challenges" that, in his view, require different ways of thinking about leadership. There are many examples of this sort of community leadership, from Greenburg, Kansas, to Lawrence, Massachusetts, and from small towns in the Mississippi Delta or Appalachia to Vernonia, Oregon. In short, the community leadership is trying to create change in many small rural places.

Our research also demonstrates that community leaders can learn from experience some of the same lessons that they can learn from more formal CLD programs. While they may not exhibit as much change on our indicators over the five-year period investigated, they report operating at higher levels than our CLD study participants. We argue that this experienced group of leaders may be a resource for developing new community leaders and program sponsors need to find ways to use them. Since small communities often do not develop new leaders to soften generational transitions, considering this resource of leader experience could be helpful in several ways. We do, however, caution against taking such an approach if the community's leadership culture is not the sort to effectively address adaptive challenges.

In this research, we make some initial efforts to examine the effects of specific educational elements commonly used in CLD programs. In fact, one of the observations we do not want to overlook is just how similar these programs are in content and format, despite their various sponsors, and how little these designs have changed in the past thirty-plus years. In the previous chapter, we examined the effects of the amount of time participants spent in the program, its content elements, its learning styles, and the effects of sponsorship on the individual-level outcomes, and determined that these factors have different effects on these outcomes. The only general conclusion we offered was that the amount of time participants spent in a program made a significant difference in the outcomes we measure at the individual level. Overall, however, our research has demonstrated that the whole of the experience has some very important and positive outcomes for individuals, organizations, and communities.

In this chapter, we address a number of issues spawned by this research that may be of particular interest to practitioners of many types. We raise these issues in the spirit of discovery and introspection with an eye toward improving what we do in several dimensions of CLD. Obviously, this is a challenging task as the context for practice is very complex: no one community is too similar to another. On the other hand, our comparative study demonstrates that communities' practice is quite similar despite community differences. How program sponsors address this situation in the future will be a major undertaking, both practically and intellectually. In this chapter, we address a set of practice issues we feel are

Leadership Principle Employed	INSTITUTIONAL STRUCTURES	COMMUNITY ORGANIZATIONS & ASSOCIATIONS	AD HOC COLLECTIVE ACTION
FORMAL AUTHORITY	X	x	x
PERSONAL INFLUENCE		X	X
RELATIONAL LEADERSHIP		X	X

Figure 6.1. Community Leadership Domains and Principles of Leadership

important as relevant to the problems of insuring the most effective designs for CLD programs and linking these programs to community outcomes.

Questions for Practitioners

ARE WE DOING WHAT WE SET OUT TO DO?

Most current community-based CLD programs aim to build community leaders' capacity for engaging in more community development work to benefit the community. This objective differs from that noted by Michael and associates (1990) in their late nineties study of Cooperative Extension CLD programs. They determined that the existing programs at that time had one of three objectives: individual or personal skills development, group management skills, or influencing public affairs (or civic engagement in a very singular form). Today, the emphasis on community betterment as an outcome for CLD programs seems to be the prevailing objective, despite some recognition that personal and group leadership skills/behaviors may be affected.

However, if community betterment is really the desired outcome, program sponsors are likely disappointed, even with the outcomes we have documented. Instead, what we have observed is that (1) the primary outcomes at the individual level are civic engagement and social cohesion, results that may eventually drive participants in a somewhat different direction; and (2) the community effects that are occurring seem to be rather disjointed events that take place "in" the community rather than being "of" the community. In other words, small groups of individuals leave these CLD programs with their own agendas and interests, mobilize others who share those interests, and start a project to make some sort of local change. Often they are successful. Further, such actions may often approximate what Heifetz and Linsky (2002) or Drath and associates (2008) suggest. But, because there is no community-wide vision to guide such actions, they are often singular and uncoordinated with other activities in the community. This does not mean the activity does not benefit community well-being in some fashion. Indeed, the development of a safe house for abused families or a new children's playground would be welcome most anywhere. However, we question whether a project-driven approach unguided by any larger involvement of community citizens in the creation of a common direction produces the most desirable outcome, since it consumes valuable resources getting these unique things accomplished that might have been used elsewhere. It is certainly possible that people may later look back on these projects longingly and wish the resources were still available.

We should qualify this conclusion somewhat in recognition of the success of a few programs, supported by the Casey Foundation and cataloged by the Leadership Learning Community, that approached improving community leadership by first concentrating on pulling together a diverse group of community representatives to address a community problem (usually part of an adaptive challenge). This approach focuses on providing learning opportunities and staff-guided interventions that include discussion and reflection on the leadership learning that is taking place during the process of determining how to address the challenge. This sort of approach might be especially appropriate in communities and neighborhoods that have little existing capacity but a significant need for remediation and improvement (Hodgkin 2011).

We offer a different vision for CLD program objectives based on our research. Granted, some observers question whether civic engagement is meaningful or has been overused in ways that cover such a multitude of social, political, and cultural activities that make it difficult to determine exactly what is being described (Berger 2011). Berger argues that the term civic engagement has been used to cover so many differing scenarios that it has become essentially meaningless—we should be using precise terms, such as political engagement, social engagement, and moral engagement, to reflect the different nature of our attentiveness and energy expenditures. Berger does acknowledge that he speaks primarily of macro systems of government when he makes his distinctions, rather than of small communities where direct democracy can often come into play. We prefer to defer to Couto's (1992) distinctions that citizen leaders can sometimes act as a "shadow government," or a "parallel government," depending on elected officials' willingness and ability to act on citizen demands. In addition, we would argue that civic engagement is an outcome that reflects a willingness and a capacity of CLD participants to get involved with "public work" in the context that Boyte and Kari (1998) use the term.

In figure 6.1, we present a picture of the various contexts in which community leaders act. These distinctions are somewhat idealistic and in reality the boundaries are more often blurry. Nevertheless, we make the point that leaders need to understand how they conventionally function compared to what the contemporary settings demand of them as an approach to leadership. For example, leaders in government institutions typically rely on their statutory authority (particularly when challenged) to support their actions rather than on a more democratic participatory process. At the other extreme, citizen activists engaged in civic or public work typically rely on their relationships with other citizen leaders in collaborative efforts to achieve results. This figure represents a somewhat conventional view of how things function in small communities where resources, including capable local leaders, tend to be scarce. Nevertheless, it outlines a situation that may help focus our thinking about what sort of CLD program purpose we intend to address, which domain needs the most improvement, and which principle needs attention. Building institutional leaders' capacity to use more open, democratic, participatory processes in decision-making requires a different sort of CLD program design than building capacity in organizational leadership.

Further, we acknowledge the research that shows the importance of bridging networks among community leaders (Brown and Nylander 1998; O'Brien et al. 1991), which we call social cohesion, can be affected by CLD participation (Rasmussen et al. 2011). Drawing on their research, Brown and Nylander (1998, 75) state: "A community with many weak ties in its leadership network structure should be able to disseminate the information and resources necessary to organize collective action better than one oriented toward strong personal ties." Similarly, O'Brien and associates (1991, 1998) find that leaders in small communities with diverse vertical and horizontal networks acted as leaders in more viable places than those with less diverse networks. In other words, social cohesion in the form of bridging (and linking) social networks (Szreter and Woolcock 2004) works to build a stronger, more viable community.

Since social cohesion leads to a more viable community, CLD educational strategies should recognize more explicitly the potential of existing outcomes to lead to that cohesion, and should build more focus into curricula elements for civic actions. Thus, educators and sponsors need to give more attention to learning activities that emphasize network diversity and political education. As others (Brown 1991; Kahn 1970) point out, some rural communities have very strong, centralized power structures that tend to exclude many citizens. Such communities limit the general citizenry's democratic civic engagement. CLD programs in such communities should help participants understand their existing leadership culture, how their local decision-making system works, and how they can access or exploit that system. Both Brown (1991) and Kahn (1970) provide practical suggestions to address these challenges, and note that CLD programs that include discussions with existing community leaders about "how things work around here" are helpful for new and aspiring community leaders. It is, of course, necessary to balance such learning with discussions of the basis of democratic governance and inclusiveness so that existing power structures are not simply perpetuated. In cases where the existing power structure does not want to respond or cannot due to statutory limitations, CLD participants must also learn how to act as a parallel government, consulting political institutions as appropriate but not depending on them to solve problems. They must learn how to mobilize and manage resources to get things done, or how to enlist voters to support ballot measures and educate voters about issues.

Leadership intends change; it threatens the way things are.[1] Leaders and sponsors of CLD programs should be aware that new citizen leaders will threaten the status quo. The status quo always has its defenders—those who want to keep things just as they are or have been. Being a citizen leader requires courage and CLD sponsors who are encouraging citizen leaders to take up community challenges need to remember this and fully appreciate what they are suggesting to CLD participants (Heifetz and Linsky 2002).

For CLD program sponsors, this is also important in another way, as programs initiated without the support of the local power structure often do not find a foothold in a community. These programs need legitimacy or public political sponsorship from existing community leaders, which communicates to other citizens that they approve of and look forward to the changes from the program.

How does a program sponsor obtain this kind of political support? First, they must make sure that the existing leadership understands that the participants are being prepared as the next generation of community leaders and that political support will help ensure their legacy in the community. One of the failings of most rural communities is that no attention is paid to leadership transitions from one generation to the next (Pigg 2002). Second, sponsors must invite existing leaders into the planning effort to make sure that the program design and content will address community needs. Third, they must invite existing leaders to have a prominent role in sponsorship, from helping to select participants to making the inaugural speech at the opening session to guest lecturing to presenting graduation certificates at the closing one. There are likely other ways to convince existing leaders that these new citizen leaders are not a threat but potential partners for getting things done that most everyone agrees need to be done in the community but for which there is insufficient leadership to accomplish (e.g., Heifetz and Linsky 2002). Remember, as a program strategy, a CLD program tries to broaden the network of weak ties that relationships with the existing power structure can mobilize, but using citizens who have a somewhat different sense of empowerment and civic responsibility.[2]

The intended result of a revised CLD program strategy might be an enhanced civic infrastructure. This civic structure involves processes for developing and considering alternative solutions for difficult problems in which all citizens are welcomed. It includes the decision-making procedures necessary to sort out which possible solution makes the most sense in the current environment and includes the capacity to implement that solution. The civic infrastructure involves processes of imagination, dialogue, priority setting, scenario building, planning, and public administration that are often not considered legitimate elements of governance, especially in small communities. A healthy civic infrastructure allows solutions to emanate from the grassroots and from the top equally, and leads to developments that are more broadly supported by the community as a whole and are likely to be more innovative and sustainable (Morton 2003).

HAVE YOU MOBILIZED EMPOWERING SPONSORSHIPS?

As we argue above, a CLD program experience empowers participants, but taking advantage of this psychological change means taking a few extra steps in program organization. We suggest above that it is important for existing leaders to help select participants in the program, participate in the opening and closing events, and even appear on the program in selected components as knowledgeable teachers and mentors. We can take that a step further and suggest that, since these programs are usually expensive to implement and raising funds from sources other than the participants themselves can ensure those participants are more diverse, soliciting sponsorships from local employers and institutions can be important for several reasons.

First, sponsorships empower the participants symbolically by communicating to them that the community supports their self-development effort and recognizes the importance of having good leaders available. Second, the material support is important to many who give up their hours to participate and take time away from work at an employer's expense; if that same employer encourages employees to participate, it conveys that this is an important experience for the business/organization as well as the community—and a number of studies show that participants are likely to use leadership skills learned in CLD programs first and most often in their jobs (Bolton 1991; Ohnoutka et al. 2005). Lastly, sponsorships build collective ownership of the CLD process, communicating to all the citizens that organizations and businesses in the community recognize the leadership deficit and intend to reduce it by welcoming anyone who wishes to participate as the sponsorships will (help) support their participation.

HAVE YOU EXAMINED PROGRAM DESIGN STRATEGIES?

If CLD programs refocus on enhancing a civic infrastructure on the basis for a new leadership culture, then it stands to reason that current program design strategies need examination. We showed in chapter 5 that various elements of current program designs, when tested against the individual outcomes, seem to have marginal or inconsistent effects. Further, we noticed that most of the programs we examined used program strategies initially designed thirty or more years ago when we understood leadership differently. One of the authors also attended a recent conference of leadership program organizers and, in a session on program design, noticed the elements discussed were similar to those in the programs we investigated—and just as dated.

Making the necessary changes does not require a complete overhaul. As Brown and Nylander (1998) note, there remains a place to emphasize leaders' psychological and cognitive attributes as is shown in our outcome for Personal Growth and Efficacy, or what Meehan and associates (n.d.) call "inner work." However, this comes with a caveat—as they note, "leadership (program) participants want to believe that they are an asset for tackling problems in their community and not the problem that needs fixing" (Meehan et al. n.d., 4). But, now is a good time to start some experimentation and innovation in program strategy, including the appropriate evaluation to determine if desired outcomes are achieved. In keeping with our notion that a particular type of leader development is necessary to support collaborative leadership, we offer some suggestions for collaborative learning. To support the notion of building a stronger civic infrastructure, we offer some ideas for learning how to become politically engaged, either with political institutions or through organizations and activities dedicated to public work. Finally, we briefly review new community-based leadership development approaches that are quite different than those we have studied and that deserve greater attention and, perhaps, replication in ways appropriate to local contexts.

HOW CAN WE FOSTER COLLABORATIVE LEARNING?

Developing the kind of socially cohesive networks that support collaborative leadership requires broadening one's network of weak ties. This means learning more about people in your community and learning to appreciate diversity and how it may contribute to problem solving. Collaborative leadership also means learning that leading is a social process among equals and not a hierarchical structure—a process that is open, fluid, and inclusive. Learning these ideas may not be easy and may require multiple approaches. You might develop a personal, psychological appreciation for how different people are, as well as how people may (in reality) view you through the use of a tool like the Myers-Briggs or True Colors instruments, followed by open, honest discussion about the results and how they can be interpreted, is a good place to begin instilling an appreciation for different types of people with different ways to approach problems. But, it is only through working together in problem solving that these differences and their contributions to collaboration become concrete. Chrislip and Larson (1994) and Bryson and Crosby (1992) write extensively about how collaboration should operate, with good examples to draw from as case studies. Peter Senge and associates (1994) have multiple exercises in collaborative learning that support these case studies. Going further, this is a good place to incorporate a project into the curriculum. For instance, the participants could make a list of possible projects (via brainstorming or World Café processes), setting priorities and choosing several projects that they can tackle as collaborative teams then organizing themselves based on the qualities they have learned to appreciate in others. We also suggest finding examples, if possible from within the community or from nearby communities, that represent this sort of collaboration and arranging discussions with the involved community representatives about how they proceeded, obstacles they overcame, and how they managed the task collaboratively.

ARE YOU TEACHING THE POLITICS OF CIVIC ENGAGEMENT?

There are at least two perspectives on how to learn to become politically engaged (Berger 2011; Wren 2007). The liberal perspective emphasizes the individualistic nature of American democracy and encourages citizen education (about issues and candidates) and voting, petitioning, voter registration, and so forth. This approach focuses on the representative institutions constitutionally adopted to govern *for the people*. It suggests that CLD educators use tools like study circles to help participants learn about an issue and the various options for resolution, including policy options. Knowledgeable voters are then better prepared when they enter the voting booth to vote confidently based on a candidate's stance on issues of concern to them. Participants can learn about other aspects related to the representative institution by working with experienced campaign organizers, and trainers are available to assist with this process. Often, engaging other citizens by registering them to vote and urging them to get to the polls or to vote for a specific candidate is better handled in tandem with someone more experienced, at least to start. The National Community Development Institute's political advocacy and policy intervention training has been lauded for its effectiveness in this arena (Meehan et al. n.d.).

A second approach, known as communitarian, argues that despite individualistic tendencies, Americans recognize the common good and will work collaboratively toward it, especially when faced with problems that affect the general population or, at least, a large portion of it. The difficulty here is determining what the common good is, as there may often be disagreement about which solution fits it best. Further, this process may be complicated by complex or messy problems that do not have an optimum solution or technical answer (Heifetz 1994). The collaborative approaches mentioned above are likely to work best in this context. In addition, encouraging and assisting CLD participants to find roles as leaders in voluntary associations will help give them experience with the development of collaborative leadership and working for the common good on a small scale. Finally, this might be a good opportunity to reintroduce exercises and discussions about community visioning as a way to determine what is commonly thought of as good for this community in the future. What we have in mind here is not necessarily that CLD participants develop a vision for their community (although as an exercise this might be a learning device), but that they learn about how to conduct a community-based visioning process (Walzer 1996). There are a number of useful techniques for this, and a CLD planning committee should be able to determine which is most appropriate for its community.

DO YOUR PROJECTS PROVIDE AN AUTHENTIC VEHICLE FOR LEADER DEVELOPMENT?

Some of the CLD programs we studied included a class project as part of the learning experience. Many other programs use this element as a sort of experiential learning process as well as a community betterment exercise. The trouble is, most of these projects do not seem to be significant as they do not have enough time or resources to really make an impact. Many program sponsors question the desirability of retaining this element as part of the design strategy.

However, there are other community-based programs that are not generalized leadership development programs but focus on a specific issue or project as a vehicle for leader development. The Leadership in Action Program sponsored by the Annie E. Casey Foundation in Baltimore is a good example (Meehan et al. n.d.). Although this specific project, improving early childhood education, brought together existing institutional leaders by design, the kind of leadership that emerged likely taught each participant the importance of collaboration and shared leadership. Similar approaches could be used in smaller communities by assembling collaborations of concerned citizen leaders along with institutional and organization/association leaders to build the sort of network of resources necessary to address the problem. Together, they can be challenged to learn to work across their boundaries, discover and appreciate diversity, expand the weak ties that constitute their working networks, innovate and devise new solutions, and combine assets in order to need less external assistance. This is an exercise in strengthening the civic infrastructure. We are reminded of the slogan of a small hardware store in Austin, Texas, that says: "Together you can do it yourself."[3] The store's owners loan customers the tools and equipment to do a job and teach them to use the tools and materials for any DIY project they bring to them.

Aside from a singular project focus as a vehicle for developing leaders, CLD sponsors can follow our above suggestion to incorporate the project focus earlier in the curriculum and make it work much like an action learning experience, with time set aside for reflection during the process. Many important collaborative leadership experiences could be the focus of active and reflective learning activities during the process that might be more effective than the school of hard knocks.

ARE YOU ENGAGING PARTICIPANTS IN COMMUNITY ACTIVITY?

As our research shows, these community-based programs increased the breadth and depth of participants' involvement in local organizations as leaders and/ or active participant volunteers. This is invaluable to those organizations. Our research also shows that some CLD programs ensured a link between their programs and community organizations operating locally so that, as participants completed the program, they could be recruited to be volunteers or board members in these organizations. Moore (1988) notes that some larger municipalities have CLD programs in which the sponsor maintains an active placement program for participants that the participants acknowledge at the beginning of the program; it is up to the participant which organization she volunteers to serve with, but know from the beginning that service is expected.

In a small, rural community, a placement program should be relatively easy. Sponsors should be able to identify local organizations and associations and their needs for leaders in a variety of roles. They could maintain an annual directory of such opportunities and offer CLD participants specific opportunities that fit their individual interests and abilities. Building such relationships with other organizations would be a good way to develop financial sponsorships for a CLD program and involvement in a program planning committee. It would also be important to track these individuals to facilitate networking over time.

DO PROGRAM EVALUATION EFFORTS FOCUS ON THE RIGHT TARGET(S)?

The research reported here underscores the importance of emphasizing program theory as a guide to focusing program evaluation activity. We have demonstrated that participation in CLD programs leads to individual, sometimes idiosyncratic effects. Numerous studies cited here demonstrate various types of these effects in several ways. Our research shows that the individual effects are related to each other in a logical, reasonable fashion and should be treated as a related set of effects. Brown (1991) and Rasmussen and associates (2011) go a step further and argue for a greater emphasis on the network effects of participation. Given the prominence of social cohesion or bridging social capital in our results, we agree this network effect should be more comprehensively evaluated.

In addition, as we attempted here, program sponsors and evaluators need to pay more attention to CLD programs' longer-term, community effects. Our study is only a beginning and much more work needs to be done, especially as our study is limited to community-based programs that aim at general community development. As with our discussion above about refocusing the educational strategy, sponsors need to be clear about their program theory and express their desired outcomes in clear, unambiguous language. Then, evaluators need to select and measure corresponding indicators after the program's completion. An unclear time-lapse factor is involved here; we used a two-to-three-year time-lapse framework, which captured a great deal of activity resulting from CLD participant leadership. However, some activities take longer to get organized and produce results could be important to include in any study. Practically speaking, it may take five years or more to see results in some areas like economic development (Emery and Flora 2006).

ARE YOU RECRUITING MORE DIVERSE PARTICIPANTS FOR PROGRAMS?

Recruiting participants is often a difficult task. Sponsors frequently end up with participants that are too homogeneous to fully represent the community. Sometimes this results from the educational strategy as people with Latino, Native American, or Asian backgrounds may not relate to the typical approach offered (Meehan et al. n.d.). For example, in a recent study on the Lakota Sioux, Gambrell and Fritz (2012) demonstrate the dimensions of the cultural differences faced by those Native Americans interested in leadership development in this culture. More immediately, financial barriers and time constraints often prevent citizens from taking a serious interest in opportunities to participate. Some citizens may also not view themselves as leaders or as having leadership potential and may therefore ignore the general invitation. These opportunities have to become personalized and targeted in the recruitment process, with special efforts to ensure each participant feels welcomed and valued as an individual who can contribute to the community.

Alternatively, the project approach, which begins with a community problem or issue and invites citizens with an interest in that issue to help resolve it and generate solutions may offer a different way to build collaborative leadership skills among citizens with diverse backgrounds. Care has to be taken to keep the focus on the issue or problem even as leaders' development takes place, but taking time to reflect on the process is a good starting point. Such an approach also calls for well-trained organizers and consultants to observe and intervene in the process with a consistent message about the leadership learning that needs to take place (Parks 2005).

Reforming CLD Program Efforts

In this chapter, we have challenged several types of practitioners to examine their program efforts for developing community leaders. We have demonstrated that the results of these programs, as they currently operate, need to be redesigned to take greater advantage of the results already evident. More specifically, many existing CLD programs that rely on outdated and marginally relevant thinking about leadership development need to acknowledge these programs' effects and make better use of the invigorated sense of civic engagement produced. In addition, more explicit attention to how bridging networks can build a sense of social cohesion in the community, which itself is a resource for taking action, is warranted.

It is our argument, more fully developed in subsequent chapters, that enhanced civic engagement targeting public work in a context of community development, coupled with a reinforced set of bridging social networks, represents an enhanced civic infrastructure. This is particularly the case when the newly strengthened networks include institutional and organizational actors who work alongside citizens concerned for their community's future. Reforming CLD program designs to leverage current practice with greater emphasis on the actual outcomes produced is necessary on the grounds of both efficiency and effectiveness. In the next chapter, we explicate this perspective and our arguments in support of it more fully.

Part Two

A CONCEPTUAL FRAMEWORK FOR COMMUNITY LEADERSHIP
DEVELOPMENT IN ACTION

7.

New Directions for Community Leadership Development

Earlier in this volume, we described the impact of community leadership development (CLD) programs on the individual participants. Those who participated in CLD programs displayed significantly greater scores in the six leadership outcome indices constructed through the responses to surveys: Personal Growth and Efficacy, Community Knowledge, Community Commitment, Shared Future and Purpose, Social Cohesion, and Civic Engagement. In other words, CLD program participants emerged with increased individual leadership capacity. The point of our effort, however, has been to address the impact of these programs on community.

While the development of individual capacity through leadership training is a positive thing, a long tradition of community development literature (e.g., Flora and Flora 2013; Green and Haines 2012) demonstrates that improving individuals' skills does not necessarily lead to positive community outcomes. Our task was to try to determine what impact, if any, could be attributed to leadership training of individuals through CLD programs. For that, we used a statistical path model (figure 4.2) to link participation in CLD programs to outcome measures in the form of changes in community capital assets. Interestingly, the path model indicates that growth of individual capacities (community knowledge and personal growth and efficacy) only led to the development of community capitals when mediated through broader community engagement (such as through community knowledge and community commitment). The path model shows that the key contributors to community capital development were indeed civic engagement and social cohesion.

This being the case, it is important to see if our findings might add to literature on civic engagement. How is civic engagement related to rural community development? Might our research help us better understand the need to improve engagement and how to go about it?

Civic Engagement and the Mother Science

In order for individual residents to make changes in their communities, they have to engage in community activities. In a very real sense, this involves getting engaged in the public sphere or the community's civil society. This involvement often requires knowing something about community politics and how they work. Such understanding is central to de Tocqueville's notion of the "Mother Science." Being engaged in civic activity means working with others on a project that benefits the community rather than private interests. It means effectively communicating the benefits of a proposed action to the community, perhaps linking the proposal to existing activities. It may also mean developing partnerships with local officials or the leaders of community organizations that control resources necessary for success. Someone who is engaged in civic activity can be motivated by many things, but often an interest in the community's long-term general well-being plays an important role.

Citizens' engagement in the community's civic life is a central feature of what the National Civic League calls the community's civic infrastructure (Parr 2008). The civic infrastructure refers to the structures and processes that govern the community and the ways in which residents live and work together. It includes the institutions and organizations in the community, as well as the rules by which residents abide to achieve collective goals as effectively as possible. The civic infrastructure also includes residents' capacity to engage these institutions and organizations as both individuals and also in groups that may be loosely organized to collaborate or challenge positions on issues that affect the public. Being civically engaged often means making public what otherwise might be kept private, such as the conversion of a piece of open land that might have uses for both public and private benefit. Governing the community and public life is not the exclusive purview of government institutions. In fact, as the president of the Kettering Foundation argues, governing is a general responsibility of all citizens and we abdicate this responsibility to others and to these institutions at our (possible) peril (Mathews 1999).

When it comes to civic engagement, voting for representatives in government positions is insufficient. Civic engagement means that citizens are involved directly in governance and in the decision-making process that produces collective action. This further implies that individuals are directly involved in formulating policy in preparation to enact or implement it through decision-making. Civic engagement requires knowledge and skill and confidence (or self-efficacy) to produce actions and policies that are effective and inclusive of diverse ideas and values.

At the community level there are many opportunities for civic engagement, yet experience shows that few residents are interested in such involvement until some proposed action or policy is perceived as a threat to the status quo. For example, participation in local elections is often very low and many candidates run unopposed for election. Yet, if things are to change and communities are to improve, that status quo must be abandoned and new ways of thinking and acting must be considered. As Bennis and Nanus (1985) argue, citizens who consider taking a leading role must have courage to deal with the complexity of modern society and be able to establish credibility in the face of multiple and diverse interests.

Civic engagement has many dimensions and manifests in many ways. Direct involvement in local government activity is certainly one form of such engagement, but even here it may take several forms—holding office, serving on an appointed commission, making a presentation on a local issue at a city council meeting, or volunteering for a government-sponsored activity (Martin and Wilkinson 1985). Beyond direct involvement like this, there are many other ways to be civically engaged. Residents serve in many capacities in local organizations—some in civic organizations, some in institutional organizations (e.g., parent-teacher associations or church-related organizations), some with service organizations for youth such as scouting, and some as volunteers with food banks, homeless shelters, or hospice centers. Some people coach youth sporting activities. In some communities, there may be a general expectation that every resident should help better the community, and many people find opportunities to be involved while others do not. Other communities are known as activist communities, with various interest groups actively advocating for or against certain policies, such as the siting of waste disposal facilities nearby, the siting of environmentally threatening power generating stations, or the operations of parental counseling organizations in the community. Almost any activity individuals carry out that aims to produce collective benefit or change might be considered civic engagement. However, individual efforts, such as an individual arguing against a property zoning decision or other policy that directly affects his or her private interest, may not be civic as they aim primarily at preserving individual rather than collective interests.

Whenever such collective actions take place, leadership is required.[1] All of the individuals involved in such an episode must come to mutual agreement on their purpose and objectives, on the strategy and tactics they will use to achieve them, and how to implement their plans. Without leadership, such decision-making is unlikely to occur in any effective manner. Without leadership, such collectives are little more than mobs. While mobs can be effective in forcing change, strategically organized efforts with leadership that engages diverse interests and mobilizes resources are more likely to succeed. Our research demonstrates that some of those who score highly on our index of Civic Engagement (as an outcome of a CLD experience they've had) go on to make a significant impact on their community. An appropriate CLD design is organized in a manner so it supports the development of an increased capacity for civic engagement in individual participants. The elements of the CLD experience that contribute to this increased capacity are important, and are a curriculum with diverse content, an active learning design, and adequate opportunities for social networks to develop along with multiple opportunities for participants to share empowering experiences.

The Mother Science Expanded

What many readers of de Tocqueville overlook is his analysis of the role of moral philosophy in maintaining the fundamental principles of equality and liberty that comprise the American democratic system. As we understand these moral principles today, they underscore the importance of what it takes to come to collective agreement in a civil matter and have a reasoned discourse about the complex problems we face in a global society. The nature of diversity in the population represented by the founding members of the American democracy and today's multicultural society have only a little in common. Even in rural places where the image is of bucolic sameness, we find growing numbers of immigrants from various countries and, more recently, more emigrants from urban and suburban life looking for an alternative that is better for themselves and their children.

What this means is that the Mother Science of association and the importance of relationships needs to expand to include an appreciation and acceptance of diversity in all its dimensions. This facet of our relational interactions is a moral one that we term "social cohesion" and is another important outcome of the CLD experiences we studied.

Community leadership programs are based on the belief that rural communities in the United States need to return to de Tocqueville's (2000) Mother Science, namely people's basic capacity to mobilize themselves to solve community problems. In de Tocqueville's depiction, unlike European communities, rural American community residents in the first half of the nineteenth century were neither beholden to nor dependent on central government or local patronage structures to solve life's daily problems. Instead, they came together to find innovative ways to address emerging needs and problems on their own, usually out of necessity.

People in early American rural communities had initiative, and that, as much as anything, accounted for the can-do attitude that formed the iconic American ethos. As David Levine (2011) notes in the introduction to his book *The Capacity for Civic Engagement*, this is indeed a rhetorical narrative that American politicians and national leaders (including President Obama in 2008) turn to repeatedly. As Americans, we thrive because of a "spirit of patriotism, of responsibility, where each of us resolves to pitch in and work harder and look after not only ourselves but each other." (Barack Obama's Chicago 2008 victory night speech, quoted in Levine 2011, 1).

Recent work by researchers and practitioners associated with the Kettering Foundation explore the notion of an "ecology of democracy." Such an idea distinguishes between the roles of collaboration, deliberation, and direct action in a democracy (Kemmis and McKinney 2011). In this view, collaboration is best used for problem solving and deliberation for issue resolution when the problems are more complicated and the solutions less obvious. Direct action is often via emergent self-organizing groups to address local problems readily solved using local resources. This ecological view tends to replace conventional discussions of power and influence as the central features of leadership with notions of networking and shared purpose, where resources can be identified and mobilized among people who are no longer willing to depend on others to get something done (Wheatley and Frieze 2009). We found a large number of these direct action events that were former participants of CLD programs organized and implemented. Examples of direct action events include construction of community centers, arts centers, and cultural education centers; celebrations; health programs; educational programs for youth in areas like business ethics; and many more. We identified far fewer examples of successful deliberation on issues important to communities such as development priorities, public support for poverty reduction, and so forth, meaning the ecology of democracy is rather limited in scope in the rural places we studied.

Many politicians, ministers, movement, and community leaders in the United States herald civic engagement and call for more of it. Amid the soaring rhetoric, however, are concerns about declining civic engagement dating at least to the mid-twentieth century. Community leadership programs often cite reinvigorating resident engagement to solve increasingly complex community problems as a major goal (Etuk et al. 2013). But what is does "engagement" mean, how does it relate to "capacity" and, more specifically, "community capacity," and what does any of this have to do with "power"? And what do leadership programs have to do with any of these concepts?

Answering the following questions can lead to a better understanding of civic engagement:

- What is civic engagement?
- Why do citizens engage?
- What are the forms of engagement?
- How does civic engagement relate to community development?
- How does this play out in the context of rural America?
- How does this relate to community capacity?
- How does civic engagement relate to power, specifically power in the context of rural communities?

The last question is tricky because, if leadership is ultimately about empowerment, or rather about empowering citizens to become civically engaged, is that empowerment *of* the community or empowerment of citizens *within* the community? How do either of these concepts relate to community capacity?

We address these questions as a way to better understand how CLD programs produce concrete effects. If we understand civic engagement, community capacity, power, and empowerment, we can then discuss how community leadership programs might impact a community and ultimately lead to change.

What Is Civic Engagement?

Civic engagement refers to a broad set of practices and attitudes of involvement in social and political life that converge to increase the health of a democratic society. The concept has assumed increasing importance as a means to reverse the balkanization of individual interests and the rapid disintegration of communal life. (Banyan 2007, 86)

Civic engagement is associated with activities including voting, volunteering for civil society organizations, engaging in the political process, and joining social movements (Lindahl 2011). There is a vibrant literature on civic engagement as it related to political activism, specifically in the context of democratic societies (Poston 1976). As mentioned above, the United States has long been considered to represent the first great experiment of a society where civic engagement played a critical role in the functioning of democracy. Yet, it is also true that the patterns de Tocqueville observed in early nineteenth-century America have been replicated in many other places—and there are active efforts to create conditions of civic engagement in many developing countries (e.g., Tobin 2010).

The study of civic engagement cuts across several social science disciplines, including anthropology, administrative studies, education, political science, planning, psychology, social work, and sociology. There are distinct themes associated with the study of civic engagement, including the structural factors that contribute to civic engagement (e.g., Lim and Sander 2013; Manturuk et al. 2012; Davies et al. 2012); the kinds of interventions that lead to greater civic engagement, usually related to youth development and education studies (e.g., Latimer and Hempson 2012); the relationship between civic engagement and democratic governance (e.g., Banyan 2007); the relationship between civil society and civic engagement (e.g., Putnam 2000; van der Meulen 2012); the role of education and youth programming in getting young people civically engaged (e.g., Sherod 2005); and civic engagement and community action (e.g., Smock 2005; Besser 2009; Putnam 2000; Green and Haines 2012; Flora and Flora 2013).

One of the key points here is that civic engagement can be many things. While it is often used to connote political engagement, it can also be the engagement in nonpolitical civic affairs, such as volunteering to deliver social services or organizing community activities. In our research, and using the community capitals framework (Flora and Flora 2013, 2005), we grappled with this difference through measuring the assets that CLD programs help mobilize. Specifically, we examined to what extent community leadership program graduates increase civic engagement, in what form, and to accomplish what activities. Answering these questions empirically is one thing, but we also wanted to define the reasons behind them. In addition, we considered the forms of engagement, whether there were specificities about engagement in rural America, how engagement relates to community capacity, and how engagement and capacity relate to power and empowerment.

Table 7.1
The forms of community development and their factors

Factors	Imposed	Directed	Self-help
	← • ◆ • ◆ • ◆ • ◆ • ◆ • ◆ • ◆ • →		
View of Community	Function-Based	Function Based-Associational	Association
Benefits	Structural	Structural/Interaction	Interaction
Principal Stakeholder	Private/ Government	Government/ NGO	Residents
Input	None	Limited	High
Involvement	None	Limited	High
Learning Outcome	None	Moderate	High

Note: Table 7.1 adapted from Matarrita-Cascante and Brennan (2012, 298).

Why Do Citizens Engage?

Community residents may engage civically for a variety of reasons: because they see problems in society and believe their engagement will bring about change; because they believe engagement is their responsibility to their community; because their faith or associations call them to service; because there is some status associated with service; or because they see engagement as a stepping stone to community or broader political leadership.

For social movement scholars, people engage civically to create social change through movements. It has long been established that people do not join social movements just because things have become "bad enough." Varying theories posit that movements may gain membership and viability for different reasons. Meyer and Staggenborg (1996), for instance, argue that movements become viable and, by association, people engage in them when there is a perceived opening in the political structure, yielding greater opportunities for movement success and making engagement less risky. Other scholars argue that movements emerge and gain membership when there are sufficient resources (financial, social, cultural, etc.) to be mobilized to sustain a movement (McAdam et al. 2004). Snow and Benford (1988) argue that people join movements when organizers are able to frame issues by diagnosing a problem, proposing solutions, and motivating action. Beyond framing, others note that people are likely to engage in social movements because of shared ideology and values, but also because of others in their social networks—having family and friends in the

many aims, including but not limited to initiatives to: improve the opportunities for art and cultural development; solve community conflicts; address diversity issues; and support initiatives involving built and social capital to create a more vibrant downtown or main street (Matarrita-Cascante and Brennan 2012; Flora and Flora 2013; Green and Haines 2012).

These conceptualized forms of development are, of course, ideal types. In many cases, self-development may lead to community processes that address material needs and are more expert driven. For instance, an association of community stakeholders could coalesce around the need to expand the local hospital or improve housing stock. In either case, while self-development may initiate community development efforts, these efforts may combine with more directed forms of development to ensure that the physical structures associated with the initiative meet construction standards and/or regulations. The short and long of it is that different forms of intervention can lead to different forms of civic engagement.[2]

Beyond engagement either in social movements or in response to development initiatives, community-level civic engagement may happen as part of a longstanding perceived need and/or desire to be associated with civic institutions. Putnam's (2000) data on the decline in civic engagement are relevant here. Using an impressive array of data, Putnam demonstrates in his classic *Bowling Alone* that not only had Americans' trust in government and generalized social trust fallen precipitously since the early 1970s, but membership in everything from sports clubs to labor unions to religious institutions had fallen since the 1960s. He argues that while there has been growing attention to creating civic engagement and democracy in international development since the 1980s, engagement has fallen in the United States and indeed in North America generally. Citizens turned to activities that were more personal and less concerned with civic and political life.

Others, such as Skocpol and Fiorina (1999), counter that while this might be true, the civic organizations that Putnam uses to measure engagement are problematic. Many of America's iconic civic clubs and societies that have seen falling membership were the bastions of social values that were exclusionary to particular groups and ways of thinking. Further, if civic engagement has indeed fallen, it is not so much because of individual decisions and reactions to technology as it is because of political economic structures designed to prevent that engagement.

Canadian activist David Meslin (2010) picks up this perspective and argues that a combination of the structures of local government have increasingly been designed around efficiency rather than around participation and engagement.

The clear implication is that if people had the opportunity and cultural encouragement to engage in local politics, they would. He argues that while advertising has perfected the art and science of creating interest in products and services, government and governance systems continue to perform public engagement through often poorly worded meeting announcements in the back pages of the newspaper.

Others, however, build on Skocpol and Fiorina's first point, and argue that engagement has changed rather than declined. Gibon (2006), for instance, in a report for the Case Foundation, points to evidence that participation in voluntary service activities among young people in particular has actually increased, especially in the decade after the terrorist attacks of 2001. Metaphorically, while citizens may be "bowling alone," that's in part because younger people play Ultimate Frisbee instead. It can also be said that, while people may not be as inclined to show up at the town meeting, they may be more likely to engage through posting comments online (Berger 2011).

In summary, people do not simply engage because they have grievances. Plenty of evidence in communities shows that residents' dissatisfaction may lead to disengagement rather than engagement (Morton et al. 2008). Clearly one form of civic engagement is when people are organized into community or social movements through perceived openings in the political structure, framing by organizers, cultural alignment, or social networks. People may also become engaged to achieve social acceptance or to gain status in the community. Part of Putnam's concern is that the decline of membership in civil society organizations leads to a decline of the institutions that previously facilitated this form of engagement. It is also clear, however, that the structures of development in a given community can have a significant impact on the opportunities for and extent of engagement. A final important note is that the nature of civic engagement may be changing with the ability of people to communicate both locally as well as extra-locally through the Internet and online social networks.

What Are the Forms of Engagement?

The community leadership literature has long recognized the importance of distinguishing between positional (the village, town, or city mayor, council, or others with official titles) and non-positional (informal) community leaders (Devereaux 1960). Often those who hold power and influence within a community, or even those who are essential to achieving something, are informal rather than positional leaders (Flora and Flora 2013). Classic network analysis in communities demonstrates that power often rests with influential people who do not hold official positions (Hoppe and Reinelt 2010).

As we consider civic engagement, the same principle holds. Civic engagement may exist through multiple forms, such as running for election and holding official government positions, leading civil society organizations, and holding other important nonpolitical community positions. While these are jobs, they are jobs that often come with an expectation of service to the broader community. For example, a nonpolitical school principal (or a teacher, for that matter) may interact with students and their families outside of the school setting. A principal may also enable the use of school facilities for community functions. Likewise, a high school football coach may see his duties as including participation and having the team participate in community fundraising and charity events.

There are also those who are civically engaged but hold no recognizable position in society—they simply show up and get things done (Wildavsky 1976). In some cases, these people are organized, as in Smock's examples above. In many cases, they are not so much organized as engaged through a sense of responsibility to their community. There is growing evidence that emerging community issues are increasingly addressed by community-based organizations (CBOs) that are never formalized, but rather emerge to solve a particular issue and dissipate once successful (Opare 2007). This is sort of engagement that we most often discovered the CLD participants involved in organizing. Residents engage as part of CBOs, receiving little more than, hopefully, their fellow residents' admiration and a sense of pride for achieving whatever the CBO was formed to accomplish—whether an ice cream social, a park cleanup, or a food pantry for those who are hungry in the community (O'Brien et al. 1991; O'Brien and Hassinger 1992).

One of the challenges for this trend is that CBOs are faced with growing governance complexity in actually achieving their desired goals. In the rest of this volume, we demonstrate how CLD programs can help mobilize both formal and informal civic engagement. In particular, CLD programs may empower people to make community change through creating bridging social capital and social networks, as well as through providing the human capital skills of knowledge of the political process through which resources may be allocated to solve problems and implement change (Morse and Buss 2008; Morse 2008; King and Hustedde 2001).

Citizen Engagement and Rural America

Increasing demand for rural leaders has produced new appreciation of the role of the leader, but at the same time it has revealed that very many rural communities and organizations are unable to achieve their objectives because of lack of competent leadership. One of the paradoxes of life is that where leaders are most needed, they are the least in evidence. (Sanderson 1940, 12)

For Sanderson (1940), a rural leadership crisis arose because communication and transportation was easier. Rural community residents could travel with increasing ease to urban centers in 1940, and telephones meant that surrounding farmers could communicate with other farmers without visiting town. These cultural changes from more diffuse communication and transportation technologies drove what he saw as a rural leadership crisis.

Sanderson's concerns, while couched in the institutional functionalist paradigm that was dominant in post-World War II social science, bears some resemblance to the concerns of more contemporary social scientists about the loss of civic engagement. For Putnam (2000), the civic engagement crisis has not been the lack of qualified people in areas of positional leadership, as Sanderson bemoans, but rather a deterioration of the structures that engaged citizens on a daily basis. These informal interactions created what Putnam calls "social capital," interactions of trust and reciprocity.

But, as we noted above, social capital comes in multiple forms. Bonding social capital is the relationship among those who are similar—good friends, family, those with whom one has a long-standing connection, and those who are located in different places and spaces in society. Bridging social capital is the relationship among those who are different, and with whom one is not close (Szreter and Woolcock 2004). The problem, asserts Putnam (2000), is that as society has modernized, citizens have increasingly kept to themselves—while bonding capital has survived, Americans see less of their neighbors in informal settings. Metaphorically, while we may still bowl on occasion, we do so alone or with family and existing friends, rather than in leagues that would force us to make new ones. Putnam argues that this loss of social capital in general and bridging social capital in particular means that fewer and fewer different people come together to solve large community problems through civic discourse.

Given Sanderson's concerns in the 1940s, it is not surprising that rural sociologists continue to study the extent to which decline of Putnam's concerns about civic engagement exist in rural communities as well as broader society. Besser (2009) directly addresses this question of whether national-level decline in civic engagement transferred to concerns about civic engagement in rural communities (thought to be more civically engaged than their urban and suburban counterparts). Using survey data from selected communities in Iowa's ninety-nine counties, she finds that while Iowa's rural communities still show high rates of bonding social capital, there was a dearth of bridging social capital.

Other research comes to a similar conclusion, often with a greater emphasis on the economic structure of the community as a driving variable. For example, Tolbert and associates (2002) and Lyson and Tolbert (2003) find that rural civic engagement was positively related to the local economy's structure. In other words, those communities that had more locally owned small businesses, and that tended to have a greater engagement in community affairs, had greater civic engagement. Lyson and his colleagues (2001) similarly find that communities displaying greater proportions of smaller, locally owned agricultural operations were more likely to have greater community engagement, and those communities surrounded by these smaller, locally-owned agricultural enterprises were likely to be more vibrant.

These findings are important because research indicates that civic infrastructure is positively related to the quality of public services (police, fire, water, sewer, etc.) local government delivers (Morton et al. 2008). In an era when local governments must adopt innovations, collaborations, and interlocal agreements to more efficiently deliver services to the public, civic engagement is essential to bridge expectations and these new arrangements' potential. Lacking engagement, reactions to such arrangements may include complaints, distrust, apathy toward local government, or a propensity to leave the community. Writ simply, when residents of communities disengage, it can lead to a downward spiral of deteriorating services, dissatisfaction with services, and possibly community abandonment.

Community Capacity

Community capacity is the interaction of human capital, organizational resources, and social capital existing within a given community that can be leveraged to solve collective problems and improve or maintain the well-being of that community. It may operate through informal social processes and/or organized efforts by individuals, organizations, and social networks that exist among them and between them and the larger systems of which the community is part. (Chaskin et al. 2001, 7)

CLD programs are ultimately committed to improving the community's capacity to address the issues that will advance its quality of life. As Chaskin and associates (2001) note, improving community capacity is partly about improving the knowledge and participation that is essential for civic engagement. It is also about creating the civic infrastructure that can facilitate and provide the venue for engagement. Ultimately, they argue that the development of community capacity requires a systems approach that involves analysis of:

1) Characteristics of community capacity, such as sense of community, commitment, ability to solve problems, and access to resources;
2) Levels of social agency, including accounting for individuals, organizations, and networks;
3) Community functions such as planning, decision-making, governance, production of goods and services, information dissemination, organization, and advocacy;
4) Strategies such as leadership, organizational development, organizing, and organizational collaboration;
5) "Conditioning influences," which include safety, residential stability, density of acquaintance, structure of opportunity, migration patterns, race and class dynamics, and the distribution of power and resources; and
6) Outcomes, in terms of better services, influence on decision-making, and economic well-being.

Many of these elements are central to what Morton (2003) and others (Parr 2008) enlist as important to their notion of civic infrastructure—the ability to solve problems and access resources, institutional and organizational accountability, participatory planning and decision-making in governance systems, relational leadership, equitable distribution of political power and resources, and so on. The key point is that community capacity development involves efforts within multiple domains to address important local issues.

This basic insight about community capacity development has been picked up as well by community development scholars such as Kretzmann and McKnight (1993), who developed the Asset Based Community Development framework for work in poor neighborhoods of Chicago. The framework is ultimately empowering in that it focuses on accentuating not only what is wrong in persistently poor areas, but also communities' existing tools to address those concerns. Green and Haines (2012) build on Kretzman and McKnight, referring to an asset based approach, but incorporating Flora and Flora's (2013) notion of community capitals to provide a more detailed schematic of what those assets will likely be. From this perspective, the task of capacity development is to recognize how to leverage combinations of capitals to resolve particular community issues. For example, while a community may be classified as low income, by building social capital it may be able to leverage social networks to deliver particular services such as food for the poor or to create political capital to improve its educational facilities.

Green and Haines (2012) and Flora and Flora (2013) emphasize the importance of the establishment of community indicators and measurement of change over time. Importantly, the indicators developed should not be limited to those that are easily measured. Not only are there often problems of scale in rural communities with easily available data, such as those from the US Census, but they also may not reflect key changes critical to improving community capacity. For instance, Kirlin (2003) talks about the importance of developing "civic skills"— skills as mundane as how to compose letters to government or corporate agents, how to express opinions at community or public meetings, and how to request assistance from local bureaucracies—as key to improved capacity in poor and marginalized communities.

As Chaskin and associates (2001) note, all of this must be done recognizing cross-cutting issues such as race, class, culture, and decision-making processes; issues of public participation, consensus, and legitimacy; external stimulus or constraints on community development; and ultimately issues of local-level power and control. In short, community capacity is enabled through leveraging bridging social capital (Putnam 2000; Hyman 2002; Flora and Flora 2013).[3]

Conclusion

All of this brings us back to the importance of civic engagement in fostering positive community change. While individual capacities are important, change at the community level happens through developing not only individual capacities, but also forms of civic engagement. Authors such as Chaskin point out that community capacity is contingent not so much on individual skills, but on citizens' engagement in civic affairs, forming what Morton (2003) and Parr (2008) call civic infrastructure. The key point is that CLD programs have already played some role in creating civic engagement, but recognizing the import in this area for community capacity may have implications for future program design.

In addition, we have attempted in this chapter to (1) link the empirical findings of our research that demonstrate the importance of civic engagement as an outcome of CLD participation to a broader understanding of civic engagement as a concept, and (2) develop the groundwork to pay more explicit attention to developing civic engagement as one of CLD programs' primary purposes. In doing so, we recalled de Tocqueville's view of American society as demonstrating the strengths of collaborative activity in local communities to address perceived needs—his Mother Science. However, we expanded that view by linking it more directly to learned behaviors for community leadership. We argued that community residents' civic engagement builds community capacity in the form of a stronger civic infrastructure, which supports participation and democratic decision-making as well as residents' sense of empowerment. A stronger civic infrastructure provides a long-term benefit to community viability unlike any specific project with a limited scope.

Civic engagement and a strong civic infrastructure also require another element: social cohesion. It is to this factor that we now turn in our efforts to better understand how CLD programs can affect community outcomes. We also consider how leadership development activities can produce social cohesion in a practical way. Our position is that civic engagement, by itself, could possibly remain an individual activity unless coupled with residents' recognition that they cannot obtain many of the things they value in community life on their own. Rather, they must collaborate with others, and must use networks of others in the community with the interest and talents to assist in achieving important objectives.

8.

Community Leadership Relies on Social Cohesion

If civic engagement is key to achieving important community outcomes as the result of what participants learn in community leadership development (CLD) programs, do other individual outcomes also contribute? As our research shows, citizen activists who completed the leadership development offerings acted along with others from their cohort as well as other community members to successfully complete the work that they envisioned would help the community. In our experience, there are very few occasions where the citizen activist acts alone in civic engagement episodes. The idea of the charismatic leader does not seem relevant here. Rather, these individuals seek out partners of diverse backgrounds who share a common interest in making their community a better place to live. Residents may or may not consider themselves leaders or followers, but each has something to contribute and a role to play if the venture they decide upon together will be successful. Most of the time, success means doing "public work" (Boyte and Kari 1998) by engaging in civic (political) activity even though they may not need to form a relationship with civic officials.

Leadership development also contributes to community improvements through the development of social cohesion or, as we defined it earlier, the development of bridging social capital.[1] The partnerships we describe in part 1 of this volume form not haphazardly but intentionally. They usually start with a small number of community residents who might come up with an idea in which they are really interested over coffee or breakfast. They then reach into their social networks for others they think might already be or could become interested given the right sort of communication and invitation. These social networks may be based on relationships formed in a CLD program, a church or service club, a business interaction, or even a family. In most cases, those invited to participate in this civic venture are individuals with whom the initiators have interacted, perhaps many times. This interaction has provided both knowledge of common interests and also a minimal level of trust in each other. Putnam (2000) and others argue that this knowledge is one of the basic elements of bridging social capital.

Recognizing the role that social cohesion plays in supporting collaborative partnerships strongly suggests a different definition for leadership. Certainly, the partners could all be recognized as community leaders, but this may not be necessary. It appears that, in small rural communities, many collaborators do not want to be called leaders for various reasons. This reticence to be recognized as a leader does not mean their actions are not "leaderful" (Raelin 2003). Rather, it opens an inquiry into what the terms leader and leadership really mean as reflected in these bridging relationships.

Defining Leadership

We have come to understand leadership to be relational, a social phenomena that emerges when people who share a common purpose collaborate to achieve that purpose. Our perspective is that individuals, being different in many ways, bring different attributes, knowledge, and skill sets to a relationship; the leadership that emerges is more powerful and more likely to be successful than in instances where a single individual or two or three people alone take on a community project. As Heifetz (1994) argues, leadership today must adapt in order to deal with the complexities of modern life, and adapting is often easier when many leaders collaborate, with each bringing different ideas and network resources to the relationship. In this volume, we have tried to maintain a distinction between the development of "leaders" and the knowledge, skills, and capacities they must have to engage in leadership relationships and leadership development, which is a social process more than an educational one. We believe this understanding is supported by our research findings as reported in this volume. The sense of personal efficacy that is an outcome of the leadership development experience contributes indirectly but substantially to social cohesion (see figure 2.2).

Nevertheless, we often found ourselves having to use the term "leadership development" because the practitioners who organize and implement these programmatic interventions so commonly use it. Further, it is likely that average community leaders do not understand leadership to correspond to this definition, even if they may experience it as a relationship. We hope this volume will help start a constructive discussion that distinguishes the social construct of leadership from the attributes of individuals that might support their activities as leaders in the community.

Having offered this definition and our commitment to it, we must also acknowledge that leaders often act in ways that we typically name as "leadership." When the governor of a state orders the state's National Guard units to assist with a natural disaster response, they are exercising their authority as governor and, we say, demonstrating leadership. For instances such as this, Burns (1978) coins the term "transactional leadership," or the exercise of authority and/or influence to organize resources and accomplish a concrete task. We also note that transactional leadership usually deals with problems for which solutions are already known or can be readily identified. A different sort of leadership is required when the problem people face has no ready solution and requires significant reframing and innovative thinking. This is what Burns (1978) calls "transformative leadership" and what Heifetz (1994) calls "adaptive" leadership. Following Heifetz's lead, Parks (2005, 10) defines leadership as "the activity of mobilizing people to address adaptive challenges—those challenges that cannot be resolved by expert knowledge and routine management alone." The activity Parks and Heifetz have in mind as producing leadership is usually the result of collaboration, working together, sharing resources and ideas, and discussing options and debating their advantages and disadvantages until a course of action is determined (Bryson and Crosby 1992; Parks 2005).

There is an emerging and, we feel, convincing literature that supports this understanding of leadership as a product of social interaction. This literature is found in the intersections between "field theory" (Wilkinson 1991) and the "relational" view of leadership (Drath et al. 2008; Ospina and Schall 2001; Pigg 1999). Field theory derives from social interaction theory as Mead and others present it (Wilkinson 1991), and recognizes the social outcomes of interaction in communities that results in identifiable structures that act in their special fields of interest as well as the community field. Without reference to field theory, Paxton (2002, 259) makes a similar distinction between community residents' actions that are "tied to the wider community . . . and those that are not." It is reasonable to postulate that this same interaction also creates leadership activity (Israel and Beaulieu 1988). As Parks (2005, 60) notes: "Adaptive leadership requires partners, allies, and confidants—for perspective, support, information, building coalitions." These partnerships form and grow using the social cohesiveness that develops with interaction among community residents and represents a diverse resource base from which mobilization can be successful. Defining leadership as a collective attribute rather than an individual one has important practical implications for CLD program sponsors and practitioners.

Leadership as Relational

There has been an intermittent concern about rural community leadership since at least the World War II era, but that concern has changed in focus. While there are certainly still leadership programs intended for institutional leaders and managers, a growing number of programs are intended not so much for sitting mayors or councilors, but for a range of residents, and are intended to empower them to address community problems and concerns. The goals of these programs depends on their sponsors, and may range from educating up-and-coming business people to be better leaders to diversifying participation in solving community problems (Ramsay, Reed, and Vandenberg 1998).

Other things have changed since the end of the war era as the "commons" that comprised the "common good" is being transformed. As Parks (2005, 3) notes:

> The new commons in which we now find ourselves is both global in scope and relentlessly local in impact. In a simpler time, the village green, the market square, Main Street, the wharf, the great plaza, the town, the city, or even the nation offered a sense of a shared life within a manageable frame. Today's new commons requires participation in a more dynamic, interdependent, and vast web of life—within a frame growing increasingly *un*manageable.

Why should we worry about developing additional and better leaders in the community? Is it not sufficient to elect and appoint capable individuals to positions of responsibility and authority and expect them to fulfill their roles in capable fashion, satisfying at least the majority of the populace? The answer is an obvious "no." But sorting out the reasons behind that answer is more complicated. In our talks with community leaders, we received the impression that elected and appointed leaders are too often inadequately prepared to do their jobs and are structurally limited in their accomplishments either by statute or the restrictions of time and energy. Even in small towns and rural counties, the complexities of governing today are greater than many leaders imagine when they decide to run for office. The amount of time it takes to govern effectively is immense, especially if resources are as constrained as they often are.

There is, perhaps, another reason why it is important to develop new leadership in communities: to the extent that command and control leadership is no longer adequate or desirable for addressing today's adaptive challenges, leaders must learn and accept new models. Many times those we elect and expect to provide leadership in making progress on adaptive challenges—what Schall (1995) calls "the mess"—find that the authority they could formerly call upon to mobilize resources toward solutions simply does not exist. At the least, their authority alone is not sufficient to address these challenges successfully. Nevertheless, they continue to act in many cases as if the command and control model is still the proper approach. Parks (2005) argues that this model is part of a larger myth that was largely unexamined until the past couple decades, and that remains largely unexamined at the local level and in vernacular settings. Drath and his colleagues (2008) refer to this myth as a "leadership culture" comprised of a set of values and beliefs about the relationship between authority and leadership that is no longer useful and, perhaps, is even damaging to efforts to make the sort of progress toward community betterment rural communities need. Others also address the need to abandon the old myth and create a new one. Books such as *Complexity* (Waldrop 1992), *Leadership and the New Science* (Wheatley 1992), *Force for Change* (Kotter 1990), *Getting Things Done When You Are Not in Charge* (Bellman 1992), and *Tempered Radicals* (Meyerson 2001) all indicate concern with the old myth, and some take the next step of describing the new myth necessary to address today's complex "swamp" issues. Drath and associates (2008) and Heifetz and Linsky (2002) arguably take the challenge of new myth development the farthest in their respective works. Heifetz, for example, has been developing and applying his approach in the classroom and in consulting work for more than twenty years (Parks 2005). To us, the approaches these two sources represent are compatible in many ways, and often appear to differ more in terminology than in basic concepts. The underlying idea from both approaches is a rejection of formal authority as the primary source of leadership in recognition of its relative ineffectiveness making progress in swamp issues.

So, it is not unusual for individuals in formal leadership roles to have to form collaborative relationships with others in the community—civic groups, service clubs, faith-based organizations, youth groups, or even ad hoc resident groups—to get things done. This sort of collaboration requires "relational leadership," a form of leadership that recognizes that each participant has something to contribute at some point in the process, and that each participant may be a leader at some point and a follower at others (Bryson and Crosby 1992; Ospina and Schall 2001). The idea recognizes that no single person has all the answers and that strength and innovation come from diverse groups of individuals committed to solving the same problem and acting in concert to that end.

Further, it may often happen that ordinary people in the community with leadership skills and inclinations, along with impatience with the lack of action from formal leaders, may take things in their own hands and do what de Tocqueville lauded 200 years ago: join together to get something done that satisfies their immediate motives. In this collective action, they exercise relational leadership. The "leadership" emerges as a social phenomenon of the shared intention and interaction (Rost 1991; Graen and Uhl-Bien 1995). In fact, this is the sort of leadership we discovered that most often occurred as the result of CLD programs and that delivered a range of benefits to rural communities in which leaders resided.

The relational view of leadership has been linked to a change in the basic idea that underlies our thinking about leadership. This basic idea is reflected in three elements: leader, follower, and common goals (Drath et al. 2008). The idea existing in the relationship among these three elements is that leader directs followers, who work to accomplish the common goal the leader established. This idea forms the basis for the existing leadership culture (the old myth) in most organizations and communities. We often speak of the need for leadership to give us the proper direction so things will change in the direction we desire. This culture spawns a dependency on leaders that often cannot be met. Heifetz (1994) argues this is especially true when the problem or issue facing the community is complex and not readily solved by ordinary technical approaches. Instead, we need an adaptive approach with diverse input from a broad spectrum of collaborators, each of whom may help set direction. The collaborators must then determine how each contribution might fit together to comprise a satisfactory solution.

Such interaction does not happen normally. People must recognize that technical solutions do not offer a satisfactory response to important issues and feel empowered to act independently. A small group may call a larger group into being using their community social network, and this group then begins to generate ideas to address the identified issue. This social process is "leadership" (Drath et al. 2008; Ospina and Schall 2001) and emerges from an interactive process that illustrates a new basic conception—that leadership is a process of agreeing upon a *direction*, creating *alignment*, and establishing *commitment* among those involved. Through interaction, a direction is agreed upon and the group's purpose is clarified; those involved identify what they want to accomplish and how they want to proceed, and then get on with it. Through interaction, each participant aligns with this direction and with partners, and creates a shared value system regarding the work to be done. Through interaction, the participants strengthen their existing commitment to the community with a new commitment to accomplishing their specific purpose. What emerges from this process is leadership, a social attribute that all participants create and share.

In this sense, then, we can define leadership as a relationship of a specific type—one that is based on "direction, alignment and commitment" (Drath et al. 2008). Becoming an effective participant in the sort of social process this definition envisions may not come naturally and may require learning. Some of these things are what we now recognize as leaders' attributes: working collaboratively, knowing how to develop consensus, being a good communicator, knowing how to plan and organize an activity, and so forth. The way that someone deploys these attributes in a relationship makes a difference in our understanding of what constitutes leadership.

Although he uses somewhat different language, Heifetz (as described in Parks 2005) speaks to a similar idea. His teaching emphasizes a distinction between authority and leadership, power versus progress, and personality versus presence. He pays less attention to an individual's power and influence and more attention to whether or not those involved in leadership progress toward solutions to adaptive challenges. Shifting the focus away from authority also shifts it away from personality and toward what Heifetz calls "presence," individuals' ability to be skillful in intervening in a variety of situations from interpersonal to global. This ability to be present, to comprehend what is happening in the complex system related to the adaptive challenge, and to make choices about when and how to intervene to help the group make progress is critical to leadership success.

The community aspect of this relationship is understood through field theory as applied to setting direction and creating alignment and commitment. As is well known, field theory distinguishes the community field from those that represent specific and more narrowly defined interests such as the economy, education, health care, public safety, and so forth. In order for community change to occur, the participants in these civic activities must be able to define their direction in relationship to the direction in which the community wants to go. One can imagine that this process often involves establishing a community vision. Indeed, our research finds that while individual participants may learn why community vision is important and, perhaps, a bit about what function such vision may serve, the shared purpose and future outcome has little relationship to the civic engagement or social cohesion outcome and, later in the analysis, little effect on the community outcomes we measured.[2] The individuals in the projects and activities we studied appeared to agree upon a direction in a limited fashion, but that direction did not appear to be explicitly related to any broader community direction.

Alignment also is created through interaction and can be accomplished with the community field's enhancement in mind. Program sponsors can address this task by making sure participants are diverse and represent different community sectors or interests in addition to including those interested in the general community field. Direction and alignment are both necessary to produce "progress" toward solutions to adaptive challenges. Heifetz (in Parks 2005) provides more discussion about how progress is achieved and, at least for the classroom, makes a number of suggestions to support learning that could be adapted for CLD activities.

Finally, without commitment it seems unlikely that individuals will remain "present" in a social process that aims to bring together diverse interests and populations and systematically address what it will take to produce some leadership on complex issues. This is because:

> The discovery that the activity of courageous, adaptive leadership inevitably must take place within a field of complex systems requires a shift in perception. In the practice of adaptive leadership, what really matters is the capacity for effective participation—ways of being present that foster the building of collective strength. That is, even if one is standing in the spotlight, it is more useful to envision oneself as a resonant and responsive node in a dynamic network or field of energy and an agent of emergent possibility and progress, rather imagining oneself as simply gifted and entitled to be on top and in charge. (Parks 2005, 99–100)

Such a shift in perspective is obviously difficult and requires commitment to the task and to the individual partners, as well as a challenging degree of self-discipline.

Readers should recall that both these approaches require a group of people who interact and all remain present in the process. Each member of the group brings different resources and ideas to the process of creating a non-technical solution to adaptive challenges. Social cohesion results from this commitment and results from the efforts of individuals to mobilize their networks to bring important resources to the process. Community commitment is one of the outcomes we document as important for producing both civic engagement and social cohesion outcomes at the individual level (see table 2.1).

We do not believe the current leadership development activities are not at least partially effective. But few of the activities that became the focus of our efforts to demonstrate the community effects resulting from leadership could likely be defined as "adaptive challenges." In fact, most of the activities that we studied to determine community effects were organized by a small group committed to a specific, limited objective it felt would improve the community as captured by one or more of the Community Capitals. Most of these activities had little or no involvement of formal, institutional authorities, but instead relied on the sense of empowerment the participants in the group shared. How would things have been different if a broader network had been available to draw upon for resources and support? How would the leadership have emerged from the process? What other sorts of issues might have been addressed (such as those related to the community field)? What would the CLD activity have looked like to answer these questions? How would participation in the activity been organized? Are rural places simply so homogeneous or resources so limited that new ideas are difficult to identify? What learning activities could have been organized for participants that would reflect a different leadership culture than that to which they were accustomed?

For example, Parks (2005, 111–12) notes: "People must be drawn together into difficult work and find the strength, energy, and commitment to sustain the work across the long haul." She goes on to describe a method used in Heifetz's classes involving creative acts presented in public to classmates that reveal the diversity among the group and build acceptance and trust across difference. She concludes: "The experience of compassion and respect plays a vital role in inspiring trust and building bridges across difference. Given that factions of various kinds inevitably develop within the class as within any human group, the [creative sessions] appear to foster a new basis for common ground." This description sounds much like that Putnam (2000) uses in regards to the basis for bridging social capital.

Social Cohesion as a Basis for Community Leadership

Charles Rios recognized that he could not develop a refuge for abused women and children alone. He needed to do too many things, to mobilize more resources, and to manage more people with related interests in this project than he could alone. The whole project entailed some risk—on an individual level, financial and reputational risks to Charles—but he felt that the risks those suffering abuse faced were too great to ignore any longer. Going it alone simply was not a good idea. He needed help to get everything done successfully. He found common ground with Dan, Verna, Carlotta, and others, and they worked together, sharing the risk and the satisfaction when they made progress.

Heifetz and Linsky (2002 78) write about the need to develop relationships with partners in any community endeavor. They note:

> Partners provide protection, and they create alliances for you with factions other than your own. They strengthen both you and your initiatives. With partners, you are not simply relying on the logical power of your arguments and evidence, you are building political power as well. Furthermore, the content of your ideas will improve if you take into account the validity of other viewpoints—especially if you can incorporate the views of those who differ markedly from you. This is especially critical when you are advancing a difficult issue or confronting a conflict of values.

Here we see the confluence of leadership and social cohesion or bridging social capital. At this point, we understand there is a reciprocal relationship (Paxton 2002) between social cohesion and bridging social capital. As Schuller (2007, 17) notes in discussing social cohesion and bridging forms of social capital, we "must deal in relationships." Sometimes, these relationships may comprise leadership as defined above. A more cohesive community makes it easier to assemble and align diverse interests to support a common direction. In reciprocal fashion, bridging social capital, based as it is in relationships of generalized trust and interactions focused on the community field, can be instrumental in generating social cohesion.[3] We make the distinction in this research based on how we measured social cohesion empirically as a community effect, and argue the individual indicators in the index point more toward mobilizing diverse interests than building on intimate relationships. Leadership, as progress toward solutions to adaptive challenges, forms based on the interactions of diverse individuals representing different specific fields of interest in the community who agree upon a common direction, align themselves with others so as to achieve their purpose, and share a commitment toward the general betterment of the community and each other as they work together. As Whitham (2012) argues, this sort of social cohesion may best be developed via "gathering place networks" in which people with diverse backgrounds and life experiences (and human capital resources) may meet and get to know one another. We argue that the CLD experiences participants shared also creates networks where the value of such diversity becomes more fully appreciated.[4]

The twentieth century leadership culture that Heifetz and Drath describe may be in the process of experiencing some unintentional change as community residents recognize that the older model, the one that is related to possessing formal authority and has been described as a "leader-follower-common goal" base, just does not work with regard to many community issues. Some of these issues may, in fact, be amenable to technical solutions or at least can be addressed with

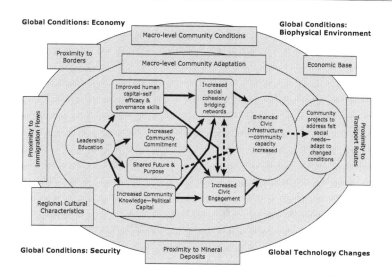

Figure 9.1. Toward a Theory of Community Leadership: The Centrality of Civic Infrastructure.

existing knowledge. We recognize that solving "technical problems" of the sort participants in CLD programs most often address is not trivial. However, it takes a different kind of knowledge to address the more pressing adaptive challenges a community might face. The important knowledge is often represented in the social cohesiveness of the community's residents as expressed in both internal and external (horizontal and vertical) networks. The development of some of this knowledge may be tacit or implicit in the CLD experience. In some cases, we can document that the curriculum devised by sponsors addresses it explicitly, though not intensively. We interpret this as a response to recent thinking about the importance of collaboration in a number of influential publications (e.g., Bryson and Crosby 1992) and in the communications from foundations and institutions to community residents.

Furthermore, we document the actual practice that CLD program participants bring to their community betterment efforts. We find the process followed to reflect many elements of the kind of process Heifetz, Drath, and others encourage, which often reflects the mobilization of differences to create direction, alignment, and commitment from among a network of people with whom the participants have developed a relationship. The process also reflects a sense of empowerment that can be effective without regard to the formal authority any member of the network does or does not possess.

We believe that the learning experiences that might allow future leaders to reject the leadership culture of the last century and build a newer one are likely insufficient. Further, if this is the case, program sponsors are missing a significant opportunity to help promote and support this kind of change. We address how they might accomplish this in the next chapter. We should note that, even if sponsors implemented the sort of changes we advocate, changing a leadership culture will require considerable time and persistence. As Heifetz and Linsky (2002, 11) note: "People don't resist change, per se. People resist loss." Giving up the norms, expectations, and behaviors tied to the old leadership culture represents a loss to many individuals. CLD program participants need to learn how to deal with such situations in order to make progress on adaptive challenges.

9.

Toward a General Theory of Community Leadership

Acknowledging the efforts of a large group organized by James M. Burns to develop a general theory of leadership and their admitted shortcomings, we too despair of being able to offer a general theory of community leadership (Goethals and Sorenson 2006). Even though we narrow the field somewhat from what Burns's group tackled, the complexity of community leadership remains substantial. At the macro level, contextual developments affect communities in different ways depending on their economic base, proximity to borders and immigration routes, location of mineral deposits or transit routes, dominant cultural characteristics, and many more factors. At the micro level, these macro effects in turn create reactions among community members based on their understanding of globalization's effects, interactions with others in the community, value system, local family members, power relations, psychological efficacy, and so forth (Hickman 2010).

Our research has produced a model of the effects of CLD programs on individuals and communities (see figure 9.1). Neither this infogram nor the discussion that follows intend to have theoretical implications. Structural path models are limited to providing a degree of explained variance, which is a function of what figure 9.1 includes. While we have noted that our research explains some of the variation in certain community capitals, and represents assets within the community, we have also noted the limitations of this research—the size of the study population, the measures used, and so forth. Much more remains to be done to fully answer questions about community effects. The one thing we do not claim to have produced is a new theory of community leadership. However, we do conclude that the five years of research, analysis, and study we have devoted to this topic have provided a number of insights that should be considered on a theoretical level as work progresses. We discuss these insights and observations in this chapter, and offer our perspectives on a general theory of community leadership beyond our elaboration of important central concepts in the previous two chapters.

Figure 9.1 illustrates the results of our analysis presented in part 1 with the addition of the idea that the "capacity" that is created by changed attitudes, knowledge, and propensities for action regarding individual civic engagement and the new bridging networks created in the CLD program is captured by enhanced civic infrastructure. This infrastructure is considered important, if not necessary, to the effective planning and decision-making, the resolution of conflicting ideas, and the development of a comprehensive (if not compelling) vision and purpose for the community that are all necessary if communities are to make relevant and appropriate changes for development purposes. Our analysis has demonstrated that individuals undergo important changes as a result of their participation in CLD activities. These changes are psychological, cognitive, and behavioral. They empower participants by preparing them to become active citizens in the community, engage in activities that produce constructive changes, and, in the process, enhance the civic infrastructure by bringing new ideas and skills to this structure and the processes involved therein. In addition, these participants join an existing network that reflects the social cohesion necessary to mobilize the existing resources and to access new resources in order to implement change. The resulting activities that propel change may happen directly as residents organize ad hoc projects or through existing organizational structures. Regardless of the path, the result is an enhanced civic infrastructure based on associations of individuals and organizations in relationships of trust and reciprocity guided by a shared purpose.

We recognize that a few of these links are not well supported in our analysis. As we discussed in chapter 4, this lack of statistical support may well be an artifact of our measurement techniques. The conceptual relationships we are not able to demonstrate statistically appear on the figure by dashed lines. The civic infrastructure concept is an addition to our thinking that resulted from our findings about how individual changes manifest in collective activity. The relationships and ideas captured by the dashed (hypothetical) lines need additional research. We discuss a number of the specific elements of this situation in more depth below. However inadequate or untested, we intend this model to capture our proposal for a theory of community development that arises from CLD activities and explains how community leadership is central to community change—a relationship that has long been argued but rarely tested empirically.

Community and Complexity

We view community as a complex adaptive system composed of structures (including institutions and norms for behavior), actors, and assets in continuous interaction (Wheatley 1992). Communities do act (Luloff and Swanson 1988; Brown 1991), and this action is typically guided by leaders who use available assets in response to changes in their situation as they understand the elements of that situation. Furthermore, leaders are affected by other leaders in the community, as well as by other citizens' opinions and actions. The community consists of structures, what Wheatley (1992) and Wilkinson (1991) call fields, that include the normal institutions we deal with as governmental bodies as well as organizations and families, but also includes the norms of behavior that govern our interactions with each other. These norms determine what is discussable, what is fair and just, what options citizens have to participate, who is included in decision-making, and so forth. Many of these structures control assets that may be necessary to support successful actions citizens desire, especially government, organizational, and business structures, although many important assets reside with individual actors in their human capital. As Wheatley (1992, 49) says, these are "unseen structures, occupying (social and psychological) space and becoming known to us through their effects."

One of the most important consequences of seeing the community as a complex adaptive system is that doing so rejects a linear view of change and substitutes a view that takes into account the impinging forces that the actions, values, assets, and motives of other citizens in the community represent. The linear view is Newtonian or mechanistic. It emphasizes the development of goals and the organization of resources to meet those goals through mobilizing followers to assist in the task. It is more attuned to a "management" view than a leadership view (Pigg 1999) and contradicts our contemporary views of leadership as a relationship requiring collaboration and shared responsibility for action. It also fails to recognize the important element of leadership work that Heifetz (1994) calls adaptive work, which is the continuous, reflexive modification of strategy and tactics necessary to achieve success in the face of the numerous and constantly changing aspects of the community environment in which leaders try to function. Bennis and Nanus (1985) noted several decades ago that complexity was one of the three major challenges facing leaders in contemporary society, a view that is perhaps best understood when we see community as an adaptive system that responds to a wide variety of effects that themselves affect leaders as they act. This complexity is more than the effects of such trends as globalization—it also is represented by the general messiness apparent in community processes related to governance and decision-making.

CLD sponsors will recognize that this view will create some uncertainty among program participants who view leadership as more like management or a leader-follower relationship. We would all like the world to be predictable. But, there is really no reason to think this would be the case in a community context any more than it is in a family or work context. Surely days and weeks may pass with little noticeable change that directly affects how we live our lives. Nevertheless, as leaders bring more people into the relationship, especially those they may not have known well before, and consider more factors as they pursue a course of action, they have to learn to be adaptive. It is likely impossible to control many of the factors that will impinge on what citizen leaders try to do (Heifetz 1994).

Different Strokes for Different Folks?

We have noted the interest of program sponsors in recruiting CLD participants that are more diverse in their demographics and we have referenced the fact that some demographic groups do not think of leadership in this same way as white Americans. We have discussed Gambrell and Fritz's (2012) valuable perspective on the Lakota Sioux, but what about the Iroquois, Blackfoot, or Osage people? Do these groups view leadership differently? If so, to what degree? Within the Lakota peoples, being a leader means something different in substantive terms than it does in other cultures. On the other hand, being an effective leader in the Lakota or white cultures means appreciating the basic values and history of your ethnic group and community (Burns 1978; Rost 1991; Wilkinson 1991). What about Latino or African American views? Martinez-Cosio (1996) argues that a universal model is possible, but only if respect is given to the motivations and cultural values of minority individuals who want to participate. She addresses primarily Latino interests and emphasizes the importance of justice to Latino people, but also notes that the term "Latino" really has little meaning today as there are so many cultures represented in this population that finding some common cultural thread may be difficult.

So, what does this mean for the researcher interested in leadership and leadership development? We feel a comparative approach is necessary to forming a general theory. Comparing programs designed explicitly for single (non-white) cultures with one that has effectively diversified its participant base but uses more conventional and universal content and approaches to leader and leadership development could be productive. Doing this will likely require a collaborative research approach with researchers in several locales representing different institutions to ensure reasonable access and comparative samples. Further, the efforts could focus primarily on participant-level outcomes to determine whether any differences could be explained by participant characteristics and curriculum strategies. However, the results could be quite revealing and informative for practitioners and sponsors alike.

Civic Education Is Needed

Civic education needs among the general population, especially the younger population, is a growing concern (Galston 2004). The results of the well-known study periodically repeated by UCLA since the 1960s show that the number of college-age adults who actually vote has declined to about one-third in presidential elections and one-fifth in congressional elections. Similarly, among this age group, only a minority think their voting makes a difference, frequently discuss politics, get political information from traditional news media, or try to keep up with politics (Galston 2004, 263). At the high school level, results reported on the National Assessment of Education Progress tests for civic education shows that 64 percent of high school seniors tested in 2010 (the most recent year administered at the time of writing) had a basic level of knowledge at best, a level unchanged since 1998.[1] Further, it is likely that this situation does not improve much as young adults join and devote their time to the work force. As they also move into community life and begin to seek an active role in their communities as leaders, where will their basic knowledge about how our system of democratic, representative government works? Since most civics classes deal with national, rather than local, structures and processes, the challenge is even greater. Although constrained in some places by statutory limits and in many places by available resources, communities often have substantial authority over nearly all aspects of individual well-being. How citizens interact with local authorities to address issues of concern may be a good measure of long-term community viability. That interaction is, in our view, mediated by the civic infrastructure of the community (Morton 2003).

Obviously, there is the question of where adults will get their civic education once they depart formal educational institutions. CLD programs, along with other adult education programs, can provide a source of such education. Our research shows that community-based CLD programs can produce civic-engagement-related outcomes, including knowledge about how local governance systems work and how to get things done in the local community, but we argue this could be significantly improved with a change in focus to acknowledge the importance of this outcome and its relationship to community well-being. Other community-based efforts are being developed and proving effective. For example, Schwinn and associates (2005) discuss "learning democracy centers," such as the Lower Outer Cape Community Coalition of Eastham, Massachusetts. These centers are the work of civic organizations able "to engage diverse members of their communities in solving their most pressing social, economic, and environmental problems" (Schwinn et al. 2005, 228). According to these authors:

> Each of these organizations helps its community master the competencies required in an inclusive, participatory democracy: valuing diversity in all its dimensions; engaging in meaningful public dialogue; understanding the systemic nature of complex problems; collaborating across organizational and sectoral boundaries; generating and implementing innovative solutions; seeking out new sources of funding and support; providing evidence that their actions are making a difference in the community's well-being; and, finally, learning from experience. (Schwinn et al. 2005, 228)

These centers are more than just deliberation arenas with enhanced participation. Resources are available for learning civic engagement skills and knowledge that are otherwise missing from the arsenal of citizen leaders who want to enact change. These centers also work to enhance local civic infrastructure.

In another experiment of the sort we envision (and mentioned above), the Annie E. Casey Foundation has supported the Leadership in Action Program in several locations, such as Baltimore (Meehan et al. n.d.). While this initiative usually engages a group of individuals occupying roles as formal leaders to collaborate and form a more effective leadership team to address a specific issue, the civic education model is a useful one that might be replicated in a different format depending on the issue being addressed. The process involves deploying educators in civic and collaboration processes that provide opportunities for active reflection and dialogue about leadership issues during the process of problem solving and action implementation.

There are fewer civic organizations where learning about civic engagement and leadership can take place, according to Skocpol (2003). Many organizations have changed their structures and now employ professional association managers to handle affairs, rather than relying on citizen leaders to do this job as before. In small communities, this may be less of a problem, as the influence of professional management tends not to reach far enough to actively intervene in organization affairs. Nevertheless, a more intentional approach to civic education would be desirable if these settings are to provide the kind of learning Skocpol claims they once provided for civic leaders. In the meantime, CLD programs may fill some of this void and could offer even more effective civic education than they do currently.

Efficacy and Empowerment

Increasing the psychological sense of efficacy, leaders' community knowledge, and building networks of weak ties is empowering to individuals as well as CLD participants' collective efficacy. Our research results demonstrate that this sense of personal growth, efficacy, and community knowledge is an important outcome in the general model of CLD outcomes. However, the model does not do justice to the suspected empowerment process beneath these outcomes.

We have argued that empowerment is a function of several individual and social processes (Pigg 2002). Empowerment involves: (1) personal growth and efficacy, (2) recognition by others, and (3) knowledge of how to remove barriers to power. Most CLD programs exhibit little explicit understanding of power and empowerment. Rather, they make an implicit assumption that knowledge is power and directly produces action; that knowing what to do is the same as knowing how to do it. While they teach and allow participants to practice personal skills, they often do not address efficacy in the broader sense. We identified few curriculum materials in use in this area. Some CLD programs address empowerment indirectly by using nomination programs, sponsors for participants, formal recognition efforts, mentoring programs, and carefully appointing the selection committee (Moore 1988). What seems to be missing is the understanding that empowering others also involves shared leadership (Kouzes and Posner 1988), and there are numerous resources available on this concept.[2]

While learning about the technical aspects of an issue in the community is important, knowing what to do about it and how are quite different areas of knowledge and skill. CLD programs' curricula often address learning about the elements of any specific issue and the different perspectives that make it difficult or contentious, but do not necessarily address how to resolve the issue. Chrislip and Larson (1994) present one effective approach. CLD program organizers can focus more on collaboration as a way to empower citizens to take action or to work more effectively with institutional representatives. Collaboration, according to Chrislip and Larson (1994, 14), operates from the premise that "if you bring the appropriate people together in constructive ways with good information, they will create authentic visions and strategies for addressing the shared concerns of the . . . community." While we might argue about who those "appropriate people" are, the notion that citizens can collaborate to devise a satisfactory solution is a means of empowering each other by sharing know-how. Kania and Kramer (2011) provide a related perspective on the effects of collaborative efforts in the notion of "collective impact."

Feeling empowered can also mean being recognized by the existing power structure and being acknowledged by others as a leader in the community. Sometimes this may come about through appointment to an agency board or election to local office. While the old boys' network seems to have shrinking power in our society, it still operates in many small rural towns (Brown 1991; Lovell 2009). Simply being introduced to local officials; talking about local situations; and sharing views about values, priorities, courses of action, and available resources can remove the sense of intimidation many citizens feel with regard to those in positions of formal authority.

Feeling empowered also means belonging to a network of other empowered individuals whom you know and trust when organizing some sort of effort in the community. This sort of bridging social capital (or social cohesion) is important when leaders feel it is time to act. It is helpful to know that there are others in the community whom leaders may call upon to join in. The people within a leader's civic network can possess important skills, knowledge, or other resources to help advance the purpose agreed upon. Rasmussen and associates (2011) demonstrate how important this social network can be in civic engagement as part of a leadership development effort.

As we think about developing civic leaders in our community, we need to think carefully about how CLD efforts will support leaders' ultimate empowerment and help to produce desired changes. Empowerment is obviously a complex psychological and social process and can be created in a number of ways. A clear strategy that fits the situation of each community and individual is essential. To return to where we began in this section, we note Larry Dennis's (1993) observation that knowledge is only power when an individual knows how to apply it, and applying it takes courage, conviction, persistence, vision, and other characteristics of effective leaders. Empowerment is more than just knowing what needs to be done or how to do it—it is the confidence needed to be successful and the self-efficacy to recognize in oneself and others the capacity or power to act in ways that lead to constructive change. Sometimes citizen leaders can empower themselves through learning and reflection; sometimes empowerment is aided by the intervention of others and CLD efforts.

The Role of Network Effects

Since one of the central effects of CLD participation is social cohesion, related to bridging forms of social capital, a general theory needs to devote attention to these network effects. A few studies undertake this task (Ricketts and Ladewig 2008; Rasmussen et al. 2011; Laumann and Pappi 1976; Brown and Nylander 1998; Sharp 2001), but none use the current methodological advances available in network analysis. All except Laumann and Pappi use qualitative data or indirect indicators of the existence of networks. Marwell and associates (1988) use a mathematical modeling technique to predict how networks might look in a community and which variety might be the most effective in mobilizing resources. Baldassarri and Diani (2007) use a more contemporary network analysis approach in two localities in Britain to test the notion that civic networks are best represented by a polycentric model of network relationships. While likely difficult to accomplish in a single location and more difficult to accomplish in comparative studies, attention to this aspect of leadership, especially with the aim of determining how it relates to collaborative leadership experiences, is important. On the other hand, if Brown's (1991) findings hold, and rural communities demonstrate highly centralized, top-down networks of leaders who make decisions for the community at large with little citizen involvement, then this sort of network analysis awakens us to the pressing need for the kind of CLD programs our research identifies as producing civic engagement and social cohesion effects as they may be associated with democratic processes.

The Community Civic Structure

Enhancing civic structure through CLD efforts increases the kinds of actions that improve collective well-being. Morton (2003) tests this general proposition and finds justification for it with regard to the quality of rural community services. Wagner (2004) and Orum and Gramlich (1999) capture the same notion using slightly different terms. Morton (2003, 105) argues:

> The civic structure of a community consists of normative expectations that

multiple individual and group actions will lead to solving collective problems in the broad community interest. Encompassing the ideas of civic culture, civic engagement and civic norms, a community with high civic structure has multiple groups that negotiate and compromise with each other to construct social, economic and political institutions that meet their collective needs. The level of civic structure reflects the capacity of communities to solve problems such as the allocation of public resources in the community interest and the facilitation of the private exchange of goods and services . . . High levels of interaction and communication across community groups and sectors expand the resources of the community by integrating different population perspectives and skills in the search for solutions to community problems . . . A civic structure has social interactions that contain a high degree of inclusiveness, tolerance for minority group perspectives, and active participation in public problem solving.

Our interpretation is that civic structure integrates the individual-level outcomes of CLD programs, or what we term civic engagement and social cohesion. Although our model analyses individual effects separately from community effects (because we have no theoretical framework or statistical method to combine them), the notion of a civic structure provides a framework for understanding how they may act together to produce community benefits that may be, in fact, greater than the individual benefits we document. In other words, civic structure is produced through increased individual capacity for civic engagement and bridging capital for social cohesion. In turn, the civic structure provides the capacity for community change that produces material benefit through collaborative activity or community leadership. This is a notion similar to Wilkinson's (1991) argument that changes in the community field must be central for community development to occur. When citizen leaders work across fields or the boundaries of specific interests in recognition of common interests (the common good), changes that benefit the entire community are evident and the civic structure is shown to be at work.

SELF-INTEREST, RIGHTLY UNDERSTOOD?

This discussion brings us back to de Tocqueville and his notion of how self-interest plays a role in the American democracy. Ever afraid of unbridled individualism and its reluctance to acknowledge what was the "common good" to all citizens, de Tocqueville (2000, 204–08) devised the notion that what was necessary in civic education was "self-interest, rightly understood." By this he meant that people who understood that their individual interests were often tied to or closely aligned with those of their neighbors were more likely to engage in political and social activity than those who did not. Those who did not understand this and stood only for their individual interests were likely to isolate themselves from other citizens, causing the community to suffer. In de Tocqueville's time, this tendency might have led to despotic conditions. In a democracy, it leads to communities that lack a strong civic structure. The communal effect is especially apparent in communities, where de Tocqueville (2000, 208) notes: "Local liberties, which cause a great number of citizens to value the affection of their neighbors and their close relations, thus continually lead men back toward each other, despite the instincts that draw them apart, and force them to help one another." As Goldberg (2001) argues, this "self-interest" principle applies to social as well as economic and personal rights.

Collaboration that addresses community well-being occurs among citizen leaders who, as individuals, may represent different fields in the community but who share the same general/civic purpose (de Tocqueville's self-interest rightly understood) or a common good (Morton 2003; de Tocqueville 2000). The difficulty we identified is that, too often, this collaboration is restricted to a few interests or a small subset of community fields—just enough to get the specific job done—and does not consider the greater community benefit. This is evident in the nature of the community outcomes we see in our model and the lack of a relationship between community development curriculum content in the programs and the individual outcomes we investigated. It is also evident in our own qualitative impressions of the kind of activities our CLD participants told us they engaged in after their learning experience. Finally, it is evident in the difficulty we have in finding an empirical relationship between our outcomes and the Shared Future and Purpose indicator. Perhaps it would be useful to think about a new CLD program strategy formulated around "direction, alignment and commitment" the central leadership principles Drath and associates (2008) pose for use with a specific issue or community purpose in mind, as is being done in the Leadership in Action Program referenced above.

In addition, we repeat our contention that community is socially constructed, an institution composed of individuals and their interactions that create norms of trust, reciprocity, and a basis for public actions—a civic structure. In practical terms, these actions are often episodic, unplanned, and accretive (in terms of the effects of changes that occur), involving civic activity that is often ad hoc, especially in small communities), and thus are in need of directed and aligned public work. Further, this kind of public work requires relational leadership (collaboration). Therefore, we also argue that community leadership is socially constructed from among those citizen leaders who recognize that common action is the only way to meet common interests (Uhl-Bien 2006). Leadership is the emergent property of the relationships formed in this set of interactions (Rost 1991; Drath et al. 2008).

RELATIONAL LEADERSHIP

Leaders who collaborate and use their individual and collective social, political, and human capital construct relational leadership. Relational leadership theory has only recently emerged as a cogent theory (Uhl-Bien 2006; Drath 2001), but has some common ideas with several other theoretical perspectives such as shared leadership (Pearce and Conger 2003). Drath (2001) takes this a step further and offers "relational dialogue" as one of the three bases for leadership, indicating that leaders construct a dialogue among themselves in order to better understand their situation and the elements that might comprise a solution (i.e., sense-making). Through that dialogue, they develop a shared commitment to action through collaboration. This perspective is similar to the one we offered in figure 6.1 for the cell labeled "collective action," in which relational leadership is the basic type of leadership participants exercise in this sort of activity.

The implication for CLD sponsors and program organizers is that the participants are not now learning leadership, but instead are learning the individual skills and attitudes of leaders that let them form the sort of collaborative relationships that become community leadership and that give them new capacity for action. Some of these relationships may involve only citizen leaders like themselves, individuals with no sources of legitimacy or authority beyond their cause, voices, and numbers. Some relationships may involve partnerships with organizations in the community or institutions that may hold formal authority. As Drath and associates (2008) note, these skills involve the ability to establish "direction, alignment and commitment" among the participating citizen leaders. Here we see a convergence with a possible theory of community change, the theory of aligned contributions (Pillsbury 2009), which describes a collaborative skill set for a group of community leaders who align themselves according to a single, desired, urgent goal and put the energy and attention of their respective organizations to work to achieve it. The goal provides direction; dialogue, compromise, and reciprocal behaviors provide alignment; and collective, shared accountability create collaboration and commitment. Using case studies from resources that feature these types of activities in learning exercises for a CLD program would be a useful tool for discussion and reflection about specific skills and how to acquire them in practice.

Heifetz, in his courses at Harvard (Parks 2005), suggests a somewhat different learning model. He uses a method he calls "case in point," where an individual's own leadership experiences provide the materials for group study and examination along with classroom presentations and dialogue with consultants and teachers. Either of these two approaches represents a substantial departure from current practice.

To refer once more to figure 6.1, the nature of leadership required in different socio-political contexts, even at the community level, is different, and each context (institutional, organizational, ad hoc collective) requires distinctive capacities. CLD participants who run for and gain elected office or are appointed to a statutory commission, for example, must learn how and when to exercise their statutory authority and when to engage with other citizen leaders regarding issues that face the community. Long-recommended civic engagement practices such as participation and consultation are too limited for modern political society, even in small communities. Local officials can learn a great deal and be assisted in material ways by authentically engaging citizens and recognizing that citizens, rather than some higher power, grant them authority. In other words, leaders in institutional settings can exercise relational leadership as well as can leaders in other settings.

Similarly, the leaders of local organizations should heed this call for greater collaboration. In an issue of the *Stanford Social Innovation Review*, in a well-regarded article entitled "Collective Impact," Kania and Kramer (2011) challenge community organizations to engage in a different kind of collaborative leadership that more effectively addresses the sort of adaptive work and "wicked problems" that technical expertise alone cannot solve. Several of the basic principles they advocate speak to the need for collaborative, relational leadership, including a common agenda, shared measurement systems, and mutually reinforcing activities. These principles cannot be established without authentic relational leadership. Local organizations could better serve as classrooms for civic education in most communities with greater attention given to the need to strengthen the civic structure of their community.

CLD NEEDS A THEORY OF COMMUNITY CHANGE

There are no theories of CLD, yet, as we have noted, many theories that might apply to it. This makes the task of theory selection for testing quite difficult, for both the researcher and the practitioner. Again, it is generally useful to separate theories regarding leader development from those regarding leadership development, and for the latter especially few theories are available for guiding research and evaluation. What we have produced in this volume is not so much a theory as a model of the relationship among specific effects related to CLD and, as our data from the comparison sites show, there is a world of leadership development that occurs apart from formal learning programs that still has not been widely investigated. We don't really know precisely how and what sort of community leadership development takes place, although we certainly might speculate on both accounts.

In this research, we followed the basic assumption that leaders do, in fact, have a direct effect on communities; that, through their actions, they produce change. Certainly, they do not act alone and, if they are truly successful, usually exploit opportunities made available to them. Still, community leaders can change their community and often make it a better place to live for some, if not all, of its citizens. Our results demonstrate the validity of this assumption and, although we had hoped for stronger statistical relationships, the logic of the model produced seems sufficiently convincing to lay the groundwork for some changes in the way we think about and practice CLD, as we discussed above. Our results also suggest some changes in the way we conceptualize our theory of community leadership.

Localism Without Limit?

Several specific aspects of CLD require theoretical attention. One of these is the relationship between citizen action and institutional governance. Our research seems to indicate that, in small rural communities, these domains of action often seem unrelated, and our data are insufficient to permit us to analyze if this may be factual. How does citizen activism become successful without government support in our democratic system? Can engaged citizens access resources that government institutions in these small communities cannot? If so, why, and what sort of resources are they? Related to this question is that of the nature of the political capital of citizen activists who organize to take on a community change task. How does a loosely organized collective of individual citizens with similar interests committed to change in its community access political capital? Is this the result of network effects? Or, do governments acknowledge their own inability to act, and therefore grant a collaborating group of citizens a form of legitimacy that creates political capital they can use to access other resources? Are there some types of change activities that government officials would rather have citizens undertake with little "official" involvement because of political or financial risk? If so, what opportunity does this create for citizens and how can they more readily recognize and seize it? All of these questions seem related to Boyte's focus on public work, and we believe that work deserves greater and more systematic attention.

While Madison and Jefferson much debated the virtues of local government

(Wren 2007), de Tocqueville (2000, 46) was unequivocal about the role of local municipal government activity in the American democracy:

> It is . . . in the municipality that the strength of free peoples resides. Municipal institutions are to liberty what primary schools are to knowledge; they place it within reach of the people; they give them the experience of the peaceful exercise of it and habituate them to make use of it. Without municipal institutions a nation may give itself a free government, but it does not have the spirit of liberty.

It is at the local level that people have the greatest direct influence over their own affairs and the greatest opportunity for meaningful participation. Citizen leaders in the community represent the foundation of the American democracy, and exercise "power with" as well as "power to" although they may have little "power over" (Boulding 1989).

However, the limits of localism are well known.[3] Localism can not only marginalize minorities but also create deeper enclaves of influence and authoritarianism that make change difficult, if not impossible, to implement (Brown 1991; Parkinson 2007). Racism and sexism still infect many localities including small, rural places. Current battles over immigration policy at state and local levels are reminders of this problem. Lovell (2009) documents the struggles of African Americans and women to find a foothold as leaders in their communities in the South. Further, the effects of globalization that have stripped national governments of some of their autonomy, replacing it with the power of international corporations and institutions, have also affected the ability of local (and state) governments to fully implement changes that would have desirable long-term effects on issues such as the environment and public health (McMichael 1996; Friedman 2000).

However, new ideas have emerged that can support local governance without exacerbating, and while perhaps even helping to overcome, some of these difficulties. The Issues Forum, initially championed by the Domestic Policy Association, provides the opportunity to frame issues in a manner that transcends locality as the only relevant aspect of a problem or solution, bringing to bear all manner of other possible perspectives. Although initially designed for use at the national level, it can be modified for local use as well. The Study Circle is another approach, as is Deliberative Dialogue (McCoy and Scully 2002), and both of these techniques for creating civic education opportunities about issues and civic engagement processes can be useful in overcoming localism.

A second area for consideration is a practical "how many citizens does it take to . . . ?" sort of focus on the nature of intentional change. This is not just a rhetorical question. Given the penchant of many commutarian writers to suggest that "more is better," we wonder if there is not a critical mass of leaders that, given the nature of community change, is sufficient or optimum for getting the job done. We acknowledge the wide variation in the nature of the task and how that may influence the number of leaders it takes to make a difference. Small communities are limited by the number of residents. Does this constrain the nature or number of the tasks they might undertake successfully? Or does it mean they will use a different strategy to organize resources than a larger community might? This question is not purely a matter of numbers—rather, people come together with different values, life histories, and talents they can bring to any activity, so the nature of the participant group may also play a role. However, this is not an insignificant question for residents determining how to get something done in their community? If recruiting a certain number of people to help is an initial constraint (or not), research should be able to give them some guidance.

MEASURING PARTICIPANT EFFECTS

The third question we feel is important if theory is to be helpful involves determining return-on-investment. As we noted in the opening chapter to this volume, many millions of dollars have been spent on CLD programs over the years and we expect that substantial amounts will be spent for years to come. Therefore, it is important to determine not only the nature but also the value of the effects on the community in which the program takes place. For example, many CLD participants get involved in activities related to local economic development that may lead to significant new investment in infrastructure, jobs, and training, as well as an increase in the local tax base (unless tax incentives attract an external investment). These kinds of changes can be easily quantified and extended over time with some degree of reliability. But they can also take a long time to materialize, and other significant changes in the community may be much harder to quantify in financial terms. How do you quantify the value of a home for abused women and children or a shelter for the homeless or an after-school program for youth whose parents are working? These sorts of activities undoubtedly have public value because they create material benefits for citizens both specifically and generally, but it may be very difficult to place a dollar value on some of these benefits. This does not mean they should be ignored, so finding ways to place some sort of value on them as the result of our efforts in evaluation and research would be most helpful. Demonstrating such value could lead to a more effective understanding of community change and leadership.

Our research demonstrates a statistically reliable, extensively tested method for measuring the participant effects of community-based programs that aim to develop leadership capacity that will enhance community development. We developed the methodology over a twelve-year period and have tested it in multiple settings. We accomplished all of this work using public funds, so the methodology is open for use by anyone with similar interests. We are confident that using the methodology in similar settings will produce similar results.

A more important question is what to do with the individual effects information, how to relate that information to the actual elements of the "treatment(s)" participants undergo so that we have a better sense of how programs produce these effects, and how contextual effects such as selection methods and community characteristics alter these outcomes. These are merely examples of the questions that research must answer if we are to better understand how the development of our community leadership theory produces these participant effects.

Of perhaps greater importance is a more complete understanding of the community effects and of appropriate methods for measuring those effects, properly linking them to the participant effects. In our view, this requires a more robust theory comprised of contributions from sociological and political sciences, as well as the ecological understanding of how contextual effects come into play. Practically speaking, a considerable difficulty arises in comparative studies, as the community effects will likely vary considerably in their specifics, especially as they manifest in community history and structure. We conducted a comparative study, using the community capitals framework (CCF) as a set of analytical categories, with limited success. Any research undertaken along the lines outlined here would have to not only determine a way to address the differences between effects but also examine the nature of the leadership that characterized the community activities in which the participants became involved: was it collaborative, or a more traditional top-down, leader-follower model? The biggest obstacle, of course, is funding, which will likely need to originate within the foundation community rather than from the public.

In spite of this inescapable difficulty, future efforts should consider notions of power in the community, especially leadership based on informal authority and influence and how citizen leaders interact with institutional authorities. Future efforts should also consider community cultures as they are expressed in values, attitudes toward change and conflict, and inclusiveness of growing diversity. Contextual factors such as local citizens' understanding of the effects of globalization and technological change would be important to consider. Couto and associates (2010) outline other factors that would be worthy of consideration in a more robust conceptualization of a program theory of community change.

Without a more robust theory, future research will tend to try to measure more than is necessary at a cost that is prohibitive. Measurement needs to be strategic: what community effects are truly important to try and capture? What contributing or limiting factors need to be accounted for in determining CLD programs' effects? We suspect that these programs will continue to be popular and that similar interventions will continue as they have for the past several decades. The need for quality leadership in our democracy is continuous. Therefore, it is imperative that we do not ignore these efforts and find ways to ensure that CLD program investments create some measure of optimum effectiveness and genuine public value.

The CLD programs in our study sample did not have any learning elements that dealt with power in the community and how it functions or is acquired. Yet, intentional change is unlikely without a clear understanding of power. Since one form of power is the formal authority statutes grant elected officials, it is important to understand how changes are created in this context. More important in rural communities are all those instances of change in which this sort of formal authority doesn't seem particularly relevant but influence and relational networks are.

It has been said that "leadership defines itself through action" (Heifetz et al. 2004). An appropriate theory of change is action-focused; that is, if you want to understand leadership, you must look for examples of actions and the factors that affected those actions. We expect that there are specific theories of community change unique to each community, along with (a number of) general theories of change that could apply to many cases. What is a CLD educator to do? A good understanding of how change happens in the community the CLD program serves, an investigation into "how things work around here," is a good starting point. Working with an advisory group composed of locals who are also concerned about local leaders' capacity to deal with the future will be helpful as they will know the specific institutional boundaries that define the existing civic structure. The educator must help this group critically address local needs in planning for a CLD effort. This will likely require discussion of power in the community, which can make some people uncomfortable. Framing this kind of discussion in terms of concrete actions and the leadership associated with those actions can be a way to avoid some of this discomfort. The information provided by Parks (2005) and Heifetz and Linsky (2002) may be especially useful in addressing this challenge.

Even as the question of power is addressed, it is also appropriate to understand that much of the leadership for the community likely takes place without the exercise of formal authority. However, leaders cannot function without a power base, so the question is one of how to create power without direct access to formal or institutional authority. Fortunately, this is one of the attributes of the American democracy that represents the genius of our founders. Amendments nine and ten of the US Constitution state that whatever power is not granted to the institutional authorities by the people continues to reside with the people. This is the source of Boulding's (1989) distinctions among "power over," "power with," and "power to." Community leaders who are not in elected positions cannot access formal authority, so they can exercise little "power over." However, they can develop "power with" other collaborators, which can contribute to the "power to" accomplish substantive changes. In these actions, they exhibit leadership. The theory of community change necessary to guide CLD programs must be based in an understanding of the context in which the program will be implemented and the competencies associated with successful leadership activity in that context. For example, the theory of change underlying the theory of aligned contributions that Pillsbury (2009) tests is implemented in a context where people who represent the primary institutions and organizations associated with a specific community issue are collaborating. The competencies are defined accordingly, and include such elements as "race and culture," "accountability," "collaboration," and "leading from the middle," each of which has a rationale attached to them that is related to the process of creating the action agenda these leaders will follow to demonstrate their leadership.

Another example is the Horizons Program, which the Northwest Area Foundation initiated to address poverty in eight states. This program enlisted communities using a theory of change, in this case the idea that knowledge of the causes of poverty, expanded community capacity for leadership, development of a vision for the community's future that includes poverty solutions, and community coaching and action consulting by external assistants will lead to eliminating poverty in that community.[4]

It is interesting that the Horizons Program did not deal explicitly with power in its implementation, while the theory of aligned contributions deals with it through recruitment of the institutional participants. Our research shows that many of the activities in which local leaders became involved required them to mobilize or access political capital. This capital comes in a variety of forms, and more research is needed to identify those that community leaders use or create most often. In very few cases, however, does it appear that leaders organized activities that required formal authority as a form of political capital. Clearly, they were able to make changes in their communities without "power over," but our research does not clearly specify the nature of the power they actually used.

Nevertheless, CLD programs will need to address how/when leaders can act without authority and act effectively (Heifetz and Linsky 2002). This element needs to be part of the theory of change incorporated into the program's curriculum or learning strategy.

COMMUNITY EFFECTS ARE DIVERSE

As we note above, CLD programs' possible community effects are as diverse in their particularistic nature as the contexts in which they occur. We tried to use the CCF to capture the complexity of community change in the nature of each specific activity we studied in the treatment sites. In each case, it took three or four of the capitals to begin to describe the full nature of the local activity. Nevertheless, the framework proved able to capture the nature of most all of this activity and categorize the specifics in order to analyze them in constructive ways. While not perfect by any means, we recommend an analytical tool like the CCF as a starting point for understanding the nature of community effects. On the other hand, the CCF does not appear to include a way to capture what we report in chapter 3 regarding the increasing breadth and depth of CLD participants' involvement in community organizations. Though we can classify these structures into one of the CCF's categories, we can do little beyond that. It would be helpful to have a better sense of how CLD participants affected these organizations because of their learning experiences.

As a starting point, we suggest a sort of grounded theory approach that begins with a more complete examination of the community activities and the nature of the leadership associated with each before tracing the leaders back to a CLD experience. Since we are reasonably confident of what the individual effects of that learning experience are likely to be, focusing the research energy and resources on better understanding the nature of the leadership activity "in process" and its results may lead researchers to a broader and different set of categories for analysis than the use of the CCF. This approach would also provide an opportunity to examine how each citizen leader engaged in the collaboration, contributed, interacted, and so forth, thereby better characterizing the actual nature of the leadership. Questions about the role of power and institutional authority, partnerships with local organizations, network effects, resource availability, and leaders' adaptability could be addressed directly by devoting research resources here first. Finally, this sort of approach would permit within community comparisons of treatment effects. Without this sort of intensive study, developing a general theory will likely fail.

Leadershipitis

Kenneth Ruscio (2004, 2–3), in his book on the leadership dilemma, states:

> We are not always consistent in diagnosing our present situation or proposing remedies for the condition of modern politics. It is especially problematic when the prescription for what ails democracy is blithely presented as "better leadership." If we think leadership can solve our problems, or if we want better leaders, we need first to understand the particular forms of democracy we endorse. Different principles of democracy—different aspirations—impose distinctly different kinds of obligations and responsibilities on leaders.

We do not offer a solution to Ruscio's dilemma, but we do understand its implications and present some of them in this volume. There is little doubt that those who search for better leaders and leadership capacity will continue to provide financial support for efforts to achieve these ends, but too often without an explicit, shared understanding of what leadership means or what sort of democracy program organizers envision. That situation is understandable, but it is time that we take the obvious next steps and move from simplistic attributions of leadership causality and effects to a more complete understanding of community change and citizen leaders in democratic processes. Further, we are encouraged by our findings that a democracy based more concretely on a reconstruction of de Tocqueville's notions of the central importance of "association" provides a direction in which to move to satisfy Ruscio's concerns (Goldberg 2001).

The empirical research in part 1 on the community effects of CLD efforts has a number of results that should provide some initial guidance for the sort of next steps we envision. Our research demonstrates that six specific outcomes result from community-based CLD efforts, even when these efforts are comprised of diverse curricula. It demonstrates that the education is effective when compared to leaders who learn by experience only, although experiential learning should also be considered in thinking about leader development. Additionally, these six outcomes are not independent of each other, but form a set of structured relationships in which Civic Engagement and Social Cohesion (bridging social capital) appear to be the most interesting outcomes.

Community organizations see effects from CLD participation as well. As this study documents, participation in leadership development challenges participants to broaden and intensify their relationships with community organizations. The data show that CLD participants take on new leadership roles in the organizations to which they already belonged and join new organizations where they might use their capabilities and interests among others with similar interests. These organizational relationships continue to provide opportunities for citizen leaders to further hone leader skills like negotiation, goal setting, networking, collaboration, and others. These organizations are informal leadership schools and should be encouraged and supported as valued parts of the civic structure. As Putnam (1993b) argues, strong organizations are associated with good civic governance.

We would note, as Berger (2011) does, that not all of these organizations have a civic purpose, if "civic" is understood as related to political activity. Many of them likely provide some sort of community service, but usually play an indirect or even independent role in local political affairs. On the other hand, in small rural places, local governments and community organizations often collaborate to get things accomplished. Our point, however, is that leaders' experiences in these organizations are good preparation for excursions into the political arena when necessary. So, being able to point to the effect of CLD programs on organizations is, potentially, an important one in a civic sense where community change is a topic of interest.

Civic Engagement as an individual outcome (composed of attitudinal and cognitive dimensions) appears to be one significant link between an individual's participation in CLD programs and community effects. The research shows that, using the CCF, there are significant changes in social capital, political capital, and natural capital. The model produced also shows that Civic Engagement is a function of Personal Growth and Efficacy (indirectly), Community Knowledge (directly and indirectly), and Commitment (directly). While the variances in the model produced are small and likely an artifact of the measurement used, they are significant statistically.

Likewise, Social Cohesion as an individual outcome has a significant explanatory effect on human capital and financial capital. Social Cohesion is also related to Personal Growth and Efficacy (directly and indirectly), Community Knowledge (indirectly), and Commitment (directly). As a complete model, these two variables have significant effects on five of the seven community capitals.[5]

Our conclusion is that CLD programs do have a significant effect on communities where they are held. These effects are represented by changes in the community capitals and result from the variety of activities and projects participants in CLD programs pursue after their learning experience is completed. We cannot quantify this effect with the present data, even though that would be desirable. The anecdotal evidence is clear that considerable value was created and a substantial return-on-investment (ROI) resulted from most if not all of the investments made by sponsors of these CLD programs. Our research shows that not only that participants highly value the experience individually, but also that key informants in the community had little trouble identifying community projects and activities that had occurred in the previous two-to-three year period and identifying many of the individual leaders associated with them. In other words, activities of CLD program alumni were highly visible and other leaders considered them beneficial to the community. The ROI question seems easy enough to answer in at least a rough manner. Assuming that most CLD programs might have cost sponsors and participants together a total of less than $25,000,[6] the development of a regional cultural event that draws several thousand tourists who spend money in the community, the expansion of a sports program for community youth through the construction of new facilities with community donations and fundraising activities, or the establishment of shelter with community donations would easily account for at least a 1:1 ROI. Similar examples could be identified. Better data would likely produce even more attractive results for the ROI, but these data is rarely collected by local program sponsors, though we recommend they do so in the future.

One of the important observations we make in this research is that these community activities were the result of people who collaborated to mobilize community assets and get something changed in their community. As the results show, sometimes this required building a relationship with political institutions in order to access political capital, perhaps in the form of a grant or a zoning approval. In many cases, however, no government institutions were formally involved and people acted without support or interference to achieve their objectives. They exercised relational leadership directed toward a shared purpose. Thus, we also conclude that much of our attention to leadership is not to be discounted in community change.

Nevertheless, our research suggests that much more could be happening if CLD programs were to re-examine their purpose and take into account the actual outcomes they do or do not produce. Applying these results would suggest, as we have discussed above, a reformulation of the CLD curricula to include a greater focus on "politics" or "public work" as Boyte and Kari (1998) describe. According to Boyte (2004, xi) "politics" derives from the Greek word, *politikos,* which means "of the citizen . . . the activity of amateurs, not specialists [*like politicians or bureaucrats*]." As Aristotle argues in *Politics*, politics involves the negotiations of a pluralist world, people of different views, interests, and backgrounds interacting in order to accomplish some task. "*Politics is the opposite of relations based on similarity.*"[7] Developing a stronger curriculum around collaborative learning activities targeting the sort of topics that are directed to how community politics works "in this community" and how to acquire political capital, influence local decision-makers, identify the most effective forms of participation in public affairs, frame issues so that civic dialogue can occur, build coalitions of individuals and organizations with diverse interests, and address other related topics seems a reasonable addition to the learning.

Contextual factors matter (even though we do not measure their effects here) and sponsors need to recognize this fact when organizing CLD programs. This is also true for historical factors, many of which may support increased leadership capacity and community change. Different leadership principles may be appropriate for different situations, so leaders and partners in collective action must be able to wield or draw upon many types of skills within themselves or within the group (see figure 6.1). Not every leader has to have a complete skill set if all the collaborators commit to the same outcome. If the right leaders mobilize as partners in the endeavor, the challenges can be met.

Further, we recognize that community affairs, even in small communities, are often messy and complicated, and grow increasingly so with globalization and technological change. Communities *will* adapt to these changing conditions. The question is whether citizens can join together as leaders and direct such adaptations, or whether they will be left scrambling in their wake. Community leaders cannot control the future, but they can control how the community reacts to it through political, collaborative actions that leverage the community's diverse assets rather than relying on a few technicians for solutions that are often limited by experience and linear in nature. The most successful solutions may be those that arise from a full recognition of the disequilibrium the community faces and the broad experiences and knowledge of all citizens, rather than only a few.

We are confident in the collaboration of citizen leaders. We know of enough places where this relational leadership approach is already working, despite considerable challenges. Our research documents some of those places and events. We can do more; indeed, if prospects for a healthy democracy are in doubt, we must do more, and the best starting point is the community. Leadershipitis is neither a disease nor a condition, but a solution.

Notes

PREFACE

1   This research was supported financially by a generous grant from the
    US Department of Agriculture, National Institute for Agriculture, under
    grant No. 2006-35401-17560. In addition, the institutions employing
    each of the authors allowed us to allocate the time and institutional
    resources necessary to accomplish the research and we are grateful for
    that support.

INTRODUCTION

1   See, for example, the extensive meta-evaluation by Avolio et al. (2009) that
    reviewed 200 studies in formal organizations, business, and non-profits,
    with most studies focused on individual effects such as skills, knowledge,
    attitudes, or perceptions.
2   Most of this theoretical literature has been widely discussed in other places
    and we did not deem it necessary to rehash that treatment here. Further,
    much of this literature does not directly relate to community leadership
    or the role of community leaders in community action, so it is difficult to
    link any discussion of this literature to this research. We feel it is important
    to address this deficiency in the literature, but doing so is not our purpose
    in this volume.

CHAPTER ONE

1   All individual names used in this volume are fictitious.

CHAPTER TWO

1   We recognize that not all residents of the community are citizens, even in rural communities. However, there are instances when citizenship status is an important element of political capital and central to being able to accomplish community interventions, so we often use this term when appropriate. In other cases, we use the term "resident" when citizenship status is not critical to the discussion.

2   The topic of bridging and bonding social capital and their advantages and disadvantages are discussed more fully in part 2 of this volume.

3   These and other US Census data were obtained from the census.gov data site online from tables composed by US Census Bureau staff for public use.

4   Significance in this case may also be a function of the large number of respondents in the study.

CHAPTER THREE

1   We recognize that not all community change results in material benefits or improvements of some sort and that the community capitals can be deployed for maintaining status quo as easily and effectively as for change.

2   We obtained an early, pre-publication copy of this work from one of the professionals who collaborated with Magis.

3   One state (four sites) from the Phase I study of individual effects was omitted from the Phase II study of community effects due to difficulties experienced in gaining access to sites for data collection.

4   Portions of this section come from Pigg et al. (2013) and are used with permission from the editor of *Community Development: Journal of the Community Development Society.*

5   Obviously, this procedure produces only raw frequencies rather than any sort of standardized measure.

6   See the Institute for Digital Research and Education, n.d., Los Angeles: UCLA Statistics Consulting Group (http://www.ats.ucla.edu/stat/spss/topics/logistics_regression.htm) for additional explanation.

7   Another possibility is that the independent variables may be highly inter-correlated; however, that is not the case in this model, so the reduced variation from the transformation of these variables is most probably the explanation.

8   Such self-organizing efforts appear to conform to the notion that communities may behave as "complex adaptive systems" in collectively responding to internal and external conditions identified as opportunities or threats, as a number of complexity theorists such as Wheatley (1992) and Innes and Booher (1999) posit.

9   Some of the curricula may have contained content related to Kretzmann and McKnight's (1993) asset-based approach that we feel is similar in concept to the CCF.

CHAPTER FOUR

1   Race and ethnicity are not included in this analysis because, among those programs included in the study, the incidence of participation by individuals who were not Caucasian is extremely small.

CHAPTER FIVE

1   As we will discuss later, some proposed changes are not considered desirable by enough members of the community and so leadership is encouraged in many ways to oppose such change and protect the status quo. Such episodes highlight the tensions within communities and among community leaders. They also emphasize how important it is for leaders to be sensitive to residents' priorities and the values that represent their community.

2   This section adapted with permission from Pigg (forthcoming).

3   Quoted with permission from a speech given by Jim Hightower to the 75th Annual Meeting of the Rural Sociological Society, 27 July 2012, Chicago, IL.

CHAPTER SIX

1   As we will discuss in the last chapter, this collective action may, in a real sense, constitute leadership itself.

2   We present this observation in a related, but somewhat different, manner in the next chapter.

3   As we discuss in this volume, we use the term social cohesion to describe this form of social capital, so as not to confuse readers in discussing our analysis of the effects of CLD programs.

CHAPTER SEVEN

1   Szreter and Woolcock (2004) propose that social cohesion is a function of three types of social capital, two of which are externally focused: bridging and linking. Linking social capital reflects vertical linkages with people and resources external to the community or organization.

2   Portions of this section have been adapted from Pigg, et al (2013) and are used with permission from the editor of *Community Development: The Journal of the Community Development Society*.

3   This is not to say that other factors, such as the degree of bonding social capital, may affect social cohesion. In fact, in small communities, it may be empirically difficult to distinguish the relative effects of bonding and bridging social capital (Leonard and Onyx 2003; Schuller 2007).

4   We do not measure the presence or strength of these networks as others have tried to do (Rasmussen et al. 2011), but we frequently found that participants mentioned this effect in their qualitative responses to the questionnaire we used or in interviews we conducted about the community effects. Future research needs to more fully explore this sort of "network effect." For example, it seems plausible to define three types of bridging social capital: *social* as relationships based on somewhat casual or infrequent interactions such as business transactions or meetings at a local restaurant; *linking* as relationships that connect people across explicit vertical power differentials such as interactions between client and authorities in various institutional settings (Szreter and Woolcock 2004); and *civic* as relationships among individuals meeting in local civic associations or across associational lines in collaborative activity (Whitham 2012). Each of these could logically form the basis of social cohesion, and leadership may emerge from relationships within or among all these types of interaction. The important points are that these relationships indicate difference and that some combination of each may be suitable for achieving progress toward solution of adaptive challenges.

CHAPTER EIGHT

1   The NAEP Civics test applies mostly to national civics topics.

2   Portions of this section have been adapted from Pigg, et al (2013) and are used with permission from the editor of *Community Development: The Journal of the Community Development Society*.

3   Localism refers to the notion that the political decisions that matter most to individuals are made locally by institutional leaders as well as the notion that these decisions are those over which local residents may have the most influence in relation to institutional leaders.

4   An example of this program can be found at that also provides an example of Drath's principles for action: "direction, alignment and commitment."

5   It is possible there were insufficient numbers of cases in the two community capitals without any relationships to record any effects.

6   The most expensive programs we investigated reported charging about $500 per participant as an enrollment fee and raised additional funds from various sponsors (as well as using in-kind contributions) to support their CLD programs that, in sum, likely amounted to less than $25,000. Some programs were much less expensive.

7   Italics added.

CHAPTER NINE

1   Adapted from Magis (2008) using multiple sources.
2   Might come from the original survey as well as key informants.
3   From existing databases.

Appendix A: Community Leadership Development Survey Form

This study addresses the effects of participation in community leadership development (CLD) education activities in communities. The purpose is to determine what individual and community effects occur and how they may be linked. This project involves gathering data through the completion of an online survey.

Based on referrals from local program organizers, CLD program participants are invited to participate in the survey. Participation includes responding to questions posed in the online survey about the nature and scope of each individual's participation, motives for leadership, what they may have learned and how they may have applied this learning. The survey normally was completed in about twenty minutes. The survey was conducted using Survey Monkey with a response rate of over 60 percent following Dillman and associates' (2009) recommendations for online survey administration.

Participants are requested to provide their name and phone number at the end of the survey so that a follow-up interview may be scheduled to determine the nature of their leadership activity in the community in more depth.

This study was funded by United State Department of Agriculture and it was a collaborative project among the University of Missouri at Columbia, University of Illinois at Urbana-Champaign, and The Ohio State University. Use of the instrument is permitted for application in other settings as may be appropriate. For more information, contact :

Dr. Kenneth Pigg
Rural Sociology
120 Gentry Hall
Columbia, MO 65211
piggk@missouri.edu

SECTION 1: KNOWLEDGE, SKILLS, AND EXPERIENCE

Consider each of the following items carefully as they describe you as you are or as you feel today. Based on how each item applies to you, please indicate your level of agreement or disagreement by circling the appropriate number following each statement. Circle "1" if you strongly agree; circle "4" if you strongly disagree.

Strongly Agree	← • • • • • →	Strongly Disagree

1. I have knowledge of local, county, and state resources.

| 1 | 2 | 3 | 4 |

2. I strive to improve the quality of life in my community.

| 1 | 2 | 3 | 4 |

3. I talk optimistically about the future of my community.

| 1 | 2 | 3 | 4 |

4. I feel that I could do as good a job in public office as most other people.

| 1 | 2 | 3 | 4 |

5. I seek out different perspectives to generate new ideas.

| 1 | 2 | 3 | 4 |

6. I know how to assess and tackle problems in systematic ways

| 1 | 2 | 3 | 4 |

7. I am involved in my community.

| 1 | 2 | 3 | 4 |

8. I understand my community's structure and dynamics.

| 1 | 2 | 3 | 4 |

9. I envision exciting new possibilities for my community.

| 1 | 2 | 3 | 4 |

10. I have understanding and patience when working with others.

| 1 | 2 | 3 | 4 |

| Strongly Agree | ← • ◆ • ◆ • ◆ • → | Strongly Disagree |

11. I know the difference between management and leadership.

    1   2   3   4

12. I try to deepen personal relationships with others

    1   2   3   4

13. I am confident of my ability to work together with others to solve my community's problems.

    1   2   3   4

14. I get to know people in their different roles.

    1   2   3   4

15. I value the contributions that others make in my community.

    1   2   3   4

16. I appreciate local businesses.

    1   2   3   4

17. I am aware of all the needs in my community.

    1   2   3   4

18. I have confidence that my community will achieve its goals.

    1   2   3   4

19. I consider myself to be well qualified to participate in public issues.

    1   2   3   4

20. I try to learn more about people's backgrounds.

    1   2   3   4

21. I know the steps needed to obtain broad-based support for activities in my community.

1   2   3   4

Strongly Agree	← • • • • • →	Strongly Disagree

22. I understand the implications of local issues.

1	2	3	4

23. I seek to forge connections and strengthen personal and professional bonds among members of my community.

1	2	3	4

24. I aim to improve my consensus building skills

1	2	3	4

25. I strive to make this community a better place for everyone.

1	2	3	4

26. I am a leadership role model for others in my community.

1	2	3	4

27. I feel I have a good understanding of the important public issues facing our community.

1	2	3	4

28. I have a sense of community ownership.

1	2	3	4

29. I articulate a convincing vision for the future of my community.

1	2	3	4

30. I move out of my comfort zone and learn to grow.

1	2	3	4

31. I know how to change things in my community.

1	2	3	4

32. I strive to increase my analysis and reasoning skills.

1	2	3	4

SECTION 2: KNOWLEDGE, SKILLS, AND EXPERIENCE II

Consider each of the following items carefully as they describe you as you were BEFORE your participation in the community leadership program. Based on how each item applies to you, please indicate your level of agreement or disagreement by circling the appropriate number following each statement.

Strongly Agree	← • ◆ • ◆ • →	Strongly Disagree

1. I have knowledge of local, county, and state resources.

       1   2   3   4

2. I strive to improve the quality of life in my community.

       1   2   3   4

3. I talk optimistically about the future of my community.

       1   2   3   4

4. I feel that I could do as good a job in public office as most other people.

       1   2   3   4

5. I seek out different perspectives to generate new ideas.

       1   2   3   4

6. I know how to assess and tackle problems in systematic ways.

       1   2   3   4

7. I am involved in my community.

       1   2   3   4

8. I understand my community's structure and dynamics.

       1   2   3   4

9. I envision exciting new possibilities for my community.

       1   2   3   4

10. I have understanding and patience when working with others.

       1   2   3   4

Strongly Agree	← • ◆ • ◆ • →	Strongly Disagree

11. I know the difference between management and leadership.

       1   2   3   4

12. I try to deepen personal relationships with others.

       1   2   3   4

13. I am confident of my ability to work together with others to solve my community's problems.

       1   2   3   4

14. I get to know people in their different roles.

       1   2   3   4

15. I value the contributions that others make in my community.

       1   2   3   4

16. I appreciate local businesses.

       1   2   3   4

17. I am aware of all the needs in my community.

       1   2   3   4

18. I have confidence that my community will achieve its goals.

       1   2   3   4

19. I consider myself to be well qualified to participate in public issues.

       1   2   3   4

20. I try to learn more about people's backgrounds.

       1   2   3   4

21. I know the steps needed to obtain broad-based support for activities in my community.

       1   2   3   4

22. I understand the implications of local issues.

       1   2   3   4

| Strongly Agree | ← • • • • • → | Strongly Disagree |

23. I seek to forge connections and strengthen personal and professional bonds among members of my community.

     1   2   3   4

24. I aim to improve my consensus building skills.

     1   2   3   4

25. I strive to make this community a better place for everyone.

     1   2   3   4

26. I am a leadership role model for others in my community.

     1   2   3   4

27. I feel I have a good understanding of the important public issues facing our community.

     1   2   3   4

28. I have a sense of community ownership.

     1   2   3   4

29. I articulate a convincing vision for the future of my community.

     1   2   3   4

30. I move out of my comfort zone and learn to grow.

     1   2   3   4

31. I know how to change things in my community.

     1   2   3   4

32. I strive to increase my analysis and reasoning skills.

     1   2   3   4

SECTION 3: QUALITIES OF LEADERS AND COMMUNITIES

Please indicate your level of agreement or disagreement with each of the following items by circling the appropriate number. Please base your responses on your own personal observations.

Strongly Agree	← ♦ ♦ ♦ ♦ ♦ →	Strongly Disagree

1. Good community leaders consider the moral and ethical consequences of their decisions.

     1   2   3   4

2. Non-profit, civic organizations provide the most important means for expressing and actively addressing the complex needs of the community.

     1   2   3   4

3. Good community leaders usually accomplish more by exercising their authority to direct action by others.

     1   2   3   4

4. Effective community leaders help everyone believe their efforts can make a difference.

     1   2   3   4

5. In good communities, only people who know each other well can work together effectively and successfully.

     1   2   3   4

6. In good communities, leadership does not rest with one individual but with community members interchanging roles as the need arises.

     1   2   3   4

7. Effective community leaders allow others to both define and perform leadership roles.

   1   2   3   4

8. Leadership is automatically vested in those with formal authority.

   1   2   3   4

| Strongly Agree | ← • • • • • • → | Strongly Disagree |

9. Good followers don't make good leaders.

       1   2   3   4

10. It is just as much the task of every citizen to help the community reach its goals as it is the task of government officials.

       1   2   3   4

11. Good community leaders assist organizations and their members to think and act in new ways.

       1   2   3   4

12. Good community leaders encourage and work with followers to reflect on current activities and the issue(s) before them.

       1   2   3   4

13. Good community leaders know followers expect them to solve problems for them.

       1   2   3   4

14. Good community leaders help everyone learn how to develop relationships that allow for collaborative action on issues in common.

       1   2   3   4

15. Good communities are places where things are done right.

       1   2   3   4

16. The best decisions in the community are those where everyone contributes his/her best ideas and we arrive at a shared conclusion.

       1   2   3   4

17. Good leaders understand that what is best for every individual in the community is best for the community as a whole.

       1   2   3   4

18. Good community leadership results from a citizen-centered, problem-oriented, deliberative public decision-making.

       1   2   3   4

| Strongly Agree | ← • • • • • → | Strongly Disagree |

19. Good community leadership is not about individual contributions but what citizens accomplish together.

| 1 | 2 | 3 | 4 |

SECTION 4: INVOLVEMENT IN COMMUNITY ORGANIZATIONS

We are interested in learning how people are involved in local organizations and the nature of the leadership they provide. Below are listed some examples of organizations (by type) that might be in your community. Please use these examples as a guide and enter the names of specific organizations in which you are involved in response to the questions below. Also listed are descriptions of the possible extent of your involvement in these organizations. Use these categories to help us understand how you have been contributing to the betterment of your community through these organizations.

Samples of Organizations in the Community

1. Committees, commissions, task forces, etc. created to deal with a local community problem, e.g., health care, attract industry, etc.
2. Elected or appointed governmental offices, e.g. city council, county supervisor, etc.
3. Local/national community service organizations concerned with health, education or welfare, e.g., PTA, United Way, American Cancer Society, Scouts, 4-H
4. Business organizations, e.g., Chamber of Commerce
5. Professional Organizations, e.g., American Medical Association, Pork Producer's Association
6. Clubs and Social Organizations, e.g., Elks, Shriners
7. Cultural Associations, e.g., Choral society, Art Institute
8. Churches and Religious organizations, e.g., Baptist Church, Knights of Columbus
9. Political Parties, organizations and clubs, e.g., Young Democrats, Sierra Club, National Farmers Union
10. Veterans and patriotic organizations, e.g., American Legion, VFW
11. Other organizations

Extent of Community Involvement

Active member—Mark this if you attend most meetings.

Leadership role—Mark this if you hold a leadership position such as president or secretary or if you chaired a committee.

Please complete the following questions.

1. Write in the name of the three specific organizations or committees in which you are currently involved where you feel you are making the greatest contribution or impact. (See boxes above for examples.) You may be involved in other organizations not listed.

1–1

1–2

1–3

2. Circle the number that best corresponds to the extent of your current involvement in the organizations that you mentioned in question 1.

Committee/ Organization	Inactive Member	Active Member	Leadership Role
1–1	1	2	3
1–2	1	2	3
1–3	1	2	3

3. Write in the name of the three specific organizations or committees in which you were involved *PRIOR TO* your leadership development learning experience where you feel you made the greatest contribution or impact. (See boxes above for examples.) You may be involved in other organizations not listed.

3–1

3–2

3–3

4. Circle the number that best corresponds to the extent of your previous involvement.

Committee/ Organization	Inactive Member	Active Member	Leadership Role
3–1	1	2	3
3–2	1	2	3
3–3	1	2	3

5. In what way do you think your role(s) as a leader in these organizations (in 2 above) has benefited from your participation in the leadership development activity in which you have participated? (Check all that apply below.)

a. Changed my attitudes about working with others

b. Improved the skills I now practice that are required of leaders

c. Made it easier to get things done in these organizations

d. Helped me improve the community by addressing recognizable needs

e. Encouraged me to seek more leadership responsibility in these and/or other organizations

f. Changed my expectations about what can be/might be accomplished to improve my community

6. How do you know the committee or organization you provide leadership to has benefited? Please describe:

7. How has the community benefited from the work of your committee or organization? Please describe:

SECTION 5 DEMOGRAPHICS

Please mark an X in the appropriate answer or fill in the blank.

1. Please write in your age on your last birthday.

2. Please circle your gender.   M   F

Race/Ethnicity: Of the following choices, all races are Non-Hispanic except for (6) Hispanic.

1. White.

2. Black or African American.

3. American Indian and Alaska Native.

4. Hawaiian or Pacific Islander

5. Asian

6. Hispanic

7. Other

4. Please indicate the number of years you have lived in your community.

☐   Years

5. Do you have immediate family members living in your community?

☐   1. Yes

☐   2. No

6. Please select the one that best describes your employment status.

☐   1. Employed full time

☐   2. Employed part time

☐   3. Self-employed

☐   4. Unemployed/out of work

7. Marital status

☐   1. Single/ never married

☐   2. Married/Significant other

☐   3. Separated

☐   4. Divorced

☐   5. Widowed

8. Did you vote in the last local election?

    1. Yes

    2. No

    2. Don't know / Not sure

9. Highest Education Level

    1. 8th grade or less

    2. Some high school/did not graduate

    3. High school graduate/GED

    4. Vocational/technical or Business school

    5. Some College

    6. College Graduate

    7. Post-college/Graduate work

10. What was your total household income for 2006?

    1. 8th grade or less

    2. At least $10,000 but less than $20,000

    3. At least $20,000 but less than $30,000

    4. At least $30,000 but less than $50,000

    5. At least $50,000 but less than $75,000

6. At least $75,000 but less than $100,000

7. More than $100,000

8. Don't know/Not sure

9. Refused

SECTION 6: YOUR THOUGHTS AND OPINIONS ABOUT IMPROVING LEADERSHIP

Please write your thoughts and comments for the following questions. Feel free to continue on the next page if needed or to attach additional pages.

1. Looking back on this community leadership development program, what aspect was the most beneficial to you and your community?

2. Do you feel participation in this leadership development program was worth your time and effort?

1. Yes

2. No

3.   Why or Why not?

END OF THE SURVEY

Thank you for taking the time to complete this questionnaire. Your assistance in providing this information is very much appreciated. If there is anything else you would like to tell us about this survey, please do so in the space provided below as needed.

In order to extend our understanding on your community leadership experience, we would like to be able to interview you. If you are willing to have us contact you for the interview please provide your information (name, phone number, county name, and email address) to ruralcommunity@missouri.edu or provide them in the following box.

Appendix B:

Checklist Representing Community Capitals, for Use with Key Informants[1]

NATURAL CAPITAL	PRESENT	NOT PRESENT
• Community maintains selected natural amenities like open space for residents' use.	☐	☐
• Community maintains selected natural amenities like parks for residents' use.	☐	☐
• Local government acts to protect/preserve sensitive environmental areas in community.	☐	☐
• Agricultural areas are valued by local residents (non-farmers).	☐	☐
• Streams in the community are environmentally safe (not on EPA distressed list).	☐	☐
• Some form of natural capital used instrumentally/explicitly in local community activity (list, e.g., methane from a landfill).	☐	☐
• Community leadership actively seeks to improve air quality.	☐	☐
• Community leadership actively seeks to improve landscaping of public areas.	☐	☐
• Community leadership actively seeks to improve soil conservation.	☐	☐
• Community leadership has enacted a land development policy to protect/conserve natural capital.	☐	☐

HUMAN CAPITAL	PRESENT	NOT PRESENT
• Our community utilizes women in leadership roles.	☐	☐
• Our community utilizes youth in leadership roles.	☐	☐
• Our community utilizes people from diverse socio-economic, religious, and ethnic backgrounds in leadership roles.	☐	☐
• The community supports leadership development program(s) that includes women, youth, minorities, and people from diverse socio-economic, religious, and ethnic backgrounds.	☐	☐
• Elected leaders offer opportunities for residents to participate in governance activities (i.e., serve on local appointed boards or commissions).	☐	☐
• There is a local degree granting university, college, or community college.	☐	☐
• High school graduation rates are higher than the state norm.	☐	☐
• Local employers encourage/support OJT experience.	☐	☐
• There are accessible local worker training/adult vocational ed programs.	☐	☐
• Local employers generally consider the available workforce capable and skilled.	☐	☐
• Local group(s) write their own proposals for project funding.	☐	☐
• Community exhibits commitment to meeting basic human needs of residents through program intervention(s).	☐	☐
• Some form of human capital used instrumentally/explicitly in local community activity (list: e.g., sufficient quality and availability of healthcare or day care services).	☐	☐

CULTURAL CAPITAL	PRESENT	NOT PRESENT

Sense of Pride

	PRESENT	NOT PRESENT
• The community sponsors a cultural festival inviting surrounding communities to participate/enjoy activities.	☐	☐

CULTURAL CAPITAL continued	PRESENT	NOT PRESENT
• The community claims a distinctive cultural heritage/history (overt signage present).		
• Local public artworks demonstrate cultural heritage.		
• Local tourism program focused on cultural attributes of local area (e.g., heritage tourism program).		
• Community has a local art museum.		
• Community has a local historical society.		
• Local library has a historical section/collection or a cultural focus.		
• The community has local cultural/ethnic organizations.		
• The community has successful local ethnic restaurants or other businesses.		
• The local government supports cultural activities (via funding or applications for and administration of funding from other sources, policy re: community planning activities, sustainability measures, etc.).		
• Local institutions such as schools, ED organizations, support cultural activities.		
• Our community supports, maintains, and promotes art facilities that welcome everybody.		
Sense of Attachment		
• The community supports diverse perspectives, and honors and respects the values and cultures of all community members.		
• People generally live in the community for a long time and claim it as home.2		
• Some form of cultural capital used instrumentally/explicitly in local community activity (list). _____ _____ _____		

FINANCIAL/BUILT CAPITAL	PRESENT	NOT PRESENT
Environment and Infrastructure		
• Community supports and maintains a sound (conforms to all of the national goals) and vigorous main-street/downtown (an active committee working).	☐	☐
• Community supports a variety of recreational facilities for all.	☐	☐
• Water and sewer system quality—recent CWA or SDWA violations?	☐	☐
• The community has a modern public electric utility that has sufficient capacity to meet demand and minimizes environmental degradation.	☐	☐
Built Capital		
• Our community has safe, affordable housing that is available to all residents.	☐	☐
• Community has developed a new city park for organized recreation activities (like sports) in the last 5–10 years.	☐	☐
• Local streets and roadways in good condition.	☐	☐
• Bridges in the community are in good repair.	☐	☐
• Sidewalks and bike paths in the community are in good repair.	☐	☐
• Community library exists for local users (not a mobile service).	☐	☐
• Community owns and operates a public internet service for residential and business use.	☐	☐
• Community has identified older buildings and/or brownfield sites for economic/residential redevelopment activities.	☐	☐
• Community has an active industrial/business park.	☐	☐
• Community has commercial property available for business location or expansion.	☐	☐

FINANCIAL/BUILT CAPITAL continued	PRESENT	NOT PRESENT
• Community operates a business incubator.	☐	☐
• Some form of built capital was used instrumentally/explicitly in community activity (list, e.g., community-owned property donated for community center, local facility used to house internet provider services, community property for vegetable gardens, etc.).	☐	☐
Financial Capital		
• Locally owned banking institutions in the community (more than one).	☐	☐
• Alternatives to conventional banking institutions exist, e.g., credit unions.	☐	☐
• A local community foundation exists that is actively supported in the community.	☐	☐
• Local fundraising events usually successful and easily organized.	☐	☐
• Entrepreneurial ventures are encouraged and financially supported by the community.	☐	☐
• Community exercises its bonding capacity.	☐	☐
• Community has received recent federal grants/loans.	☐	☐
• Community offers financial or regulatory incentives for business development.	☐	☐
• Community offers financial or regulatory incentives for business expansion.	☐	☐
• Community works to reduce effects of poverty, e.g., supports community homeless shelters and/or food banks.	☐	☐
• Local tax proposals generally approved by voters (school/city/etc.)	☐	☐
• Some form of fiscal capital used instrumentally/explicitly in community activity (list, e.g., local banks contribute to cultural festivals or memorials).	☐	☐

SOCIAL CAPITAL	PRESENT	NOT PRESENT
Mediating Institutions		
• Community organizations welcome and engage women.	☐	☐
• Community organizations welcome and engage youth.	☐	☐
• Community organizations welcome and engage minorities and people from diverse socio-economic, religious, and ethnic backgrounds.	☐	☐
• Welcome Wagon or other similar activity exists in the community targeting new residents to make them feel welcome and get oriented.	☐	☐
• Community organizations are active sponsors of community events.	☐	☐
• Community organizations include civic, spiritual, service, and recreational/cultural interests (i.e., represent diverse purposes).	☐	☐
• Some form of social capital used instrumentally/explicitly in community activity (list, e.g., civic groups raise money for local cultural or educational activities.).	☐	☐
Community Member Involvement		
• Community leaders actively recruit diverse residents to participate in community activities.	☐	☐
• Most community organizations have links to regional, state, and/or national "parent" organizations (e.g., local economic development group to AEDC or similar organization).	☐	☐
• At least one community organization exists that involves youth in active roles.	☐	☐
POLITICAL CAPITAL	PRESENT	NOT PRESENT
• Community has access to influential external political actors that control resources (e.g., state and federal elected reps are residents).	☐	☐
• Community residents demonstrate high voting rates for local elections.	☐	☐
• Community organizations can achieve goals without local government intervention, support/approval.	☐	☐

POLITICAL CAPITAL continued	PRESENT	NOT PRESENT
• Local elections see competing candidates (rather than unopposed candidates).	☐	☐
• Community exhibits commitment to meeting basic human needs of residents through policy making/intervention.	☐	☐
• Community groups/agencies seek public-private partnerships.	☐	☐
• Local government seeks consensus to resolve local issues.	☐	☐
• Project leaders exhibit the ability to independently determine their agenda—goals and methods.	☐	☐
• Groups involved in local projects manage/control their own resources.	☐	☐
• Community groups demonstrate the capability to engage local government, yet maintain their independence.	☐	☐
• Government officials treat community organizational leaders as partners rather than recipients of benefits.	☐	☐
• Some form of political capital used instrumentally/explicitly in community activity (list)	☐	☐

References

Agnitsch, K., J. Flora, and V. Ryan. 2006. "Bonding and Bridging Social Capital: The Interactive Effects on Community Action." *Community Development: Journal of the Community Development Society* 37 (1): 36–51. http://dx.doi.org/10.1080/15575330609490153.

Allen, B. L., and L. W. Morton. 2006. "Generating Self-Organizing Capacity: Leadership Practices and Training Needs in Non-profits." *Journal of Extension* 44 (6). http://www.joe.org/joe/2006december/index.php

Allen, R., and P. R. Lachapelle. 2012. "Can Leadership Development Act as a Rural Poverty Alleviation Strategy?" *Community Development: Journal of the Community Development Society* 43 (1): 95–112. http://dx.doi.org/10.1080/15575330.2011.645046.

Avolio, B.J., R.J. Reichard, S.T. Hannah, F.O. Walumbwa, and A. Chan. 2009. "A Meta-Analytic View of Leadership Impact Research: Experimental and Quasi-experimental Studies." *Leadership Quarterly* 20 (5): 764–84. http://dx.doi.org/10.1016/j.leaqua.2009.06.006.

Azzam, T., and R. E. Riggio. 2003. "Community-Based Civic Leadership Programs: A Descriptive Investigation." *Journal of Leadership & Organizational Studies* 10 (1): 55–67. http://dx.doi.org/10.1177/107179190301000105.

Baldassarri, D., and Diani, M. 2007. "The Integrative Power of Civic Networks." *American Journal of Sociology* 113 (3): 735–80. http://dx.doi.org/10.1086/521839.

Banyan, M. 2007. "Civic Engagement." In *Encyclopedia of Governance*, ed. M. Bevir, 86–87. Thousand Oaks: Sage Publications, Inc; http://dx.doi.org/10.4135/9781412952613.n53.

Bartels, L. M. 2005. "Economic Inequality and Political Representation." White paper, Department of Politics and Woodrow Wilson School of Public and International Affairs, Princeton University, http://www.princeton.edu/~bartels/economic.pdf.

Basset, Lois R., and James C. Barron. 1988. "Teamwork, Sharing Build FCL Program." *Rural Development News* 12 (3): 1–7.

Bell, Wendell, Richard J. Hill, and Charles R. Wright. 1961. *Public Leadership: A Critical Review with Special Reference to Adult Education.* San Francisco: Chandler Publishing Company.

Bellman, G. 1992. *Getting Things Done When You Are Not in Charge.* San Francisco: Berrett-Koehler Publishers.

Bennis, W., and B. Nanus. 1985. *Leaders: The Strategies of Taking Charge.* New York: Harper and Row.

Berger, B. 2011. *Attention Deficit Democracy: The Paradox of Civic Engagement.* Princeton, NJ: Princeton University Press.

Besser, T. L. 2009. "Changes in Small Town Social Capital and Civic Engagement." *Journal of Rural Studies* 25 (2): 185–93. http://dx.doi.org/10.1016/j.jrurstud.2008.10.005.

Black, A. 2007. "What Did that Program Do? Measuring the Outcomes of a Statewide Agricultural Leadership Development Program." *Journal of Extension* 45 (4). http://www.joe.org/joe/2007august/iw2.php.

Black, A., and G. Earnest. 2009. "Measuring the Outcomes of Leadership Development Programs." *Journal of Organizational and Leadership Studies* 16 (2): 184–96. http://dx.doi.org/10.1177/1548051809339193.

Bolton, E. 1991. "Developing Local Leaders: Results of a Structured Learning Experience." *Journal of the Community Development Society* 22 (1): 119–43. http://dx.doi.org/10.1080/15575339109489954.

Bonjean, C. M. 1963. "Community Leadership: A Case Study and Conceptual Refinement." *American Journal of Sociology* 68 (6): 672–81. http://dx.doi.org/10.1086/223464.

Bono, J., W. Shen, and M. Snyder. 2010. "Fostering Integrative Community Leadership." *Leadership Quarterly* 21 (2): 324–35. http://dx.doi.org/10.1016/j.leaqua.2010.01.010.

Boulding, K. 1989. *Three Faces of Power.* Thousand Oaks: Sage Publications.

Boyte, H. C. 1989. *CommonWealth: A Return to Citizen Politics.* New York: The Free Press.

Boyte, H. C. 2004. *Everyday Politics: Reconnecting Citizens and Public Life.* Philadelphia: University of Pennsylvania Press. http://dx.doi.org/10.9783/9780812204216.

Boyte, H. C. 2009. *Civic Agency and the Cult of the Expert.* Dayton, OH: The Charles F. Kettering Foundation. http://kettering.org/publications/civic-agency-cult-exp/.

Boyte, H. C., and N. N. Kari. 1998. *Building America: The Democratic Promise of Public Work.* Philadelphia: Temple University Press.

Briggs, Xavier de Sousa. 1998. "Brown Kids in White Suburbs: Housing Mobility and the Multiple Faces of Social Capital." *Housing Policy Debate* 9 (1): 177–221.

Brown, R. B. 1991. "How Do Communities Act? Unique Events and Purposeful Strategies in the Formation of an Industrial Base in Rivertown." *Agriculture and Human Values* 8 (4): 46–55. http://dx.doi.org/10.1007/BF01530654.

Brown, R. B., and A. B. Nylander, III. 1998. "Community Leadership Structure: Differences between Rural Community Leaders' and Residents' Informational Networks." *Journal of the Community Development Society* 29 (1): 71–89. http://dx.doi.org/10.1080/15575339809489774.

Bryson, J. M., and B. C. Crosby. 1992. *Leadership for the Common Good: Tackling Problems in a Shared Power World.* San Francisco: Jossey-Bass.

Burns, J. M. 1978. *Leadership.* New York: Harper and Row.

Burt, R. S. 2002. "The Social Capital of Structural Holes." In *The New Economic Sociology: Developments in an Emerging Field,* ed. M. F. Guillén, 148–90. New York: Russell Sage Foundation.

Chaskin, R. J., P. Brown, S. Venkatesh, and A. Vidal. 2001. *Building Community Capacity.* New York: Aldine De Gruyter.

Chrislip, D. D., and C. E. Larson. 1994. *Collaborative Leadership: How Citizens and Civic Leaders Can Make a Difference.* San Francisco: Jossey-Bass.

Christenson, J. A., and J. W. Robinson. 1990. *Community Development in America.* 2nd ed. Ames, IA: Iowa State University Press.

Clarke, M., and J. Stewart. 1998. *Community Governance, Community Leadership and The New Local Government.* York: Joseph Rowntree Foundation.

Cook, James B. 1985. *EXCEL: An Experiment in Community Enterprise and Leadership Development.* Columbia, MO: Dept. of Community Development, University of Missouri.

Couto, R. A. 1992. "Defining a Citizen Leader." *Public Leadership Education: The Role of Citizen Leaders.* Dayton, OH: Kettering Foundation. 6: 3–9.

Couto, R. A. 1999. *Making Democracy Work Better: Mediating Structures, Social Capital and the Democratic Prospect.* Chapel Hill, NC: The University of North Carolina Press.

Couto, R. A., S. H. Hall, and M. Goetz. 2010. "Community Change Context." In *Leading Change in Multiple Contexts: Concepts and Practices in Organizational, Community, Political, Social and Global Change Settings,* ed. G. R. Hickman, 121–49. Thousand Oaks: Sage Publications.

Crowe, J. A. 2006. "Community Economic Development Strategies in Rural Washington: Toward a Synthesis of Natural and Social Capital." *Rural Sociology* 71 (4): 573–96. http://dx.doi.org/10.1526/003601106781262043.

Dahl, R. A. 1982. *Dilemmas of Pluralist Democracy: Autonomy vs. Control.* New Haven, CT: Yale University Press.

Davies, I., L. Bennett, B. Loader, S. Mellor, A. Vromen, S. Coleman, and M. Xenos. 2012. "Four Questions about the Educational Potential of Social Media for Promoting Civic Engagement." *Citizenship Teaching & Learning* 7 (3): 293–306. http://dx.doi.org/10.1386/ctl.7.3.293_1.

Day, D. V. 2011. "Leadership Development." In *The Sage Handbook of Leadership,* ed. A. Bryman, D. Collinson, K. Grint, B. Jackson, and M. Uhl-Bien, 37–50. Thousand Oaks: Sage Publications.

de Tocqueville, A. 2000. *Democracy in America.* Trans. Stephen D. Grant. Indianapolis: Hackett Publishing Co. http://dx.doi.org/10.7208/chicago/9780226924564.001.0001.

de Tocqueville, A. 1836. *Democracy in America.* London: Saunders and Ottley Press.

Dennis, L. 1993. *Empowering Leadership.* Portland, OR: Rising Tide Publications.

Devereaux, Edward C., Jr. 1960. "Community Participation and Leadership." *Journal of Social Issues* 16 (4): 29–45. http://dx.doi.org/10.1111/j.1540-4560.1960.tb00410.x.

Dillman, D., J. Smyth, and L. Christian. 2009. *Internet, Mail, and Mixed-Mode Surveys: The Tailored Design Method.* New York: Wiley.

Dillon, Michele. 2012. "Forging the Future: Community Leadership and Economic Change in Coös County, New Hampshire." The Carsey Institute at the Scholars' Repository. Paper 174. Durham, NH: The Carsey Institute, University of New Hampshire. Accessed 8 July 2013. http://scholars.unh.edu/carsey/174.

Drath, W. 2001. *The Deep Blue Sea: Rethinking the Source of Leadership.* San Francisco: Jossey-Bass.

Drath, W.H., and C. J. Paulus. 1994. *Making Common Sense: Leadership as Meaning-Making in a Community of Practice.* Greensboro, NC: Center for Creative Leadership.

Drath, W. H., C. D. McCauley, C. J. Paulus, E. Van Velsor, P. M. G. O'Connor, and J. G. McGuire. 2008. "Direction, Alignment, Commitment: Toward a More Integrative Ontology of Leadership." *Leadership Quarterly* 19 (6): 635–53. http://dx.doi.org/10.1016/j.leaqua.2008.09.003.

Dubin, Robert. 1979. "Metaphors of Leadership." In *Crosscurrents in Leadership*, ed. James G. Hunt and Lars L. Larson, 225–38. Carbondale, IL: Southern Illinois University Press.

Earnest, Garee W. 1995. "Developing Community Leaders: An Impact Assessment of Ohio's Community Leadership Programs." Ohio State University Extension 1993–1995, 1995. ERIC. Accessed 5 October 2012. http://eric.ed.gov/?q=Earnest%2c+Garee+1995&id=ED388808.

Earnest, G. W. 1996. "Evaluating Community Leadership Programs." *Journal of Extension* 34 (1). http://www.joe.org/joe/1996february/rb1.php.

Ehmke, C., and R. Shipp. 2007. "Community Directed Leadership Programs in Wyoming." *Journal of Extension* 45 (2). http://www.joe.org/joe/2007april/iw3.php.

Elliott, James R., and Jeremy Pais. 2006. "Race, Class and Hurricane Katrina: Social Differences in Human Response to Disaster." *Social Science Research* 35 (2): 295–321. http://dx.doi.org/10.1016/j.ssresearch.2006.02.003.

Emery, M., and C. B. Flora. 2006. "Spiraling Up: Mapping Community Transformation with Community Capitals Framework." *Community Development: Journal of the Community Development Society* 37 (1): 19–35. http://dx.doi.org/10.1080/15575330609490152.

Emery, M., E. Fernandez-Baca, I. Gutierrez-Montes, and C. B. Flora. 2007. "Leadership as Community Capacity Building: A Study of the Impact of Leadership Development Training on Community." *Community Development: Journal of the Community Development Society* 38 (4): 60–70. http://dx.doi.org/10.1080/15575330709489819.

Etuk, L. E., M. L. Rahe, M. S. Crandall, M. Sektnan, and S. Bowman. 2013. "Rural Leadership Development: Pathways to Community Change." *Community Development: Journal of the Community Development Society* 44 (4): 411–25. http://dx.doi.org/10.1080/15575330.2012.761639.

Fear, F. A., L. Vandenberg, M. Thullen, and B. Williams. 1985. "Toward a Literature Based 1985 Framework for Community Leadership Development." Paper presented at Annual Meeting of the Community Development Society, Logan, Utah.

Fear, Frank A, Manfred Thullen, and Lela Vandenberg. 1987. "Leadership Theory-Practice Linkages in Community Leadership Development: The Case of the Cooperative Extension Service." Extension policy paper. East Lansing: Michigan State University Cooperative Extension.

Flora, C. B., and J. L. Flora. 1988. "Characteristics of Entrepreneurial Communities in a Time of Crisis." *Rural Development News* 12 (2): 1–4.

Flora, C. B., and J. L. Flora. 2005. "Theory and Practice of the Capitals Framework." Unpublished manuscript. Ames, IA: Iowa State University.

Flora, J. L., C. B. Flora, and S. Fey. 2003. *Rural Communities: Legacy and Change.* 2nd ed. Boulder, CO: Westview Press.

Flora, J. L., and C. B. Flora. 2008. *Rural Communities: Legacy and Change.* 3rd ed. Boulder, CO: Westview Press.

Flora, J. L., and C. B. Flora. 2013. *Rural Communities: Legacy and Change.* 4th ed. Boulder, CO: Westview Press.

Fredricks, S.M. 1999. "Exposing and Exploring State-Wide Community Leadership Training Programs." *Journal of Leadership & Organizational Studies* 5 (2): 129–42. http://dx.doi.org/10.1177/107179199900500211.

Fredricks, S. M. 2003. "Creating and Maintaining Networks among Leaders: An Exploratory Case Study of Two Leadership Training Programs." *Journal of Leadership & Organizational Studies* 10 (1): 45–54. http://dx.doi.org/10.1177/107179190301000104.

Friedman, T. L. 2000. *The Lexus and the Olive Tree.* New York: Farrar Straus Giroux.

Galston, W. A. 2004. "Civic Education and Political Participation." *PS: Political Science & Politics* 37 (2): 263–6.

Gambrell, K. M., and S. M. Fritz. 2012. "Healers and Helpers, Unifying the People: A Qualitative Study of Lakota Leadership." *Journal of Leadership & Organizational Studies* 19 (3): 315–25. http://dx.doi.org/10.1177/1548051812442749.

Gardner, J. W. 1968. *No Easy Victories.* New York: Harper & Row.

Gardner, J. W. 1995. *Leading Minds: An Anatomy of Leadership.* New York: Basic Books. With Emma Laskin.

Gasteyer, S., and T. Araj. 2009. "Empowering Palestinian Community Water Management Capacity: Understanding the Intersection of Community Cultural, Political, Social and Natural Capitals." *Community Development: Journal of the Community Development Society* 40 (2): 199–219. http://dx.doi.org/10.1080/15575330903012288.

Gaventa, J. 1980. *Power and Powerlessness: Quiescence and Rebellion in an Appalachian Valley.* Urbana, IL: University of Illinois Press.

Gershon, D. 2009. *Social Change 2.0: A Blueprint for Reinventing Our World.* West Hurley, NY: High Point.

Gibon, C. 2006. *Citizens at the Center: A New Approach to Civic Engagement.* New York: The Case Foundation. Accessed 31 January 2013. http://casefoundation.org/sites/default/files/citizens-at-the-center.pdf.

Gittell, R., and A. Vidal. 1998. *Community Organizing: Building Social Capital as a Development Strategy.* Thousand Oaks: Sage Publications.

Goethals, G. R., and G. L. J. Sorenson, eds. 2006. *The Quest for a General Theory of Leadership.* Northampton, MA: Edward Elgar Publishing. http://dx.doi.org/10.4337/9781847202932.

Goldberg, C. A. 2001. "Social Citizenship and a Reconstructed Tocqueville." *American Sociological Review* 66 (2): 289–315. http://dx.doi.org/10.2307/2657419.

Goodwin, J., and J. M. Jasper. 2009. *The Social Movements Reader: Cases and Concepts.* 2nd ed. Malden, MA: Wiley-Blackwell.

Graen, G. B., and M. Uhl-Bien. 1995. "Relationship-based Approach to Leadership: Development of Leader-Member Exchange (LMX) Theory of Leadership over 25 Years: Applying a Multi-level Multi-domain Perspective." *Leadership Quarterly* 6 (2): 219–47. http://dx.doi.org/10.1016/1048-9843(95)90036-5.

Granovetter, M. 1973. "The Strength of Weak Ties." *American Journal of Sociology* 78 (13): 60–80.

Green, G. P. and A. Haines. 2002. *Asset Building and Community Development.* Thousand Oaks: Sage Publications.

Green, G. P., and A. Haines. 2012. *Asset Building and Community Development.* 2nd ed. Thousand Oaks: Sage Publications.

Grint, K. 2005. "Problems, Problems, Problems: The Social Construction of 'Leadership.'" *Human Relations* 58 (11): 1467–94. http://dx.doi.org/10.1177/0018726705061314.

Gutierrez-Montes, I., M. Emery, and E. Fernandez-Baca. 2009. "The Sustainable Livelihoods Approach and the Community Capitals Framework: The Importance of System-Level Approaches to Community Change Efforts." *Community Development: Journal of the Community Development Society* 40 (2): 106–13. http://dx.doi.org/10.1080/15575330903011785.

Hartley, J., and J. Benington. 2011. "Political Leadership." In *The Sage Handbook of Leadership*, ed. A. Bryman, D. Collinson, K. Grint, B. Jackson, and M. Uhl-Bien, 203–14. Thousand Oaks: Sage Publications.

Hawkins, Robert L., and Katherine Maurer. 2009. "Bonding, Bridging and Linking: How Social Capital Operated in New Orleans Following Hurricane Katrina." *British Journal of Sociology* 40 (6): 1777–93.

Heifetz, R. 1994. *Leadership without Easy Answers.* Cambridge, MA: The Belknap Press.

Heifetz, R., and M. Linsky. 2002. *Leadership on the Line: Staying Alive through the Dangers of Leading.* Boston: Harvard Business School Press.

Heifetz, R. A., J. V. Kania, and M. R. Kramer. 2004. "Leading Boldly." *Stanford Social Innovation Review* (winter). http://www.ssireview.org/articles/entry/collective_impact.

Hickman, G. R. 2010. *Leading Change in Multiple Contexts: Concepts and Practices in Organizational, Community, Political, Social, and Global Change Settings.* Thousand Oaks: Sage Publications.

Higgins, Elizabeth, and McCorkle, C. 2006. "The Development of a Rural Community Capacity Index-Based on Cornelia Flora's Community Capital Framework." Paper presented at the Community Development Society Annual Conference St. Louis, MO.

Hodgkin, S. 2011. "Participating in Social, Civic, and Community Life: Are We All Equal?" *Australian Social Work* 64 (3): 245–65. http://dx.doi.org/10.1080/0312407X.2011.573798.

Hoppe, B., and C. Reinelt. 2010. "Social Network Analysis and the Evaluation of Leadership Networks." *Leadership Quarterly* 21 (4): 600–19. http://dx.doi.org/10.1016/j.leaqua.2010.06.004.

Howell, Robert E., Ivan Lee Weir, and Annabel Kirschner Cook. 1979. *Public Affairs Leadership Program: An Impact Assessment of Programs Conducted in California, Michigan, Montana, & Pennsylvania*. Battle Creek, MI: W. K. Kellogg Foundation.

Hughes, E. T. 1998. "Leadership Development Program Serves as a Change Agent in Community Development." *Journal of Extension* 36 (2). http://www.joe.org/joe/1998april/iw2.php.

Hunter, F. 1953. *Community Power Structure: A Study of Decision Makers*. Chapel Hill, NC: University of North Carolina Press.

Hyman, J. B. 2002. "Exploring Social Capital and Civic Engagement to Create a Framework for Community." *Applied Developmental Science* 6 (4): 196–202. http://dx.doi.org/10.1207/S1532480XADS0604_6.

Innes, Judith E., and David E. Booher. 1999. "Consensus Building and Complex Adaptive Systems: A Framework for Evaluating Collaborative Planning." *Journal of the American Planning Association* 65 (4): 412–23. http://dx.doi.org/10.1080/01944369908976071.

Israel, G. D., and L. J. Beaulieu. 1988. "Community Leadership." In *American Rural Communities*, ed. A. E. Luloff and L. E. Swanson, 181–202. Boulder, CO: Westview Press.

Isserman, A. 2005. "In the National Interest: Defining Rural and Urban Correctly in Research and Public Policy." *International Regional Science Review* 28 (4): 465–99. http://dx.doi.org/10.1177/0160017605279000.

Kahn, S. 1970. *How People Get Power: Organizing Oppressed Communities for Action*. New York: McGraw-Hill.

Kania, J., and M. Kramer. 2011. "Collective Impact." *Stanford Social Innovation Review* (winter). http://www.ssireview.org/articles/entry/collective_impact.

Kemmis, Daniel, and Matthew McKinney. 2011. *Collaboration and the Ecology of Democracy*. Dayton, OH: The Charles F. Kettering Foundation.

King, B., and R. Hustedde. 2001. *Strengthening Civic Engagement in Community Decision-Making*. University of Kentucky Cooperative Extension Service. Southern Rural Development Center. http://files.eric.ed.gov/fulltext/ED455080.pdf.

Kirk, Philip, and Anna M. Shutte. 2004. "Community Leadership Development." *Community Development Journal: An International Forum* 39 (3): 234–51. http://dx.doi.org/10.1093/cdj/bsh019.

Kirlin, M. 2003. *The Role of Civic Skills in Fostering Civic Engagement*. The Center for Information & Research on Civic Learning and Engagement, University of Maryland. http://www.civicyouth.org/PopUps/WorkingPapers/WP06Kirlin.pdf.

Kotter, J. 1990. *Force for Change: How Leadership Differs from Management*. New York: The Free Press.

Kouzes, J., and B. Posner. 1988. *The Leadership Challenge: How to Get Extraordinary Things Done in Organizations*. San Francisco: Jossey-Bass.

Kretzmann, J. P., and J. L. McKnight. 1993. *Building Communities from the Inside Out: A Path toward Finding and Mobilizing a Community's Assets*. Evanston, IL: Center for Urban Affairs and Policy Research, Northwestern University.

Langone, C. A., and F. R. Rohs. 1992. *Community Leadership a Force for Future Change: An Impact Assessment of Georgia's Community Leadership a County Perspective Program*. Athens: University of Georgia, Cooperative Extension Service.

Langone, C. A. 1994. "Building Community Leadership." *Journal of Extension* 30 (4). http://www.joe.org/joe/1992winter/a7.php.

Latimer, C., and K. M. Hempson. 2012. "Using Deliberation in the Classroom: A Teaching Pedagogy to Enhance Student Knowledge, Opinion Formation, and Civic Engagement." *Journal of Political Science Education* 8 (4): 372–88. http://dx.doi.org/10.1080/15512169.2012.729447.

Laumann, E. O., and F. U. Pappi. 1976. *Networks of Collective Action: A Perspective on Community Influence Systems*. New York: Academic Press.

Leighninger, M. 2006. *The Next Form of Democracy*. Nashville, TN: Vanderbilt University Press.

Leonard, R., and J. Onyx. 2003. "Networking Through Loose and Strong Ties: An Australian Qualitative Study." *Voluntas: International Journal of Voluntary and Nonprofit Organizations* 14 (2): 189–203.

Levine, D. 2011. *The Capacity for Civic Engagement: Public and Private Worlds of the Self*. New York: Palgrave Macmillan. http://dx.doi.org/10.1057/9780230118157.

Lewin, K. 1948. *Resolving Social Conflicts: Selected Papers on Group Dynamics*. New York: Harper & Brothers.

Lim, C., and T. Sander. 2013. "Does Misery Love Company? Civic Engagement in Economic Hard Times." *Social Science Research* 42 (1): 14–30. http://dx.doi.org/10.1016/j.ssresearch.2012.07.004.

Lindahl, N. 2011. *Graduation with Civic Honors: Unlock the Power of Community Opportunity*. Lincoln, NE: iUniverse.

Littrell, D.W., and D. Hobbs. 1989. "The Self-Help Approach." In *Community Development in Perspective*, ed. J.A. Christenson and J.W. Robinson, 48–68. Ames, IA: Iowa State University Press.

Lovell, D. M. 2009. "Leading in the Mississippi Delta: An Exploratory Study of Race, Class and Gender." Unpublished PhD dissertation, Columbia, MO: University of Missouri, Dept. of Rural Sociology.

Lowndes, V. 2004. "Getting on or Getting By? Women, Social Capital and Political Participation." *British Journal of Politics and International Relations* 6 (1): 45–64. http://dx.doi.org/10.1111/j.1467-856X.2004.00126.x.

Luloff, A. E., and L. E. Swanson, eds. 1988. *American Rural Communities*. Boulder, CO: Westview Press.

Lyson, T., and C. Tolbert. 2003. "Civil Society, Civic Communities and Rural Development." In *Challenges for Rural America in the Twenty-First Century*, ed. D. L. Brown and L. E. Swanson, 228–40. State College, PA: Penn State Press.

Magis, K. 2010. "Community Resilience: An Indicator of Social Sustainability." *Society and Natural Resources: An International Journal* 23 (5): 401–16. http://dx.doi.org/10.1080/08941920903305674.

Manning, R. 1998. "A Care Approach." In *A Companion to Bioethics*, ed. Helga Kuhse and Peter Singer, 98–106. Malden, MA: Blackwell Publishers.

Manturuk, K., M. Lindblad, and R. Quercia. 2012. "Homeownership and Civic Engagement in Low-Income Urban Neighborhoods: A Longitudinal Analysis." *Urban Affairs Review* 48 (5): 731–60. http://dx.doi.org/10.1177/1078087412441772.

Marquart-Pyatt, Sandra T., and Peggy Petrzelka. 2009. "Digging the Dugway: Understanding Involvement in Local Politics." *Community Development: Journal of the Community Development Society* 40 (3): 262–74. http://dx.doi.org/10.1080/15575330903091670.

Martin, K. E., and K. P. Wilkinson. 1985. "Does Leadership Development Intervene in the Relationship between Public Affairs Participation and Socio-economic Status?" *Journal of the Community Development Society* 16 (2): 97–106. http://dx.doi.org/10.1080/15575338509490064.

Martinez-Cosio, M. 1996. "Leadership in Communities of Color: Elements and Sensitivities of a Universal Model." *Journal of Leadership & Organizational Studies* 3 (1): 65–77. http://dx.doi.org/10.1177/107179199600300107.

Marwell, G., P. E. Oliver, and R. Prahl. 1988. "Social Networks and Collective Action: A Theory of the Critical Mass." *American Journal of Sociology* 94 (3): 502–34. http://dx.doi.org/10.1086/229028.

Matarrita-Cascante, D., and M. Brennan. 2012. "Conceptualizing Community Development in the Twenty-First Century." *Community Development: Journal of the Community Development Society* 43 (3): 293–305. http://dx.doi.org/10.1080/15575330.2011.593267.

Mathews, D. 1999. *Politics for People: Finding a Responsible Public Voice.* 2nd ed. Dayton, OH: The Charles F. Kettering Foundation.

McAdam, D., J. McCarthy, and M. Zald. 2004. *Comparative Perspectives on Social Movements: Political Opportunities, Mobilizing Structures, and Cultural Framings.* Cambridge, UK: Cambridge University Press.

McCoy, M. L., and P. L. Scully. 2002. "Deliberative Dialogue to Expand Civic Engagement: What Kind of Talk Does Democracy Need?" *National Civic Review* 91 (2): 117–35.

McMichael, P. 1996. *Development and Social Change: A Global Perspective.* Thousand Oaks: Pine Forge Press.

Meehan, D., N. Castañeda, and A. D. Salvessen. n.d. *The Role of Leadership in Place Based Initiatives.* Oakland: Leadership Learning Community. Report for the California Endowment. Accessed 11 September 2012. http://leadershiplearning.org/system/files/TCE_public_scan_final_060911.pdf.

Meslin, Dave. 2010. *Local Motion: The Art of Civic Engagement in Toronto*. Toronto: Coach House Books.

Meyer, D. S., and S. Staggenborg. 1996. "Movements, Countermovements, and the Structure of Political Opportunity." *American Journal of Sociology* 101 (6): 1,628–60. http://dx.doi.org/10.1086/230869.

Meyerson, D. E. 2001. *Tempered Radicals: How People Use Difference to Inspire Change at Work*. Boston: Harvard Business School Press.

Michael, J. A., M. C. Paxson, and R. E. Howell. 1990. *Developing Leadership among Extension Clientele*. Pullman, WA: Washington State University Cooperative Extension. October.

Mills, R. C. 2005. "Sustainable Community Change: A New Paradigm for Leadership in Community Revitalization Efforts." *National Civic Review* 94 (1): 9–16. http://dx.doi.org/10.1002/ncr.78.

Molnar, J. J., and W. D. Lawson. 1984. "Perceptions of Barriers to Black Political and Economic Progress in Rural Areas." *Rural Sociology* 9 (2): 261–83.

Moore, C. 1988. *A Colorful Quilt: The Community Leadership Story*. Indianapolis, IN: National Association of Community Leadership Organizations.

Morse, R. S. 2008. "Developing Public Leaders in an Age of Collaborative Governance." In *Innovations in Public Leadership Development*, ed. R. S. Morse and T. F. Buss, 80–100. Armonk, NY: M. E. Sharpe.

Morse, R. S., and T. F. Buss. 2008. *Innovations in Public Leadership Development*. Armonk, NY: M. E. Sharpe.

Morton, L. W. 2003. "Small Town Services and Facilities: The Influence of Social Networks and Civic Structure on Perceptions of Quality." *City & Community* 2 (2): 101–20.

Morton, L. W., Yu-Che Chen, and R. S. Morse. 2008. "Small Town Civic Structure and Interlocal Collaboration for Public Services." *City & Community* 7 (1): 45–60. http://dx.doi.org/10.1111/j.1540-6040.2007.00240.x.

North Central Regional Interest Network on Community Leadership Programs (NCRIN). 1984. *Extension Community Leadership Programs in the United States*. Ames, IA: North Central Regional Center for Rural Development.

Northouse, P. G. 2004. *Leadership: Theories and Practices*. London: Sage Publications.

O'Brien, D. J., and E. S. Hassinger. 1992. "Community Attachment among Leaders in Five Rural Communities." *Rural Sociology* 57 (4): 521–34. http://dx.doi.org/10.1111/j.1549-0831.1992.tb00477.x.

O'Brien, D. J., A. Raedeke, and E. W. Hassinger. 1998. "The Social Networks of Leaders in More or Less Viable Communities Six Years Later: A Research Note." *Rural Sociology* 63 (1): 109–27. http://dx.doi.org/10.1111/j.1549-0831.1998.tb00667.x.

O'Brien, D. J., E. W. Hassinger, R. B. Brown, and J. R. Pinkerton. 1991. "The Social Networks of Leaders in More and Less Viable Rural Communities." *Rural Sociology* 56 (4): 699–716. http://dx.doi.org/10.1111/j.1549-0831.1991.tb00453.x.

Ohnoutka, L., L. Waybright, A. Nichols, and P. Nestor. 2005. "Leadership, Teaching, Self-Efficacy, and Networking: Untapped Benefits of Membership in Extension Volunteer Networks." *Journal of Extension* 43 (3). http://www.joe.org/joe/2005june/rb2.php.

Opare, Service. 2007. "Strengthening Community-Based Organizations for the Challenges of Rural Development." *Community Development Journal: An International Forum* 42 (2): 251–64. http://dx.doi.org/10.1093/cdj/bsl002.

Orum, A. M. and Gramlich, J. 1999. "Civic Capital and The Construction (and Reconstruction) of Cities." *Colloqui* 45–54.

Ospina, S., and E. Schall. 2001. "Leadership (Re)Constructed: How Lens Matters." Paper presented at the APPAM Research Conference, Washington, DC. November. http://leadershiplearning. org/system/files/LEADERSHIP%20%28RE%29CONSTRUCTED.pdf.

Parkinson, J. 2007. "Localism and Deliberative Democracy." *Good Society* 16 (1): 23–9. http://dx.doi. org/10.1353/gso.0.0001.

Parks, S. D. 2005. *Leadership Can Be Taught*. Boston, MA: Harvard Business School Press.

Parr, J. 2008. "Civic Infrastructure: A New Approach to Improving Community Life." *National Civic Review* 97 (2): 18–22. http://dx.doi.org/10.1002/ncr.210.

Paxson, M. C., R. E. Howell, J. A. Michael, and S. K. Wong. 1993. "Leadership Development in Extension." *Journal of Extension* 31 (1). http://www.joe.org/joe/1993spring/rb2.php.

Paxton, P. 2002. "Social Capital and Democracy: An Interdependent Relationship." *American Sociological Review* 67 (2): 254–77. http://dx.doi.org/10.2307/3088895.

Pearce, C. L., and J. A. Conger, eds. 2003. *Shared Leadership: Reframing the Hows and Whys of Leadership*. Thousand Oaks: Sage Publications.

Pigg, K. 1999. "Community Leadership and Community Theory: A Practical Synthesis." *Journal of the Community Development Society* 30 (2): 196–212. http://dx.doi. org/10.1080/15575339909489721.

Pigg, K. 2001. *EXCEL: Experience in Community Enterprise and Leadership*. Columbia, MO: University of Missouri Extension.

Pigg, K. 2002. "Three Faces of Empowerment: Expanding the Theory of Empowerment in Community Development." *Journal of the Community Development Society* 33 (1): 107–23. http:// dx.doi.org/10.1080/15575330209490145.

Pigg, K. Forthcoming. "Developing Leaders for Community Leadership and Civic Engagement." *SRDC Civic Engagement Series*. Mississippi: Mississippi State University, Southern Rural Development Center.

Pigg, K., S. Gasteyer, and K. Martin. 2009. *Impact of Leadership Development Education Programs on Individual Participants: Summary Report*. Preliminary Research Report on USDA/CSREES/ NRI Project No. 2006-35401-17560.

Pigg, K., S. Gasteyer, K. Martin, G. Apaliyah, and K. Keating. 2013. "The Community Capitals Framework: An Empirical Analysis." *Community Development: Journal of the Community Development Society* 44 (4): 492–502. http://dx.doi.org/10.1080/15575330.2013.814698.

Pillsbury, J. B. 2009. *Theory of Aligned Contributions: An Emerging Theory of Change Primer.* Arlington, VA: Sherbrooke Consulting Inc. http://www.sherbrookeconsulting.com/products/TOAC.pdf.

Poston, R. W. 1976. *Action Now! A Citizen's Guide to Better Communities.* Carbondale, IL: Southern Illinois University Press.

Provus, Malcolm. 1971. *Discrepancy Evaluation.* Berkeley, CA: McCutchan.

Putnam, R. D. 1993a. "What Makes Democracy Work?" *National Civic Review* 82 (2): 101–7. http://dx.doi.org/10.1002/ncr.4100820204.

Putnam, R. D. 1993b. *Making Democracy Work: Civic Traditions in Modern Italy.* Princeton, NJ: Princeton University Press.

Putnam, R. D. 2000. *Bowling Alone: The Collapse and Revival of American Community.* New York: Simon and Schuster. http://dx.doi.org/10.1145/358916.361990.

Putnam, R. D., and L. M. Feldstein. 2003. *Better Together: Restoring the American Community.* New York: Simon and Schuster.

Raelin, J. A. 2003. *Creating Leaderful Organizations: How to Bring out Leadership in Everyone.* San Francisco: Berrett-Koehler Publishers.

Ramsay, K., B. Reed, and L. Vandenberg. 1998. *Community Leadership Development: A Guide for People Who Want to Make a Difference.* East Lansing, MI: Michigan State University Extension. http://archive.lib.msu.edu/DMC/Ag.%20Ext.%202007-Chelsie/PDF/commleadership.pdf.

Rasmussen, C. A., J. Armstrong, and S. A. Chazdon. 2011. "Bridging Brown County: Captivating Social Capital as a Means to Community Change." *Journal of Leadership Education* 10 (1): 63–82. http://dx.doi.org/10.12806/V10/I1/RF4.

Raudenbush, Stephen W., Anthony S. Bryk, and R. T. Congdon. 2002. *Hierarchical Linear Modeling.* Thousands Oaks: Sage Publications.

Reinelt, C., P. Foster, and S. Sullivan. 2002. *Evaluating Outcomes and Impacts: A Scan of 55 Leadership Development Programs.* Battle Creek, MI: W. K. Kellogg Foundation. http://www.wkkf.org/resource-directory/resource/2006/08/evaluating-outcomes-and-impacts-a-scan-of-55-leadership-development-programs.

Rencher, Alvin C. 2002. *Methods of Multivariate Analysis.* New York: John Wiley & Sons, Inc. http://dx.doi.org/10.1002/0471271357.

Ricketts, K. 2005. "The Importance of Community Leadership to Successful Rural Communities in Florida." Unpublished PhD dissertation. University of Florida, Dept. of Agricultural Education. http://etd.fcla.edu/UF/UFE0009802/ricketts_k.pdf.

Ricketts, K., and N. T. Place. 2009. "Making Communities More Viable: Four Essential Factors for Successful Community Leadership." *Journal of Extension* 47 (2). http://www.joe.org/joe/2009april/iw2.php.

Ricketts, K. G., and H. Ladewig. 2008. "A Path Analysis of Community Leadership within Viable Rural Communities in Florida." *Leadership* 4 (2): 137–57. http://dx.doi.org/10.1177/1742715008089635.

Robinson, J. W., Jr., and G. P. Green, eds. 2011. *Introduction to Community Development: Theory, Practice, and Service-Learning.* Thousand Oaks: Sage Publications.

Rohs, R. F., and C. A. Langone. 1993. "Assessing Leadership and Problem-Solving Skills and Their Impacts in the Community." *Evaluation Review* 17 (1): 109–15. http://dx.doi.org/10.1177/01 93841X9301700108.

Rossing, Boyd E., and Daryl K. Heasley. 1987. "Enhancing Public Affairs Participation through Leadership Development Education: Key Questions for Community Development Research and Practice." *Journal of the Community Development Society* 18 (2): 98–116. http://dx.doi.org/10.1080/15575338709490028.

Rost, J. C. 1991. *Leadership for the Twenty-First Century.* Westport, CT: Praeger.

Ruscio, K. P. 2004. *The Leadership Dilemma in Modern Democracy.* Northampton, MA: Edward Elgar Publishing.

Sampson, R. J. 1999. "What 'Community' Supplies." In *Urban Problems and Community Development*, ed. R. Ferguson and W. Dickens, 241–92. Washington, DC: Brookings Institution Press.

Sandelands, L. E. 1990. "What Is so Practical about Theory: Lewin Revisited." *Journal for the Theory of Social Behaviour* 20 (3): 235–62. http://dx.doi.org/10.1111/j.1468-5914.1990.tb00185.x.

Sanderson, D. 1940. *Leadership for Rural Life.* New York: Association Press.

Sandfort, J., and L. Bloomberg. 2012. "InCommons: Supporting Community-Based Leadership." *Community Development: Journal of the Community Development Society* 43 (1): 12–30. http://dx.doi.org/10.1080/15575330.2011.645045.

Sandmann, L. R., and L. Vandenberg. 1995. "A Framework for 21st Century Leadership." *Journal of Extension* 33 (6): 1–9. http://www.joe.org/joe/1995december/a1.php.

Schall, E. 1995. "Learning to Love the Swamp: Reshaping Education for Public Service." *Journal of Policy Analysis and Management* 14 (2): 202–20. http://dx.doi.org/10.2307/3325150.

Schauber, A. C., and A. R. Kirk. 2001. "Impact of a Community Leadership Program on the Volunteer Leader." *Journal of Extension* 39 (3). http://www.joe.org/joe/2001june/rb2.php.

Scheffert, D. 2007. "Community Leadership: What Does it Take to See Results?" *Journal of Leadership Education* 6 (1): 174–89. http://dx.doi.org/10.12806/V6/I1/RF9.

Schuller, T. 2007. "Reflections on the Use of Social Capital." *Review of Social Economy* 65 (1): 11–28. http://dx.doi.org/10.1080/00346760601132162.

Schwinn, C. J., J. T. Kesler, and D. R. Schwinn. 2005. "Learning Democracy Centers: Where the Public Works." In *The Deliberative Democracy Handbook: Strategies for Effective Civic Engagement in the Twenty-First Century*, ed. John Gastil and Peter Levine, 228–36. San Francisco: Jossey-Bass.

Senge, P., et. al. 1994. *The Fifth Discipline Fieldbook.* New York: Doubleday.

Sharp, J. S. 2001. "Locating the Community Field: A Study of Interorganizational Network Structure and Capacity for Community Action." *Rural Sociology* 66 (3): 403–24. http://dx.doi.org/10.1111/j.1549-0831.2001.tb00074.x.

Sherod, L. 2005. "Civic Engagement." In *Encyclopedia of Applied Development Science*, ed. C. B. Fischer and R. M. Lerner. http://knowledge.sagepub.com.proxy1.cl.msu.edu/view/applied-devscience/n97.xml?rskey=OvHHJK&row=2.

Skocpol, T., and M. P. Fiorina, eds. 1999. *Civic Engagement in American Democracy*. Washington, DC: Brookings Institution and Russell Sage Foundation.

Skocpol, T. 2003. *Diminished Democracy: From Membership to Management in American Civic Life*. Norman, OK: University of Oklahoma Press.

Smock, K. 2005. *Democracy in Action: Community Organizing and Urban Change*. New York: Columbia University Press.

Snow, D. A., and R. D. Benford. 1988. "Ideology, Frame Resonance, and Participant Mobilization." *International Social Movement Research* 1: 197–217.

Stoecker, R. 1998. *Defending Community: The Struggle for Alternative Redevelopment in Cedar-Riverside*. Philadelphia: Temple University Press.

Stofferahn, C. W. 2012. "Community Capitals and Disaster Recovery: Northwood, ND Recovers from an EF 4 Tornado." *Community Development: Journal of the Community Development Society* 43 (5): 581–98. http://dx.doi.org/10.1080/15575330.2012.732591.

Sturtevant, V. 2006. "Reciprocity of Social Capital and Collective Action." *Community Development: Journal of the Community Development Society* 37 (1): 52–64. http://dx.doi.org/10.1080/15575330609490154.

Summers, G. F. 1986. "Rural Community Development." *Annual Review of Sociology* 12 (1): 347–71. http://dx.doi.org/10.1146/annurev.soc.12.1.347.

Swinney, J., C. Lang, and R. Runyan. 2012. "An Exploration of Rural Community Branding Efforts from the Perspective of Community Residents." *International Journal of Rural Management* 8 (1–2): 35–47. http://dx.doi.org/10.1177/0973005212461984.

Szreter, S., and M. Woolcock. 2004. "Health by Association? Social Capital, Social Theory, and the Political Economy of Public Health." *International Journal of Epidemiology* 33 (4): 650–67. http://dx.doi.org/10.1093/ije/dyh013.

Tackie, N. O., H. J. Findlay, N. Baharanyi, and A. Pierce. 2004. "Leadership Training for Transforming the Community: A Participatory Approach." *Journal of Extension* 42 (6). http://www.joe.org/joe/2004december/rb3.php.

Thullen, M., W. J. Kimball, and B. C. Wiggins. 1981. *Planning, Organizing, Conducting and Evaluating Community and Organizational Leadership Programs*. East Lansing, MI: Department of Resource Development, Michigan State University.

Tiepoh, M., and B. Reimer. 2004. "Social Capital, Information Flows, and Income Creation in Rural Canada: A Cross-Community Analysis." *Journal of Socio-Economics* 33 (4): 427–48. http://dx.doi.org/10.1016/j.socec.2004.04.007.

Tobin, K. 2010. "Civic Education in Emerging Democracies: Lessons from Post-Communist Poland and Romania." *Journal of Research in International Education* 9 (3): 273–88. http://dx.doi.org/10.1177/1475240910382996.

Tolbert, C. M., M. D. Irwin, T. A. Lyson, and A. R. Nucci. 2002. "Civic Community in Small-Town America: How Civic Welfare Is Influenced by Local Capitalism and Civic Engagement." *Rural Sociology* 67 (1): 90–113. http://dx.doi.org/10.1111/j.1549-0831.2002.tb00095.x.

Uhl-Bien, M. 2006. "Relational Leadership Theory: Exploring the Social Processes of Leadership and Organizing." *Leadership Quarterly* 17 (6): 654–76. http://dx.doi.org/10.1016/j.leaqua.2006.10.007.

Van der Meulen, M. 2012. "Civic Engagement Measured in Square Metres: Church and Civil Society in a Dutch Suburb." *Social Compass* 59 (4): 552–69. http://dx.doi.org/10.1177/0037768612449966.

Vandenberg, L., Frank A. Fear, and Manfred Thullen. 1988. *Research Practice Linkages in Extension Leadership Development Programs: Focus on Community Leadership Development Programs.* A Report to the North Central Regional Center for Rural Development. Ames, IA: Iowa State University.

Wagner, W. E., III. 2004. "Beyond Dollars and Cents: Using Civic Capital to Fashion Urban Improvements." *City & Community* 3 (2): 157–73. http://dx.doi.org/10.1111/j.1535-6841.2004.00074.x.

Waldrop, M. M. 1992. *Complexity: The Emerging Science at the Edge of Order and Chaos.* New York: Touchstone.

Walzer, N., ed. 1996. *Community Strategic Visioning Programs.* Westport, CT: Praeger.

Wheatley, M. J. 1992. *Leadership and the New Science: Learning about Organization from an Orderly Universe.* San Francisco: Berrett-Koehler.

Wheatley, M. J., and D. Frieze. 2009. "Using Emergence to Take Social Innovations to Scale." *Kettering Review* 27 (2): 34–8.

Whitaker, L. D., ed. 2006. *Women in Politics: Outsiders or Insiders?* Upper Saddle River, NJ: Pearson Prentice Hall.

Wildavsky, A. 1976. "Leadership in a Small Town." In *Leadership and Social Change*, 2nd ed., ed. W. R. Lassey and R. R. Ferdandez, 325–35. La Jolla, CA: University Associates.

Wilkinson, K. 1991. *The Community in Rural America.* New York: Greenwood Press.

Williams, M. R., and V. M. Wade. 2002. "Sponsorship of Community Leadership Development Programs: What Constitutes an Ideal Partnership?" *Journal of the Community Development Society* 33 (2): 61–71. http://dx.doi.org/10.1080/15575330209490093.

Whitham, M. M. 2012. "Community Connections: Social Capital and Community Success." *Sociological Forum* 27 (2): 441–57. http://dx.doi.org/10.1111/j.1573-7861.2012.01325.x.

Wituk, S., S. Ealey, M. J. Clark, P. Heiny, and G. Meissen. 2005. "Community Development through Community Leadership Programs: Insights from a Statewide Community Leadership Initiative." *Community Development: Journal of the Community Development Society* 36 (2): 89–101. http://dx.doi.org/10.1080/15575330509490177.

Woolcock, M., and D. Narayan. 2000. "Social Capital: Implications for Development Theory, Research, and Policy." *World Bank Research Observer* 15 (2): 225–49. http://dx.doi.org/10.1093/wbro/15.2.225.

Wren, J. T. 2007. *Inventing Leadership: The Challenge of Democracy.* Northampton, MA: Edward Elgar Publishers. http://dx.doi.org/10.4337/9781847207241.

Young, F. W. 1999. "A Neo-Durkheimian Theory of Small Communities." *Sociologia Ruralis* 39 (1): 3–16. http://dx.doi.org/10.1111/1467-9523.00090.

Zacharakis, Jeff, and Jan Flora. 2005. "Riverside: A Case Study of Social Capital and Cultural Reproduction and their Relationship to Leadership Development." *Adult Education Quarterly* 55 (4): 288–307. http://dx.doi.org/10.1177/0741713605277370.

Index

A

adaptive challenges, 120, 157, 160, 163
African American, 168, 179
aligned contributions, theory of, 176, 183
alignment, 24, 176
analysis of variance, 101
Appalachian, 102, 107, 114
Asset Based Community Development, 150
association, 185
associations, 2, 57, 61, 129
community, 2
attributions, 7, 185
authority, 29, 123, 155, 156, 157, 159, 163, 169, 172, 176, 177, 181, 182

B

balkanization, 140
binary logistic regression, 64
built capital, 82

C

capacity, 18, 53, 60, 71, 98, 121, 123, 140, 149, 166, 176, 181, 182, 185, 188
leadership, 135
change, 124, 151, 164, 167, 173, 176, 178, 180, 186
change, theory of, 182
citizen participation, 1, 107
civic capacity, 12
civic education, 169, 177
civic engagement, 2, 9, 10, 11, 17, 18, 29, 31, 57, 67, 71, 77, 78, 87, 92, 97, 121, 124, 136, 149, 153, 166, 170
antecedents of, 3
Civic Engagement, 37, 45, 49, 89, 97, 113, 138, 185
civic engagement, types of, 137
civic infrastructure, 10, 69, 93, 125, 126, 129, 136, 149, 166, 170
civic structure, 29, 60, 62, 68, 174, 182, 186
civil society, 141, 143, 147
coaching, 21

About the Authors

KENNETH PIGG has been helping community leaders become more effective change agents in their community for more than forty years as a specialist with the Cooperative Extension Service in Kentucky and Missouri and has served on a number of national panels and projects dealing with community change and leadership.

KEN MARTIN is Chair of the Department of Extension and Associate Director, Programs for Ohio State University Extension.

STEPHEN P. GASTEYER is an Associate Professor of Sociology at Michigan State University.

GODWIN T. APALIYAH is the The Ohio State University Extension's Community Development Educator and the Director of Economic Development, Fayette County.

KARI KEATING is a Teaching Associate in Agricultural Leadership Education at the University of Illinois.